OUR HOUSE IN THE CLOUDS

~

BOOK THIRTY-ONE

Louann Atkins Temple Women & Culture Series

Books about women and families, and their changing role in society

Our House in the Clouds

Building a Second Life in the Andes of Ecuador

~

JUDY BLANKENSHIP

University of Texas Press, Austin

The Louann Atkins Temple Women & Culture Series is supported by Allison, Doug, Taylor, and Andy Bacon; Margaret, Lawrence, Will, John, and Annie Temple; Larry Temple; the Temple-Inland Foundation; and the National Endowment for the Humanities.

LIBRARY OF CONGRESS
CATALOGING-IN-PUBLICATION DATA

Blankenship, Judy
   Our house in the clouds : building a second life in the Andes of Ecuador / by Judy Blankenship. — 1st ed.
      p.   cm. — (Louann Atkins Temple women and culture series ; book 31)
      ISBN 978-0-292-73903-1 (cloth : alk. paper) — ISBN 978-0-292-74527-8 (pbk. : alk. paper)
      1. Cañar (Ecuador : Province)—Description and travel. 2. Cañar (Ecuador : Province)—Social life and customs. 3. Blankenship, Judy, 1941– 4. Americans—Ecuador—Biography. 5. Community life—Ecuador—Cañar (Province) I. Title.
   F3741.C25B53 2013
   986.6—dc23   2012025778
doi:10.7560/739031

~

For our families in el norte,
our family of friends in el sur,
and
for my mother, to whom
I dedicate this book
Adelene Blankenship, 1920–2012,
my first reader, my biggest fan.

CONTENTS

~

PART TWO

where we are

~

I envy those
who live in two places:
new york, say, and london;
wales and spain;
l.a. and paris;
hawaii and switzerland.

there is always the anticipation
of the change, the chance that what is wrong
is the result of where you are. i have
always loved both the freshness of
arriving and the relief of leaving. with
two homes every move would be a homecoming.
i am not even considering the weather, hot
or cold, dry or wet: i am talking about hope.

I BELIEVE THE BEST PARTS OF LIFE are often those unexpected twists and turns that you could never have imagined—at least, those that turn out well. In my case, the strangest turn has been a long love affair with a high mountain town in a remote corner of South America, in a country called Ecuador, in a place known as Cañar.

The affair began serendipitously enough in the early nineties. I'd worked six years in Central America for a Canadian development agency, CUSO (roughly analogous to the Peace Corps), based in Costa Rica. One lucky day during my first year there, I met the man who would become my husband, Michael Jenkins, at the Flor y Mar hostel in the cloud forest of Monteverde. We were the only non-birders at the communal dinner table of eco-tourists who'd come

seeking the resplendent quetzal, a famously difficult bird to spot despite iridescent green feathers, a red belly, and a long tail. Our eyes met over the table as
one of the guests actually got up, flapped his arms, and did an imitation of a
quetzal song. The next morning, Michael invited me to take a walk to see the
dead sloth he'd spotted the day before. A tree had fallen with the sloth attached.
I couldn't resist: I figured I would receive such an invitation only once in my
lifetime.

I was a documentary photographer tied to a full-time job as a CUSO coop-
erant with a local popular education organization, Alforja. Michael was a foot-
loose traveler from Portland, Oregon, making his meandering way to Brazil.
After a few weeks lingering in Costa Rica, I suggested he stay a little longer for an
Easter weekend climb of Mt. Chirripo, the country's highest mountain at 12,533
feet. We were a small group, with a guide, but it was a difficult few days of blisters, asthma attacks, bad knees, and one very cold night bivouacked when we
didn't make it to the refuge. When Michael and I came down the mountain three
days later, we'd agreed on a future together. Soon after, he went back to Portland
to put his affairs in order. (Will he really return? I remember wondering many
times during the month he was gone. His shoes left beneath the bed reassured
me.) Then we settled in to live together in San José for the next five years.

At the end of my last CUSO contract, and after twenty years working full
time, I yearned for a free year to concentrate on my own photography, to create
a cohesive set of images around a single subject. My vague dream: to record
the daily life of a highland indigenous community in South America. Luckily,
Michael shared my romantic notions and love of adventure, along with an aver-
sion—at least for the moment—to settling into the rat race of late twentieth-
century life en *el norte*.

We gave ourselves a year. Without funding, but with enough savings to live
on, we chose Ecuador as our destination because it is a small peaceful country
in the northwest corner of South America with plenty of mountains and a then-
reported Indian population of 40 percent. We figured we had an advantage in
being fluent in Spanish (ignorant of the fact that Quichua is the native language
of Andean peoples) and having hardy dispositions that thrived on physical challenge. So, we naively thought, we would simply land somewhere, look around a
few days to find our village, and settle in (maybe even without electricity or running water, an exciting prospect). There, we further naively thought, we would
be warmly welcomed by the villagers as interested *extranjeros*, strangers, who
had come to contribute their energies and skills.

Michael's volunteer work in Costa Rica had been with a local foundation, Sol de Vida, building solar ovens with women's groups and promoting a

high-efficiency wood cookstove, called the Varney Stove. He wanted to check out possibilities in Ecuador. My contribution, I hoped, would be to serve as a sort of village photographer: chronicling the life and events of a community and giving back photos of fiestas, rituals, weddings, baptisms, funerals.

What's that proverb about the gods laughing at those who make plans? Nothing turned out as we imagined, at least in the short term. In March 1991 we landed in Cuenca, the beautiful colonial city in the south of Ecuador. We checked into the Crespo Hotel, far too expensive for our modest means, and began our search. This was pre–Internet days, so it was not possible to do online research that would have quickly informed our quest. Instead, Michael and I simply got on a different bus each day and rode into the countryside, returning tired and discouraged every afternoon.

"The *indígenas* don't live around here," a local finally told us. "The Cañaris are in the province to the north, and the Saraguros are in the south." But by then Michael and I were out of energy, patience, and good humor with one another, having moved to a much humbler and cramped hotel room after a couple of weeks. Plus, we'd fallen in love with Cuenca, one of the most beautiful and best-preserved colonial cities in South America, with its narrow cobblestone streets, magnificent architecture, interior courtyards, and inviting public plazas with fountains, domed churches, and cloistered monasteries. We placed a newspaper ad saying two Americans wanted to rent a house and, within days, we had several offers. So, in place of the rustic thatched-roof adobe hut in the country where I had imagined us, we ended up in an exquisite 1940s modernist house with parquet floors, a sweeping staircase, a chandelier in the dining room, bidets in the bathrooms, terraces overlooking the Tomebamba River, and two heavy black Bakelite telephones that actually worked—all for three hundred dollars a month. In short order, and with the landlord's permission, Michael had torn up the lawn, planted a vegetable garden, and built a darkroom in the maids' quarters.

In search of a photography project in Cuenca, I used a CUSO contact to meet a sociologist, Livia Cajamarca. She invited me to take photos for her thesis project, interviewing rural mestizo women whose husbands had migrated to the United States. I didn't know it then, in 1991, but the wave of transnational migration from southern Ecuador to the eastern United States was building momentum and would grow exponentially in the next decade. I would come to fully grasp all its ramifications many years later in Cañar.

I tried to capture in images the stories of poor, mostly young women left behind to raise children and manage crops while their husbands lived in Queens and worked in low-paying, unskilled jobs in Manhattan, or on construction projects in New Jersey. I took a few photos, but my heart was not in it.

Months later, a chance invitation from another academic in Livia's group, Patricio Carpio, to participate in a research project in the neighboring province of Cañar changed my luck. Two hours north of Cuenca on the Pan-American Highway, the highland town of Cañar lies at 10,100 feet in a valley surrounded by mountains. There, a newly formed indigenous organization, INTI (National Institute of Indigenous Technology), had agreed to participate in a survey on the effects of development projects on indigenous communities. My volunteer job was to train two young Cañari men, José Miguel Acero and Antonio Guamán, to use cameras and tape recorders to photograph their informants and record oral histories.

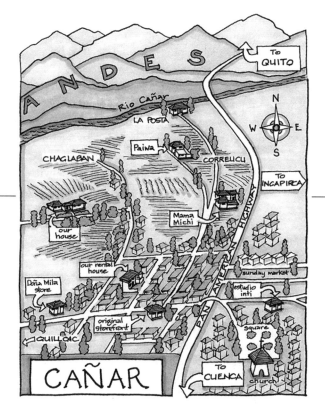

I will never forget my first visit to Cañar, when I sat through a chilly, all-day meeting in—yes, a thatched-roof adobe house—with a very reserved group of Cañari men and women, who, these many years later, are still our friends. But that day I was only a tall, thin gringa who seemingly appeared out of nowhere and so was refused her first request to take a photo. During a break in the meeting, one of the participants, Vicenta, sat in the sun on a grassy hummock spinning wool with a drop spindle. A beautiful shot! When I asked if I could take a photograph, she slowly shook her head, without even looking up, and continued spinning. I left my cameras in their case, but this image joined another "untaken" shot from that day that is forever etched on my brain: a group of three or four children sitting on the ground in front of an enormous cactus alongside a wooden gate, looking at a book. Today, I am reminded of that moment every time I walk by that cactus and that gate, both now old and tumbledown, not far from where we live.

I came back to Cuenca excited, telling Michael that I'd found the indigenous village we'd imagined, though a less romantic, homelier place than our fantasy.

I insisted he come with me to the next meeting to demonstrate his cookstove and meet my new acquaintances: the wonderful Chuma sisters, who seemed to be the activist heart of the community: Mercedes (Mama Michi), Vicenta, Mariana, María Juana and the matriarch, Mama Vicenta, and Mama Michi's son, José Miguel, my new photography student, who would eventually become the first indigenous professional photographer in Cañar.

Our year in Cuenca was quickly over, but we couldn't leave because we finally had the opportunity we'd been hoping for when the directors of INTI paid us a formal visit to invite us to collaborate with their organization. We kept the house in Cuenca, but rented a small storefront in Cañar, where I gave photography lessons on Sundays and Michael worked on a terracing project and promoted his small woodstove as an alternative to open fire cooking. (Everyone professed to love it, but no one wanted to spend the five dollars to buy it. Besides, someone would politely point out with a sweep of the arm, wood was plentiful and free with all the eucalyptus trees around.) By the end of the second year, I was able to make a set of portraits of our Cañari friends and indigenous life that captured something of what I'd come looking for.

Then it was time to return to the United States and engage with all the requisites of the American Dream: jobs, a house, vehicles, credit cards, and—of course—debts and a mortgage. But a piece of our hearts remained in Cañar, and in the next few years we began returning to Ecuador for visits, short and long. In 1997 for the baptism of our goddaughter, Paiwa, the child of my photography student José Miguel and his wife Estela; in 1998 to mount an exhibit of the Cañari portraits at the ethnographic museum in Cuenca and teach a course; in 2000–2001 for a Fulbright grant, when Michael and I lived for the first time in Cañar (*Cañar: A Year in the Highlands of Ecuador* tells that story); and in 2005 for a second Fulbright to create an interactive program on Cañari culture with local groups and the Smithsonian's National Museum of the American Indian.

In June 2005, when this story opens, Michael and I are set to leave Cañar for what we assume is the last time. I have finished my last grant project, and we will soon return to Portland, resume our life there, and consider our future, which we hope includes a foothold somewhere in the Latin world. Cañar does not figure in it—too remote, too cold, too far away from family and friends—but the past several years we've made numerous exploratory trips to Mexico, looking for that "perfect" place, where we will feel at home. We haven't found it yet, but we plan to keep looking.

Then, everything changed again . . .

PART ONE

~

CHAPTER 1

Planting a Tree for Plinio

~

Plinio's velorio

IT IS A BRISK MORNING in late May 2005 when Michael and I leave our small house on the outskirts of Cañar and walk to the nearby Pan-American Highway to wait for a bus. We are on our way to the mountain village of Sisíd, where our friend, Plinio, was buried four months ago.

In January, on the very day we arrived in Ecuador, a tearful phone call from a friend in the United States told us of Plinio's death. A skilled carpenter and construction worker, he had fallen from a ladder while installing a second-floor window. No one saw him fall or could explain how the accident happened, but Plinio died the next day of severe head injuries. He was thirty-five and had been working steadily for five years since arriving in the United States as an undocumented immigrant. Plinio was not only our sweet gentle friend from Cañar, but also our compadre. We are godparents to his youngest daughter, Adelita, and in Latino culture there is no greater honor than to be asked to be a *padrino*, which implies a life-long bond of friendship and mutual help.

This morning, as Michael and I climb aboard the large yellow bus, Transporter Cañaris, the local passengers examine us with shy but curious stares. I can imagine them thinking, *Who are these two extranjeros? What are they doing in Cañar, where few travelers stop and no gringos live? And where on earth can they be going so early in the morning?*

Michael has planned carefully for this day. In his backpack, he carries a heavy marble and bronze plaque that he designed and commissioned from a gravestone maker in Cuenca, our nearest city. Etched with the name and dates of a too-short life: Plinio Quishpe, 1970–2005, the plaque will go beside the *guayllac* tree that we plan to plant today in Plinio's garden.

Michael's pack also contains a carpenter's level, a rain jacket, a Sudoku book, a pint of Zhumir (*aguardiente* or cane alcohol), and a small shot glass—the last two items essential for the small ceremony we will have with Plinio's family. In my backpack, I carry two cameras, a rain jacket, an extra sweater, a bottle of water, a tube of sunscreen, and a copy of Jane Austen's *Northanger Abbey*.

Twenty minutes later, we jump off in the small town of El Tambo, walk across the pretty town square, and wait for the local bus up the mountain. Although Sisíd is only about twenty kilometers from Cañar, it will take us more than an hour to reach the village, at around eleven thousand feet. A woman selling bananas under the *portal* where we stand is doing a thriving business, and I just have time to buy two before a small battered bus trundles around the square and comes to a stop, spewing exhaust. Michael and I climb on, ducking our heads under the low ceiling, and crowd into a tiny seat that barely accommodates our North American bottoms and bulky backpacks. We are giants in this land of small people.

Tightly packed around us, Indian women sit with sleeping babies on their backs, young children in their arms, baskets of produce between their feet, and live chickens and guinea pigs in sacks tucked under their seats. I breathe in the pungent but pleasant smell of wood smoke from cook fires, emanating from passengers' wool clothing and hair. The women, round-faced and red-cheeked, glance at us with frank curiosity, but no one speaks or shows any sign of friendliness. They assume we are passing tourists heading for Ingapirca, the much-visited complex of Cañari and Inca ruins up the mountain.

The driver makes another bone-shaking round of the cobbled streets, searching for a few more passengers before crossing the old railroad tracks and heading out of town.

View of Cañar River valley

The winding road is narrow and potholed, with chunks of the edge washed away by recent downpours. From where I sit by the window, I can't help but glance over the edge at the certain-death drops into the valley below. But I've learned by now not to obsess over dying in a bus accident in South America (which has one of the higher rates of such accidents in the world). Instead, with a mental shrug, I affect the fatalistic attitude of local folks to sudden death and other terrible misfortunes: *fue destino*—it was destiny; *fue su tiempo*—it was his/her time; and finally, the less comforting but oh-so-true *mala suerte*—bad luck.

In Plinio's case, it was certainly very bad luck. In his five years as a *migrante*, he had found good work with a building contractor, brought his wife Zulma to join him, sent money home to support their two daughters left with his mother, and begun building a house. His dream was to return to Ecuador with Zulma, tend his garden, work his crops and animals, and see his two daughters grow up.

As we climb, the longer view grabs my attention. It is a glorious day, with an intense clear sky above a magnificent panorama of serrated slate-blue mountains to the west. Layers of light clouds float between us, high on the mountain, and the deep green Cañar River valley far below. White stucco or adobe houses with red or blue roofs sprinkle the patchwork of fields, some with grazing cows and sheep, others with ripening barley or wheat, yet others with corn or potatoes. Clumps of olive green eucalyptus trees define the borders of the fields.

As the bus labors up and up, swerving around potholes and fallen rocks, our adopted town comes into view to the south. Cañar lies at 10,150 feet in a broad north-south valley between two parallel chains of the Andes Mountains. Established in colonial times as a market center for surrounding haciendas and small farms, the town has grown hodgepodge over the centuries, from a few cobblestone streets, adobe buildings, a church, and a square into a small city with a population of about ten thousand. Agrarian reform came late, in the 1960s and 70s, dismantling the hacienda system, and while the urban areas have grown with the mestizo population, the indigenous Cañaris remain in widely scattered hamlets in the countryside, where they have lived for millennia. Today an estimated forty thousand Quichua-speaking Cañari are scattered throughout the province.

~

A half hour later, I look up from my book to see the cluster of houses that mark the village of Sisíd. Four years ago, Michael and I spent the night here after Adelita's baptism. Though it had been Plinio's idea to ask us to be godparents, he wasn't there for the ritual in the Catholic church in Cañar. The year before, he had left from Guayaquil on a rickety fishing boat on the first step of the dangerous journey to join his brother, Nestor, in *el norte*. It's a story we've heard countless times. Six days on the open seas to reach the coast of Guatemala on a boat meant for a few fisherman but crammed with more than a hundred Ecuadorians, followed by weeks of walking and traveling by bus and truck through Central America and Mexico to the treacherous border crossing into Arizona or Texas. Coyotes, or traffickers in illegal immigrants, guide and facilitate the trip at every point, beginning with a contact in the local village who might be a neighbor or a cousin. The cost when he left, in 2000, was seven thousand dollars, paid out slowly over the weeks or months to a local coyote as Plinio made his way north. (Today the cost is twelve thousand dollars.)

Once safely across the border—and Plinio was lucky to have made it the first time—he became one of the estimated half-million Ecuadorians who have left the country since the economy collapsed in 1999. Most headed for the east coast of the United States, where one of the favorite destinations is Queens, New York, which Ecuadorians like to call their fourth largest city.

Soon after the baptism, Zulma followed her husband, leaving her daughters, then two and five years old, with Mama Julia, Plinio's mother. Zulma was not so lucky at the border crossing. She was arrested in Texas, held in detention, given a trial date, and then inexplicably released. She joined her husband in a northern city, got a job at Taco Bell with false documents, and was quietly absorbed into the estimated twelve million illegal immigrants living in the United States at that time.

I try to imagine what Zulma is going through now, in these months since Plinio's death. She must be in shock, paralyzed by insecurity and fear to have been suddenly left alone in a country and culture not her own, where she doesn't speak the language or have legal status, carrying on a lonely life circumscribed by a bus ride to and from work. We recently heard that she is planning to come back to Ecuador to join the two young daughters she's not seen in several years, but no one knows for sure. (How can she *not* come back to her girls, a part of me screams, but I tamp down that thought. I've learned not to be judgmental when I hear about mothers who leave young children to be raised by relatives while they join their husbands in *el norte*, "to preserve the marriage.")

~

"*Parada!*" Michael yells, looking up from his Sudoku book. The driver grinds to a stop and waits patiently as we struggle out of our tiny seat, shoulder our unwieldy backpacks, and push our way through a crowd of standing passengers, stepping over baskets of produce and bags of grain blocking the exit. In my rush, I knock my head on the ceiling, and as the bus pulls away, I hear laughter. This is a culture where locals do not hurry to give a hand to strangers suffering minor accidents or mishaps, though I suspect their paralysis is more out of fear and respect than disregard. And I suppose it *is* funny to see a tall gringa with an overloaded pack ungracefully trying to exit a small bus.

We walk the last half kilometer up a rough dirt track, passing an assortment of houses that reveal the past and present history of this place. Old abandoned adobe *casas* with ragged thatched roofs sit cheek by jowl with new, multi-colored, two- and three-story concrete-block houses, built with dollars sent home by migrants. Some are barely under construction, with piles of sand and gravel on the side of the road. Others were never finished, rusting lines of rebar sticking into the air above concrete walls, testament to lost or deferred dreams. Still other houses sit resplendent and seemingly complete, but empty—brightly painted on the outside but often without plumbing or kitchens or bathrooms inside. These are shells, "trophy houses," built to show a local migrant's success in the United States or Spain, a sign that he or she—or they—plan to return to the home village someday and live in a new style.

As we clamber down the rocky path to a house perched on the hillside overlooking the valley, Mama Julia herself comes out to greet us. Obviously dressed for our visit, she wears two thick wool skirts with embroidered edges—one on top of the other—a short black shawl pinned over her chest, on top of a white embroidered blouse, navy blue knee socks with "USA" woven in at calf level, oversized shoes (no doubt sent by her daughter in New York), and the ubiquitous round white hat that distinguishes Cañaris from other indigenous groups in Ecuador.

"*Descansen!*" "Rest!" Mama Julia commands as she hauls two straight-backed chairs from her kitchen and plunks them down in the uneven courtyard. Her round face creases with a smile. She is probably in her late fifties, but like many country women who spend their lives working outdoors in this harsh climate, she looks much older. Her husband died of a heart attack about ten years ago, leaving her with six children. Iliana, her oldest daughter, is married and lives nearby; another daughter and son are migrants in the United States, leaving her with two teenage daughters at home.

We catch our breath from the climb and luxuriate in the warmth of the high altitude sun. Tall eucalyptus trees surrounding the compound sway in the slight breeze and bring that wonderful acerbic scent I associate with Cañar. Mama Julia brings us cups of beer mixed with Coca-Cola, a favorite local drink that tastes wonderful to me, even at ten o'clock in the morning.

We last saw Mama Julia the day of the funeral, four months ago, when she looked thoroughly destroyed by grief and the long agonizing wait for her son's body to come home. In Andean cultures, it's believed that the newly dead's spirit must not be left in limbo, and this means a quick burial, following the proper rituals, on the third day after death. But Plinio's remains were held in the United States for an interminable three weeks while an Ecuadorian consulate mishandled or lost the paperwork. The family was crazed with despair while they waited, believing his spirit to be without rest. But their greatest fear, Iliana told me, was that her brother's body would be *botado*—meaning forgotten or lost—in the cargo area of some airport. Something similar had happened the year before to a young man from their village who had died in a construction accident in New York.

Once Plinio's remains finally arrived in the coastal city of Guayaquil, the family followed the death rites as though he had just died. A *velorio*, or vigil, was held at home the first two days and nights, and on the third day, a mass was followed by a long walking procession to the cemetery for interment, Iliana sobbing into a cell phone as she described the scene to her sister in New York. Michael was a pallbearer. As is custom, we mourners remained at the cemetery, while workmen sealed the big American-made steel casket in its niche with cement, to witness that Plinio's physical and spiritual remains were at last at rest.

But today Mama Julia is energetic and friendly. "*Más cola, Mamita?*" she keeps asking me. Like many older Cañaris, Mama Julia speaks mostly Quichua, with only a sprinkling of Spanish. Most of the time I have no idea what she is saying, but Michael and I nod and smile a lot and she seems to understand our Spanish well enough.

As we finish our drinks, Michael explains that he wants Mama Julia's help in deciding where to plant the tree and put the plaque. She nods that she understands, and the two of them take off down the road to Plinio's house. I follow a few minutes later, taking time to get my cameras ready. The family gave me permission to photograph the *velorio* and funeral, and I'm assuming I'll have permission to record this day. I catch up with them standing in the road, looking up at an unfinished two-story, white-washed house and its blank, glass-less windows and weed-filled yard. For a few years, Plinio and Zulma sent money home to start building the house, but then decided it was too much investment when they couldn't be here to oversee the work. So there it sits, a sad coda to a shattered dream of a better life. No one has mentioned what will happen to the house now.

As I come close, Mama Julia is gesturing at the house and indicating to Michael that she thinks the best place for the plaque would be high up, about second-story level, facing the road. As she speaks, I watch Michael's face. This is completely contrary to his idea of placing the plaque in the ground near the tree. But with a kindly nod he takes in Mama Julia's suggestion. Then—maybe she also sees his face—she looks uncertain, shrugs, and says, "Let's wait for Iliana to decide." Plinio's sister has promised to join us later this morning.

Mama Julia turns to go back to her house, but Michael, impatient to get started and fearing a long delay if he waits for Iliana, asks if he can start digging the hole for the tree. She nods and hurries away to her daily chores, tending to her pigs, sheep, cows, and chickens. Plus, I suspect she is preparing a meal for us.

Michael and I climb the short path to the patch of grass alongside the house where Plinio's garden used to be. I have a sudden memory of visiting him here years ago, when he proudly showed me his carefully tended vegetables, flowers, and trees—unusual for a Cañari man, whose traditional role is the rougher work of plowing, planting, harvesting crops, and wrestling with pigs and bulls.

Michael gets to work with the shovel as I settle down on a grassy knoll nearby with my book. I look out at the 240-degree view of the broad river valley below and the mountains beyond and feel a surge of pleasure, or love, or . . . something! Sheep graze in the field beside me. A radio plays faintly from a nearby house, and in the near distance the bright skirts of women tending their animals or crops dot the intense green hillsides. It's beautiful, peaceful, nearly magical. I'm suddenly aware that we are within a month of leaving Cañar, presumably for the last time, and of how much I will miss it.

"What a perfect place," I yell down to Michael. "Let's forget Mexico! Why don't we come live in Cañar instead? This is where we should be!"

"I've been thinking the same thing lately," Michael grunts, head down, shoveling dirt.

An hour later, Iliana finally arrives, along with her husband, Víctor, Mama Julia, and Mama Julia's brother, Tayta Mateo, a new player in today's scenario whom I've not met. He is a vigorous-looking man in his sixties, I'd guess, with a sweet face and serious, no-nonsense manner. During the wait, Michael has planted the tree. As everyone stands around and looks approvingly at the small, spindly *guayllac*, Michael brings out the brass plaque from his backpack and begins to read the text: "This tree is planted in memory of . . ."

"So the plaque needs to be near the tree to make sense," Iliana says, immediately grasping the situation. She turns to explain in Quichua to Mama Julia and Tayta Mateo.

"Yes," Tayta Mateo emphatically breaks in, in Spanish. "All that is good. But what we need is a *hatun rumi*, right here!" He taps the ground with his foot next to the tree. "A big stone for the plaque so it won't get overgrown with grass and weeds and no one can bother it."

I look at Michael, who is dismayed to think that the uncle's suggestion will mean a delay in his careful plan: more time, more work, and more materials. But Tayta Mateo is busily scanning the immediate landscape. "There," he says, "that one!" pointing to a cut into the hillside directly behind the house, where the tip of a rock peeks out.

Within minutes, Michael, Víctor, and Tayta Mateo are digging around the rock with shovels and a pick. Soon, a huge boulder is revealed, about four feet long and weighing hundreds of pounds.

I'm standing near enough to see that the stone is perfect for its purpose. With a two-tiered flat surface, the longer plane can accommodate the plaque, and the raised shorter end will make a perfect little bench.

"So, the *Virgincita* can go right here," says Tayta Mateo, patting the raised end.

Michael just nods helplessly and says, *"Buen idea!"* I picture Plinio's spare brass plaque keeping company with one of the gaudily painted, blue-robed ceramic virgins we see for sale in stores. But Tayta Mateo is senior man in charge now, and we must follow his vision.

In the next two hours, with Tayta Mateo giving enthusiastic directions in a mix of Quichua and Spanish, the three men roll the boulder down the slope, settle it into the ground, mix and pour a concrete base around the stone ("too much mortar," I hear Michael mutter as Tayta Mateo sloshes water to make a big puddle of cement), place the plaque on top of the stone and wipe the excess from around the marble ("too much mortar," I hear Michael mutter again).

The men stand back to admire the results.

"All it needs now is the *Virgincita*," Tayta Mateo adds.

It is late afternoon and beginning to turn chilly. Michael brings out the bottle of Zhumir and the shot glass as we gather round the tree and the plaque. Mama Julia has come back with Plinio's two young daughters, home from school. The first shot is poured onto the ground to honor Plinio and *Pachamama*, Mother Earth; then each adult takes a drink from the same glass with a nod and *salud* to each other.

After that, Mama Julia will invite us back to her house for an extended meal of roasted guinea pigs with all the trimmings, followed by a lengthy sit-about with more drinks before we go home, near evening.

But the main business of the day is done and everyone seems *contento*: Plinio's tree is planted, his plaque laid, his memory honored. And though Michael and I haven't quite settled on it yet, our future in Cañar is starting to glimmer.

CHAPTER 2

On Becoming Property Owners in Ecuador

~

The property as we first saw it

IT IS JANUARY 2006, seven months after we planted that tree for Plinio, and Michael and I are more than a little amazed to find ourselves back in Cañar, living in the same small house we rented last year. After two days hard traveling, we arrived yesterday, leaving behind our freelance jobs, family, friends, neighbors, and the sweet life we've built over the last twelve years in Portland, Oregon.

"Do you want to walk down and take a look at our land?" Michael asks tentatively as we drink our morning coffee. Sun pours through the windows and the air is warm. "Sure," I answer, but I too sound uncertain, and Michael studies my face for clues. Isn't it a bit strange that we haven't talked much about the life-changing decision we made right before we left last June to put down roots in Ecuador, build a house, and live here half the year? Maybe once back in Portland, we were at first too immersed in our "other" life—busy with jobs, catching up with friends and family—to analyze our impulsive actions. Later, we were probably too occupied getting ready to leave—renting our Ash Street house for the first time through Craigslist, preparing it for tenants, arranging financing to build the new house, deciding what to bring with us—to discuss at any length the implications of how this decision will change the rest of our lives.

All those obvious questions: How would our families react to us being so far away half the year? How on earth did we think we could build a house from scratch when we've never done it and don't even know how much it would cost, or where we would get the immediate funds for construction in this cash-only country? Maybe we were just scared, but more likely, I think, we were in a state of elation, having forced this sea change in our lives, anxious to begin the great adventure, and feeling no great need to talk about it.

Still, when we landed yesterday in Cañar, it didn't occur to either of us to rush down to the cornfield we'd impulsively bought six months ago with the last of my grant funds and a cash transfer from a nearly forgotten pension fund, the result of a three-year college teaching job in New York state ages ago. Instead, we settled into the house we've kept since last year, just down the street from the house where we spent a year six years ago, which is across the road from the two-room storefront where we first got to know Cañar, fourteen years ago.

There wasn't much settling to do. I swept the dusty tile floor in the one large room downstairs that serves as kitchen-dining-living area, discovered a mouse had taken up residence under the kitchen sink, and wiped down the counters, tables, and benches. Meanwhile, Michael unlocked a wooden trunk to bring out a prized Cañar possession: a cheap espresso maker, bought in Cuenca last year. While he walked into town to shop for the makings of dinner, I climbed upstairs to make the bed and put away my camera equipment in the filing cabinet. Later, we had a dinner of fava beans, fresh corn, potatoes, onions, and eggs. We were back to our Cañar routine and diet, and I have to say it really felt like home.

~

Home has always been a relative concept to me. I grew up in a small town in a remote corner of northwestern Colorado where my parents had settled after World War II, far from their own families—my father's in Texas, my mother's in Nebraska. My father went into business, but we were really there because he was drawn to the wide-open country of the West, where he could fish its mountain streams, hunt deer and elk with his buddies, and camp with his family. My mother went along with all that, but mostly she was drawn to the idea of Home, wherever that might be. She had grown up poor in the Depression, part of a large family who always lived in rented places, usually run-down farmhouses. Once in a home of her own—even a tiny postwar two bedroom, one bath—she wanted to stay put forever. "I've loved every house we ever owned," she still says.

But my restless father had other ideas, and he imbued my two sisters and me with the sense of a larger world out there. Adventure awaited! One year he tried to talk my mother into moving us to Alaska; another year, it was Gua temala. She always prevailed with the argument that "the girls" needed to go through school in one place. But I was on my father's side, and when at eighteen I left Craig for university, I never looked back. My sister Charlotte followed three years later, and the minute my youngest sister Sherry graduated from high school, my father's vision finally won out. My parents moved first to the Ozarks, another dream realized, but then, after a few successful business years there, he and my mother sold nearly everything, bought a travel trailer, and roamed for seven years from Mexico to British Columbia, "according to where the fishing was good," before settling into a new life in the seventies in Santa Fe, New Mexico.

During those roaming years when my sisters and I lived in far-flung places— Guadalajara, Toronto, San Francisco—we had a running joke that home was wherever mom and dad's travel trailer was parked at the moment—on a beach in La Penita, Mexico, beside Williams Lake in Colorado, on a concrete slab next to friends in Phoenix.

~

Last night after our first dinner, our Cañari lawyer, Vicente Tenesaca, dropped by to report on the details of our land transaction. A handsome, easygoing man in his mid-thirties, Vicente is indigenous, but, like many other men his age, had cut his braid when he became a professional. He works with a mestizo partner, Rafael, in a small office on the plaza in Cañar. Last June, after we came to an agreement with the sellers of the land, Rosa and Juan, and paid a *seña*, a good faith deposit, we left everything in Vicente's capable hands. While foreigners are allowed to own property in Ecuador, subject to the same laws as any Ecuadorian citizen, the process of buying and selling land involves a byzantine set of legal procedures requiring a crew of lawyers, notaries, judicial experts, property registrars, engineers, land surveyors, and tax assessors—not to mention a few small bribes here and there, a delicate but necessary part of every property transaction. A lawyer is essential in orchestrating this paperwork labyrinth, collectively called "*tramites*," to ensure that the buyer ends up with a legal *escritura*, or title. Otherwise, a title can be challenged, invalidated, or undone, and you can end up wrangling in court for years, as happened with friends of ours in Cuenca who bought an old hacienda.

As the three of us sat around our wooden table, Vicente pulled papers from his briefcase and reported the salient facts: we have purchased 945.5 square meters (10,178 square feet, about double the size of a standard residential lot in Portland) in the *comuna*, or hamlet, of Chaglaban. Our irregular-shaped property sits on a hillside just beyond the Cañar town limits. It is narrower at the top, where our street, *calle pública sin nombre* (public road without a name) passes, and wider at the bottom, where it is surrounded by fields and a long view of the river valley below.

Vicente told us that a few months ago, after he had successfully jumped though all the legal and bureaucratic hoops of the purchase, there'd been a slight *pleito* with Rosa, the wife of the couple selling the land. Once the corn was harvested and the stalks plowed under, Rosa had insisted to Vicente that Michael had given her the right to continue planting on "her" land for two years. "I was forced to hire two men to build a fence around the property," Vicente said, "but since then things have been quiet."

For some reason, neither Michael nor I asked for details of this incident. Maybe we were tired after our trip, maybe we just couldn't absorb any more information, or maybe we misunderstood the implications of the word, *pleito*, which can mean "lawsuit," but in Cañar generally means something closer to "argument."

~

Initially, it was Rosa who had offered her cornfield. On a rainy June afternoon, Michael and our old friend José Miguel had walked around this area, asking about properties for sale. It was a few days after we'd planted the tree for Plinio that we first began to seriously imagine a life here. We'd agreed to look around in the weeks left before our return to the United States. Michael and José Miguel had run into Rosa outside her house, and in response to their question, she'd swept her arm to indicate that the land beside her house was for sale, even quoting a price per square meter. "Come back tomorrow and talk to my husband Juan," she'd said.

Michael did go back, and in the following few days, he and Juan negotiated a final figure for the land. By the end of the week, the men had shaken hands and traded shots of Zhumir to seal the deal. Michael came home with the news and we were ecstatic. We could hardly believe it had happened so quickly, barely days from the time we'd decided to look for property and just weeks from our departure date. It seemed such an easy leap from dream to reality. Little did we know then how far this was from a done deal!

At the conclusion of our evening meeting with Vicente, Michael brought out the Zhumir and poured a shot of *aguardiente* to make the ritual toast: "*Salud y gracias.*"

"*Felicitaciones!*" Vicente responded. "You are now property owners in Ecuador."

As he left, Vicente handed me a thick file. "I think you'll find these documents interesting reading," he said.

~

The next morning, Michael and I are unusually quiet as we walk the short distance from our house to our land. I suspect we are fearful that our future house site will look smaller than we remember, or that the view won't be as splendid, or that we simply won't be able to imagine living here and will regret trading our longtime dream of some (undiscovered) charming colonial town in Mexico for the reality of this homely outpost in southern Ecuador. But as we come up over the crest of the hill and see the cottony clouds rolling up from the river canyon to the west, the patchwork of green and russet fields spread out below, and the deep blue backdrop of the Andes Mountains, I feel a familiar little flutter in the pit of my stomach. The place is as beautiful as I remember. Beside me, I hear Michael take a deep breath and sigh, "Yeah . . . it's good!"

We turn left to walk down our road-without-a-name, a long column of tall eucalyptus and cypress trees sway on our left with fields of wheat and corn stretching out below. We pass the house of Rosa and Juan before we reach our "field." Then we stand still in the road a few minutes and simply stare, because for the first time we can clearly see what we have bought. Last June, during negotiations with Juan and Rosa, the field was covered with their ripening corn. We had paced the perimeter of the land to get some idea of its size, tried to visualize where a house might go, but it was impossible to see around the tall corn.

We only knew we loved the view, or what we could see of it from the downhill side. We also loved the fact that we would be a ten-minute walk from town, the Pan-American Highway, and good bus service, as we are determined to live here without a car. We never had a desire to be isolated in the country, surrounded by acres of land, with privacy and quiet. Rather, we've come to live in the midst of a community.

Michael and neighbors in the fog

Today the corn is gone and six piglets and a big mama are placidly feeding on the stubble and weeds; they must belong to our neighbor to the west, Magdalena.

Not sure what to do next, we step into the stubble. The piglets scatter to a far corner of the lot and continue grazing, while the mama holds her ground as Michael studies the plat. I scuff the rich black topsoil and say it looks pretty good, but what do I know of topsoil? Michael paces the fence lines with big steps, measuring the perimeters. Truth is, we just don't know how to mark this auspicious moment. We stand still a few minutes, trying to conceive of a house here, but it's no easier than it was last year. With nothing but fields and a few scattered houses around us, it all feels very unreal. "Why don't we build up near the road?" I suggest. "That will allow us a big back garden."

"No, we should build far back on the lot, away from the road," Michael replies, consistent with our usual practice of taking opposite sides. Silence. He finally gestures toward the west and says lamely, "Well, won't it be nice to watch the sunset every evening from our living room windows?"

I hadn't noticed Rosa in her back garden, about fifty feet away, but she has spotted us and walks across the field to stand near the fence. She cradles a small white hen in one arm like a new baby, but the rest of her is dark: her short curly hair, her pants and sweater, and her mood, judging by the scowl on her face. After barely a greeting and handshakes over the fence, Rosa bursts out, "What a shame! Look how much land you have! I really regret selling it to you! Look how large a piece you have and how little I've been left with." She gestures to the field behind her, nearly upending the little hen. "It was my inheritance—and for my children. Now you're going to build an enormous house here!"

"No, no," Michael and I respond in shocked unison, shaking our heads. "It won't be large," I say feebly. "We're going to build a smallish adobe house with an interior patio." This sounds so foolish, given the enormity of Rosa's concerns. A lost legacy for her children? I am not about to respond to *that*, remembering last June.

The morning after Michael and Juan shook hands on the deal, and we were so elated, Juan came by our house, downcast and apologetic, to tell us that Rosa had decided the sale was off. "*Mi señora no quiere vender . . .*" My wife does not want to sell. He sounded definite, but looked regretful as he took off down the street.

We were terribly disappointed and a bit confused. Michael grumbled that a handshake should count for something, but in truth, we knew nothing about the local customs of negotiating and buying property. That afternoon, feeling disconsolate, we walked around near the cornfield, asking about other properties that might be for sale. We found nothing. Back home, talking it over and trying to shore one another up, we grew philosophical as we began to accept that maybe we were not destined to live in Ecuador after all.

But then, another surprise! Early the following morning, Juan came by again to say that Rosa had changed her mind. The sale was on! Could we come down to their house and talk it over? I demurred and told Michael to go alone. He loves to negotiate, but I can't stand the tension and uncertainty of the game— and I tend to get flustered. In more than one market negotiating session, I've been known to offer *more* than the asking price.

Besides, I was busy. When I look back at my June 2005 daybook, I see a two-week period that includes, "Finish up Smithsonian project, document Inti Raymi Fiesta, film the weaver Juanito Tenesaca for the ethnographic museum in Cuenca."

Only one entry, on June 12, relates to the property: "Michael does land deal with banana cake—$31,000."

That note synthesizes two weeks of seesawing negotiations, during which time Michael and Juan went back and forth on the size of the lot (at one point, he offered *more* land, a triangular piece to the north) and the price per square meter, with volatile Rosa always in the background, like a puppet master. She alternately pressured her husband not to sell, then relented, then wavered again, then convinced him to change the price. We were wildly elated one day, then down the next, with our departure date coming up fast. One afternoon, the stop-and-start dealings became even more confusing when Juan came by our house offering a basket of fresh corn (presumably harvested from the land in question). Michael, seeing an opening, responded with a visit to them with a loaf of his famous banana bread. Soon after, Rosa and Juan agreed to accept our offer.

~

And here we now stand with Rosa and her white chicken. "And by the way," she says grievously after a pause, looking directly at Michael, "I never saw a penny of that *seña* you gave my husband. Not a penny of it!" Vicente told us later that most of the good faith deposit had gone for the paperwork and taxes Rosa and Juan owed to the municipality.

Michael mumbles something indistinct but sympathetic and then, looking dreamily off into the distance, says, "Maybe someday we can buy that other smaller piece of land to the north that you originally wanted to sell."

"Never!" Rosa waves her arm excitedly. "I've already sold too much; I'll never sell any more of my land. The little that remains is for my three children." She yells as she brings her hand down on the barbed wire. "Ayiiii!" Michael and I stand speechless on the other side of the fence. "I really hurt myself on your fence," Rosa says pointedly, shaking her hand.

As Michael and I make motions to leave, Rosa's expression abruptly changes. She smiles and nods and wants to shake hands again. What a strange woman! (Later, we will hear from other neighbors who've bought land from Rosa that she is *loca*, crazy.) I tell her I hope we'll be good neighbors, and she replies that we surely will.

We start up the road with mixed feelings. As foreigners from a rich nation coming to live in a poor country, we risk being cast in the role of *aprovecho-sos*, "advantage-takers" in Spanish. Our long-term relationships in Cañar have been largely with the indigenous community, where we are known as *cola-boradores*—or, as our friend Mama Michi put it humorously years ago, "gringos without a car, Bible, or agenda." With this land purchase, however, we are in new territory, dealing with Rosa and Juan, the *mestizo* community, and a whole new set of social parameters.

~

The next morning, in the quiet of our upstairs bedroom, I take a careful look at the paperwork Vicente gave me, and in it I find clues that shed light on Rosa's reluctance to sell, resentment, and regret. The cover of the *escritura*, the legal document that records the sale, lists the sellers as "Juan Baldera and esposa." Below, in faint pencil, is written "Rosa Móntez."

The buyers are listed as "Michael Jenkins and esposa." Nothing about my name, not even in pencil. Incredible! According to the patriarchal legal system established by the Spanish five hundred years ago and still largely in force, Rosa and I, as wives, are simply legal appendages of our husbands. I suppose our names are recorded in legal documents as simply "wife" or in pencil in case we should die, get lost, or be switched for another wife.

I read on: in 1987, Rosa Móntez, then twenty-six, had worked as a domestic servant for years for a local hacienda owner, a single woman named Señorita María Sánchez. In lieu of past wages, in a custom that also goes back to the Spanish, the *patrona* ceded Rosa two hectares of land (about five acres), which includes the piece we have bought.

According to a local friend who knows about these things, Rosa was probably "given away" to Señorita Sánchez as a young girl, to be raised as a live-in maid and companion—not an unusual practice among poor mestizo families with too many girl children and too little land. Rosa would have been fed and clothed, but not educated or paid for her work. So, under law, the *patrona* granted Rosa a section of land in return for a signed document that she, Rosa, would not demand past wages.

Although probably a tiny portion of a large hacienda, Rosa's five acres represented a substantial piece of property for a young woman and in a prime location near town. Historically, the Church or large haciendas owned the best land in and around Cañar, which they continued to control after the land reform in the 1960s. Rosa, like her *patrona*, Señorita Sánchez, is mestizo, and so she inherited the privilege of living near town.

A closer look at the *escritura* reveals that Rosa is six years older than her husband, information that gives me more room for speculation. I see that Juan is not from Cañar, but from a small town in Chimborazo, the province to the north. Born in 1967, he would have been just twenty when Rosa acquired her land. His profession is given as *agricultor*, farmer, and hers as *quehacer doméstico*, meaning, loosely, "domestic worker doing whatever."

Was Juan a poor young man, an outsider in Cañar, who found opportunity in marrying an older woman who owned property? We've heard from Vicente that they have sold almost all Rosa's inherited land. We also heard that Juan bought a new truck with the money from our purchase in hopes of making a business. Did Juan pressure Rosa to sell the land, bit by bit, frittering away her windfall?

In this culture, land means everything: prestige, wealth, social belonging, and a legacy for your children. Here, you can have nothing *but* land and still be someone of consequence. We know that Rosa is left only with her house, the neighboring field, and the small triangular piece behind us. While the neighbors around them have built two- and three-story houses on land purchased from Rosa and Juan, the couple still lives with their three teenage children in a poor and cobbled-together adobe, tin, and cement-block house. They appear not to have prospered from Rosa's wealth in the form of land.

As I close the file, I feel sad. I wish these had not been the circumstances of our becoming property owners in Cañar.

~

JOURNAL, JANUARY 15

As I unpack and clean, I glance out the open gate and see a Cañari girl cautiously walking by and peering in. A few minutes later, she walks by again and I realize it is Paiwa, our beloved goddaughter. I call out to her and she comes shyly through the gate. Because it is Sunday, she is dressed in her best clothes—a bright wool skirt, embroidered blouse, a little cape pinned over her shoulders (called a *"lliglla"* in Quichua), elaborate necklace and dangling earrings, and a new round white hat. I give her a hug and we fall right into our old routine. She helps me make up the bed, politely comments on anything new we've brought (like the digital thermometer that reads 64.7), then occupies herself with games on my cellular telephone. My gifts for her will come out later.

We've known Paiwa since she was two, when we made our first return trip to Cañar to become her godparents. When she tells me she is ten years old and in fifth grade, I realize that she will be a petite adult, like almost all Cañari women. Until now, she has been tall for her age, the result of the good nutrition and care that comes from being an only child.

Later, Paiwa and I walk up to MegaMarket, Cañar's first little supermarket. It is full of country folks in town for Sunday market, buying with the dollars sent by husbands and sons and daughters in the United States. As we stand in the checkout line, I watch an old man ahead of us, dressed in a handwoven jerkin and pants. His body is bent from years of plowing and planting. He looks lost as the young woman behind the counter electronically scans the prices, rings up the balance, and quickly makes change while a helper bags the goods. The old man stands for a long moment staring at the coins in his hand, trying to take in his transformed world.

CHAPTER 3

How Much Will All This Cost?

~

Michael and architect Lourdes Abad

LAST JUNE, WHEN IT LOOKED like we were really going to buy the land, Michael made some quick sketches for a house and called an architect in Cuenca we knew slightly, Lourdes Abad. He asked her to come meet us and see the house site. An expert in adobe architecture, Lourdes had designed and overseen the construction of the beautiful three-story adobe house of our friend, Lynn Hirschkind. It was a visit to Lynn's house that convinced us Lourdes would be a good match for us, albeit for something a bit more modest. Our idea, inspired by our many visits to Mexico, was for a simple adobe house with an interior courtyard.

A few days later, Lourdes arrived at our gate in her little white Toyota pickup. We walked down to look at the land and then back to our house, where Michael made an espresso for Lourdes and laid out his simple drawings on the table. I had a meeting in town, so I left, saying I had total confidence that between the two of them they would come up with something perfect.

"I'm not so sure I can work with Lourdes," Michael said gloomily when I came home later that afternoon. "She said my square design was restrictive and proposed instead three offset rectangles that would allow for more windows, a more attractive entrance, and a more interesting layout."

"Hmm, sounds like a no-brainer," I said, which didn't endear me to Michael at the moment, but he went on to say he'd agreed when Lourdes offered to make her own drawings and come again.

During the next couple of meetings, Lourdes and Michael had some friendly stand-offs, but she continued to make improvements and adjustments that we liked. Michael wanted a big kitchen and I wanted a big studio, and, of course, the interior patio was a given, but beyond that the house would be fairly conventional, at least by North American standards: two bedrooms with baths, a laundry room, a *baño social* (half-bath for visitors), and an open living-dining-kitchen area.

We ended our last meeting with Lourdes with hugs and an agreement to work together via fax while we were back in Portland.

A contractor with many years' experience, Michael knows a thing or two about houses. He completely tore out and rebuilt our century-old Victorian house in Portland and renovated several other houses that we bought and sold during the nineties real estate boom. His specialty is the "mechanicals" of a house—electrical and plumbing systems—and the more complicated the challenge, the better he likes it.

During the next few months while we were in Portland, we faxed ideas back and forth with Lourdes until we agreed on a floor plan. With the final drawings in hand, we transferred money to her account in Cuenca and gave her the go-ahead to begin construction as soon as possible. We had no contract, and Lourdes had not yet charged us a dime, but each time we inquired about what we owed, she'd say, "Oh, we'll talk about that later."

Before we came back to Ecuador in January, Michael had shopped for plumbing and electrical parts unavailable in Ecuador, expecting to tackle his mechanicals during the next few months of construction. We even foolishly thought we might be able to move into the new house by the end of our six months. But on our first night back in Cañar, a quick phone conversation with Lourdes prepared us: the house was still on the drawing board. "I'll be there tomorrow to explain everything," she said.

Several days later, Lourdes had still not been able to make the two-hour drive from Cuenca because a strike of *transportistas*, mainly truck drivers, had blocked the Pan-American Highway. In Ecuador, it seems, every group with a complaint—be it workers, farmers, Indians, or students—calls attention to their cause by barricading or disrupting traffic on a major roadway. The Pan-American is an especially popular target, as it's the transportation artery running the length of Ecuador, connecting it with Colombia to the north and Peru to the south. Blocking it can paralyze the country until an issue is resolved. Each group has its own method. An indigenous *bloqueo* is almost always accomplished with boulders and trees rolled down from nearby hillsides and piled up across the road. Farmers and union workers march and block the streets with their banners and *pancartas* (placards). Students burn tires. Amazingly enough, protestors are rarely seriously hurt or killed. *Transportistas*, of course, used their trucks to block the highway, and I never learned what their issue was.

While we waited impatiently for Lourdes, Michael suffered agonizing fits of doubt and insecurity. "I can smell disaster coming," he said ominously one morning. Then, that afternoon: "This whole idea might have been a very large mistake." The next morning: "I'm sure we're in serious trouble here."

This "black-cloud thinking," as I call it, does not make Michael the most pleasant person to be around. But through our many years together I've learned to recognize this state as his emotional hedge against disaster: expect ruination, invite misfortune, dwell on the worst-case scenario, and things might just turn out all right. Although I didn't participate in Michael's glum game, I shared some of his doubts: Were we crazy trying to build a house so far from home? Was Lourdes the right partner for this project? Did these initial delays foreshadow an interminably long and expensive construction ordeal?

The second week, bad weather and thick fog made it too dangerous for Lourdes to drive over the mountains. We could only keep waiting.

Meanwhile, I escaped the gloom and doom at home and went on long rambling walks, taking particular notice of the country houses now that we too would be homeowners in Cañar. Fifteen years ago, when Michael and I first came to Cañar, the landscape was dotted with one- or two-story, plain adobe houses. Most consisted of a few rooms and separate kitchen within a walled compound for animals, without running water or any amenities other than electricity, sometimes wires strung from a neighbor's house. The families living in these traditional houses were largely indigenous farmers, following the seasonal cycles of planting and harvesting to provide enough to feed themselves with a little surplus to exchange in the market for other goods. Crops were corn, potatoes, peas, barley, and wheat. These country folks were poor, but their livelihoods were stable as long as the economy stayed steady.

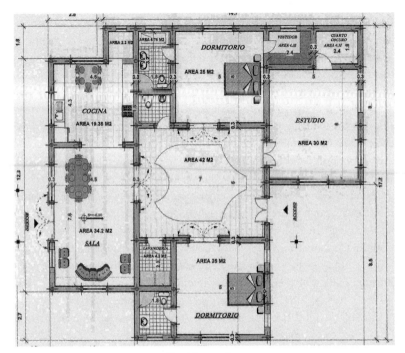

Final house plan

All that changed in the late nineties with catastrophic inflation, when small-scale agriculture could no longer support a family and men began to leave as migrants in search of work, followed by brothers, wives, sons, and daughters.

Now, the first thing a visitor notices is new but empty two-, three-, and sometimes four-story houses dotting the green fields, made of cement block and painted bright colors. These are *casas migrantes*, migrant houses built in stages as money is sent home from wages earned in restaurant kitchens in Manhattan, construction projects in New Jersey, cleaning hotel rooms in Madrid, or working fields in rural Spain. Distrustful of banks, with little agricultural land left to buy, and inexperienced in investments or business, the indigenous migrants put their money into what they understand best—a house to return to someday. Many are "trophy" houses built to impress the neighbors, with turrets and balconies, brightly painted on the outside, unfinished inside.

Michael and I are trying to do something different here—a simple one-story made with local materials. All we know so far from our conversations with Lourdes is that our adobe house will be labor-intensive and take much longer than the cement block houses we see go up around us in three or four months. I wonder if we have any idea what we are getting into.

~

Lourdes finally calls early one morning to say she is coming despite the continuing bad weather. Michael runs up to the market for fresh bananas to make banana bread. Then he opens the outer gate of our walled entrance and sits by the window with his electronic chess game where he can keep an eye on the street. He's relaxed a bit the last couple of days, and I don't hear any more predictions of imminent ruin.

About ten thirty, Lourdes pulls up in her little truck and climbs out with her arms full of sheaves of plans, a shy smile on her round face.

"*Al fin*," I say, as I stoop down to give her a hug. The first thing you notice about Lourdes is that she is tiny—maybe four feet ten—and then you immediately forget it because her presence is anything but small. A graduate of the University of Cuenca and expert in earthen architecture, Lourdes has directed the conversion of many historic buildings and churches in the region to museums and cultural spaces. She's even busier as a restoration architect since the city of Cuenca was declared a UNESCO World Heritage City in 1999.

Michael makes coffee and serves his banana bread while Lourdes apologetically explains the delay in starting the construction. She recounts the long frustrating drama of trying to find in Cañar an experienced *maestro* (foreman)

A traditional bahareque *house*

whom she felt she could trust. She was waiting for one builder she knows to finish a job, but it was taking much longer than anticipated. Finally, she said, she decided to simply wait until we came back to begin. This is her first time doing a project in Cañar, and she is being cautious.

Rolling out her papers on the table, Lourdes shows us a site plan, elevations, and detailed architectural drawings. To begin, she says, a geotechnical engineer made a soil analysis, and his tests revealed that the subsoil on our land is not the right consistency for making adobe bricks. This means we will not have the traditional adobe house we had hoped for.

Instead, Lourdes proposes we build a *bahareque* house, which consists of a post-and-beam timber frame and walls made of mud and straw. She explains that the hand-tamped walls of the house will be made with a special mixture of clay-like "white" earth, organic-rich "black" earth, and fine straw. After the walls have dried—which usually takes a month—the exterior and interior walls will be finished with a mixture of mud, straw, and fermented horse manure.

"The result will look just like a house made with adobe blocks," Lourdes says, looking at us expectantly. "Warm and quiet," she adds as Michael and I sit silent, trying to take all this in.

"This sounds just like an architectural cousin of old wattle and daub," I finally say. "You know, like the houses in Jane Austen's books, where walls were built of woven wooden strips—that's the wattle—with a plaster made of lime and cow dung—the daub. I think it was in *Sense and Sensibility* where I read . . ." I trail off as Lourdes looks at me quizzically.

"Or the lath and plaster walls of our house in Portland," Michael jumps in. He's recalling the months we spent tearing out two floors of the original walls that were made entirely of thin fir strips and plaster mixed with horsehair.

Lourdes looks impatient and goes on to explain that a *bahareque* house will be better for several reasons. Number one is flexibility and stability. Ecuador, with the highest concentration of active volcanoes in the world, is a geologically unstable country. Though we rarely have earthquakes in Cañar, minute tectonic movements and frequent small tremors cause old adobe houses to crack, shift, and sometimes come tumbling down. We've certainly seen plenty of those. A *bahareque* house won't be vulnerable to seismic activity, Lourdes points out, and anyway the large rooms of our plan call for longer wall spans than adobe block walls could safely support.

As it grows late and time for Lourdes to leave, Michael hesitantly asks, "About how much do you think the whole project might cost?" She sits silent for a long moment with an inscrutable look before saying gravely, "Well, that depends on the decisions you make now . . . and down the road."

"But couldn't we have—you know—a rough estimate?" Michael laughs nervously. "Just to give us an idea, for planning . . . maybe we'll have to go home and get full-time jobs . . . ha, ha."

Another long pause, during which I have a vision of Michael going back to work as a contractor in Portland, and me dusting off my old social work résumé. Lourdes looks pained. "I'll try to give you an idea of the budget in the next week or so," she finally says.

(Later, I learn more about Lourdes that helps explain her ambivalence about money matters. One of eight children in a socially elite but not wealthy Cuenca family, she is maybe in her mid-forties and single. As is the custom with unmarried adults, she still lives in the family home with two other single, middle-aged siblings. Their parents are dead. Lourdes leads a simple domestic life, with her office on the street level and her bedroom off the rooftop terrace. She has many friends, mostly fellow architects, unmarried or divorced women her age, and her clients. Like many refined Cuencanos, Lourdes abhors discussions about money, feeling, I suppose, that "grace and beauty" come first.

Lynn gave us a more realistic clue about costs last year: she said that Ecuadorian architects generally act as their own contractors, and charge a percentage of the final costs. So we assume Lourdes wants to wait to see how it all adds up. Still, we need to have to have *some* idea before we begin.)

After Lourdes leaves, Michael is completely transformed, his confidence in our architect and in the project restored. "Let's go into town, buy a long tape measure, and go figure out the layout of the house," he says ebulliently. After the days of waiting and worrying, Michael is full of energy and optimism, wanting to do something tangible to get started. Though I never shared his deepest doubts, I am infected by his enthusiasm and am too of a mind to mark the moment with a positive gesture.

We hike into town to the hardware store, buy a fifty-foot tape measure, come back by the house to pick up the plans, a few stakes, and a roll of red twine and walk down to the land.

Meanwhile, ominous dark clouds are rolling up from the west and the day has turned suddenly cold.

"Here's where the kitchen will be and there's the dining and living room," Michael says as we stand in the middle of our field, but his broad gestures seem to take in the whole valley and mountains beyond. "Oh yes, of course," I respond vaguely, but I am having a hard time focusing, with so much undefined space. We try pacing off the rooms in the scrubby corn stalks. Michael makes measurements and lays down a few lengths of twine, but it's hard to make sense of thin lines of red twine lying crooked amidst the weeds and lumps of black soil. Also, the weather has turned really nasty, with dense fog settling around us like a cold blanket.

A distinct difference between Michael and me is that he can visualize in three dimensions—how a set of bookshelves will look, a garden landscape, an addition—but I simply cannot. I need a physical model—a miniature Styrofoam house with removable roof, changeable walls, doll furniture, tiny trees. (I made one of these, minus the doll furniture, for the house in Portland when we were preparing to move it from its original site to a new lot.)

My only impression from this exercise is that the house might be too close to a neighbor's property line, which leads to a short, tense discussion between us, but will ultimately result in the house being set back a few extra feet.

Soon a fine drizzle is falling, with sporadic showers. I try to be cheerful and helpful, but really I'm miserable, cold, and wet. Soon visibility is down to about twenty feet and darkness is falling.

Michael agrees we've had enough. We trudge back up the hill, feeling a little dispirited. Once home, I make tea, go upstairs to our bedroom, and climb onto the bed with my laptop and books. Michael comes up, changes out of his wet clothes, and joins me with his chess game. I put some music on iTunes (Bach fugues, reflecting our state of mind and the weather), and we settle with a mutual sigh into this cozy cocoon and forget for a while that we are trying to build a house in a faraway land.

~

JOURNAL, JANUARY 20

The road is rutted, as always, the houses poor and old, and even the newer migrant houses already look old. As we dip down the hill and approach the compound of our old friend, Mama Michi, we hardly recognize the place. Where is her thatched-roof kitchen, her rickety two-story adobe with the outside stairway (where I came for that first meeting in Cañar so many years ago)? What happened to the field beside her house? And where is her mother's old falling-down house that used to sit on the hill above? All gone. We find a path from the road, and as we walk in Michael calls out, "Wasiiio-oooooo . . . ." (Roughly equivalent to "Anyone home?") A small boy runs into view, looks at us in alarm, disappears, and a couple of minutes later Mama Michi appears.

"Where are we? We're lost," I say, mock plaintively. "So many changes!" I gesture at all the new buildings in and around her compound. Mama Michi grins her special grin, the front teeth gone now, and says, "You're here! *Que milagro*! Come in!"

Michael and I take turns bending down for an awkward embrace with Mama Michi, barely four feet eight, and step into her earthen courtyard. At last, I see the original L-shaped adobe house, the old kitchen on one side— its thatched roof now replaced with clay tiles—and the attached small two-story section where Mama Michi sleeps, or slept. I recall when it had an earthen floor, and how proud she was when she could afford a wooden floor once she began working as a *curandera*, a healer, and her fame began to bring in clients from near and far. I feel comforted by the familiar row of dried corn *choclos* hanging by the entrance to her room.

Two wooden chairs appear in the courtyard and Michael and I take our places, squinting into the afternoon sun. Children run in and out of door-ways. Mama Michi sits on a low step to the old kitchen, stringing red beads for a necklace.

I ask her the purpose of the new buildings.

"Well, that one is my *jambi hausi*," she says, gesturing at the largest struc-ture, a long one-story that adjoins her original adobe house. "My healing center, where I do my nighttime work with patients. I built that just after my mother died. And that one is the new kitchen, and Serafín and his wife and child live above it." She gestures at a small building across from us. "And that's where Pablo and Narcisa and their little girl live," she nods toward an expanded second floor of her original house.

I don't get a chance to ask Mama Michi where she sleeps in these new arrangements, but by the time she finishes, I have counted fourteen family members living with her, including two daughters, two sons, two daughters-in-law, and eight grandchildren.

As the sun goes down Mama Michi invites us into the new kitchen, a concrete-floored room with a sink, running water, and gas stove. She turns to Michael and asks with mock disbelief, "You wouldn't want a beer, would you?" She sends one of her grandsons to the little storefront down the road for beer while her daughter Zoila bustles around the gas stove, cooking potatoes and boiling eggs for our dinner.

CHAPTER 4

Construction Begins, *Poco a Poco*

~

Plowing in Shayac Rumi

CONSTRUCTION ON OUR NEW HOUSE finally gets underway on a Monday in late January 2006, four months, three weeks, and two days later than we had hoped. The months were those lost while we were in Portland, assuming that Lourdes was breaking ground and getting started. The three weeks was the time lapsed since we arrived in Ecuador, waiting for Lourdes, held up by bad weather and a strike, to get here from Cuenca and the days spent while Michael was hiring a *maestro*, rounding up a construction crew, and buying tools.

But it was the last two-day delay that reminded me where we are and how things will likely go while we try to build a house in the Andes.

On the day before work is to start, our newly hired *maestro*, Belesario, explains that the first rainy season of the highland year is about to begin, which means it is time to plow and plant corn or potatoes. Most Cañaris, no matter what other jobs they have, still live on agricultural time, and planting, weeding, irrigating, and harvesting take precedence over all other responsibilities.

So, as with their fathers, grandfathers, and great-grandfathers and going back centuries before that, Belesario and the workers spend several days preparing their fields with hand-hewn wooden plows pulled by yoked bulls. As the rows are harrowed, wives and daughters walk behind, heavy wool skirts tucked up and full of seed corn or small potatoes, which they drop into the ground. Sometimes toddlers sit on the edge of the field, watched over by a slightly older child or a grandparent. I've photographed this scene many times over the years, sharing in the midday meal of warm boiled potatoes, fava beans, hot sauce, with drinks in plastic cups poured from big bottles of Sprite and Coca-Cola. If it is a cold day (almost always), the men and women take a few shots of Zhumir, *aguardiente*, to warm up their bones before going back to work.

The following Monday, the five-man crew that shows up ready to work includes Belesario and his son, Pablo; José María, who will be second *maestro*; José María's brother, Santos; Santos's son, Manuel; and two young workers named Francisco and Ricardo, also related to Belesario, but I lost track of how. Apparently, when you hire a *maestro* in Cañar, he comes with a crew of neighbors and family members.

This is fine with us. Michael and I are strangers to the construction game in Cañar, and we need to trust that things will work in our favor. I think nepotism is an article of faith in this Latino world, where survival still depends on extended family members helping one another. (In fact, nepotism comes from the Latin word *nepos*, meaning "nephew.") If you have the good luck to get a job, the thinking goes, why would you *not* hire a relative if you had the chance?

Part of our security is trusting in old friends. José María, the first man Michael hired, is someone we've known slightly since our first year living in Cañar. (He and his family appear in "The Meeting," a chapter in *Cañar: A Year in the Highlands of Ecuador*.) He lives in the next hamlet over, Correucu, with his wife, Narcisa, and three young daughters—Lourdes, Sara, and María. The family is very poor, even by local standards. They have a small section of land where they plant the usual crops of corn, potatoes, and peas, and they also have a small store next to their house where neighbors stop in to buy soap, colas, cigarettes, beer, and sweets. Traditionally, José María is a weaver—like his father—and his wife, a seamstress and embroiderer, but it's impossible to make a living as *artesanos* these days, with the markets full of machine-made goods. He lost an eye in an incident in 1994 when conflict between the mestizos and the Cañari community led to the indigenous center being burned down by the townsfolk. José María was inside when a window exploded. I suspect this sweet timid man only works on construction between plantings and harvests, or when the family is desperate for money.

It was José María who suggested to Michael that his Cañari neighbor, Belesario, would be a good *maestro*. The two men came to the house one morning soon after our meeting with Lourdes. Both seemed nearly desperate for work, and the prospect of a weekly wage for a long construction project close to home would be a great stroke of luck. With a kindly round face under his worn white hat, Belesario is probably in his early forties. Quiet, confident, and well spoken, he told us he has been the *maestro* on several large projects around here, including the *casa comunal*, or community center, that serves as school and meeting place in our little hamlet, Chaglaban. "I've been doing this for twenty years," he added modestly. With a handshake, it was agreed: Belesario would be our number one *maestro*, with José María number two.

Michael and Lourdes agree to oversee the construction together. This is an unusual arrangement here in Ecuador, where the architect is almost always the general contractor. But Lourdes has never had a project in Cañar, and she feels at a disadvantage, being two hours away in Cuenca. So it makes sense for Michael, experienced in construction and living near the site, to be the daily foreman and handle the workers and the weekly payroll.

On Tuesday, anxious to get started, Belesario walks into town and brings back a "blade man," who, in a mere two hours, levels a spot for the house with his bulldozer. Total cost: sixty dollars. Michael comes home later that afternoon, excited from watching the big machine at work. "You won't believe how much earth this guy moved around in such a short time!" he says. "You gotta come down and see it!"

But once we stand on the road looking at the mountains of black topsoil ringing the hillside lot, Michael's excitement turns to worry. Have the workers been hasty with the excavation? Isn't that grade too radical for a single-story house? Shouldn't someone have staked out a guide for the blade man? Will we need a large retaining wall? Michael is suddenly sure he's made a mistake with the first stage of our house.

"Lourdes should have been here to direct it," he says, frowning. "The *maestro* didn't even have the plans at hand or know what was going on. I don't think this is going to work with the architect in Cuenca and the construction in Cañar. We might even have to start over!" Despair settles around him like a heavy cloak.

Though my impulse is to say, "Let's just fill it back in . . . the dirt is still there," I know by now not to offer a logical solution when Michael is in a black-cloud state. Best to wait for the storm to pass.

We trudge slowly back up the hill to our house. Michael calls Lourdes to say he is afraid he's been premature with the excavation. She calmly gives him two directives: (1) stop work until she can come, and (2) buy two cell phones, one for himself and one for the workers so she can communicate directly with them. That seems a common-sense response to me, but Michael doesn't calm down, and we spend a tense night as he frets and grumbles that we are off to a disastrous start.

On Wednesday morning, Lourdes comes to Cañar and gives us a preview of how she will handle the many construction crises to come. She looks over the excavation and says reassuringly that it is fine. She and the engineer will make some adjustments to accommodate the new slope of the lot. "Maybe the house will have to be split level, but in any case, we're going to need a bigger foundation wall." After a pause she adds matter-of-factly, "And that means the house will cost more."

She turns to the *maestros*, standing anxiously by, and directs them to put in stakes, stretch strings, and lay down chalk lines so the workers can begin digging the foundation footings. I hear Michael give a big sigh of relief. Someone else is in charge, at least for the moment.

Lourdes, Michael, and I go back to the house for a serious, long-overdue talk about our budget. Sitting around the table with coffee, Michael starts by saying that we can't spend more than sixty or seventy thousand, period. Lourdes doesn't change expression, but only goes on to talk about the cost in parts: how much the concrete will cost, the wood, the labor, the finish carpentry. Listening, I realize that Lourdes is not accustomed to providing a global budget for a project before it begins, and when I mention this, she says simply, "Yes, it *is* hard."

The two of them go on to make a schedule for Lourdes's visits to the construction site—three times a week to begin and while the foundation is being laid—and they agree on the salaries for the *maestros* and workers (called "*oficiales*," the local term for skilled workers, instead of *obreros*, which means common laborers.) All this helps to clarify things—except, of course, how much the total house will cost. But I can see that Michael feels better, so we don't mention the budget again.

~

But then we have one more delay that first week, Thursday being a holiday to celebrate Cañar as the *Capital Arqueológico y Cultural del Ecuador*. This new municipal fiesta—a blatant civic attempt to boost local pride and attract a bit of tourism—has recently been added to the already overcrowded pantheon of saints' days, independence days, famous-battles-won days, civic anniversary days, and other legal and religious holidays that routinely break up the work week and school year. Fiestas mean drinking, and drinking naturally leads to being *chuchaki*—hungover—so Michael gives everyone Thursday and Friday off.

The second week, construction speeds up, although it does not begin auspiciously. Monday morning, Michael goes down to find the workers standing around idle. "We left our tools with the *señora*," Belesario says, gesturing to a house down the road, "and she is gone and her house is locked." Why hadn't someone come to the house to tell Michael? He holds his tongue, charges home, grabs some money from the filing cabinet, and goes into town to buy a wheelbarrow and three shovels. Later that afternoon, when I walk down to the site, I see all the workers leveling the huge mountain of earth that the blade man had piled too high on one corner.

The next day Michael works alongside the workers to build a shed for the tools and materials; no more relying on neighbors. He comes home at five thirty, sunburned, exhausted, with aching muscles and blisters, but exhilarated. "Oh, how I love these physical manifestations of progress," he says as he sits down with a beer.

Lourdes with chalk outline of the house

On Wednesday, the workers begin digging trenches for the foundation walls, called *"cementaciones."* (I'm trying to learn all these new Spanish construction terms, but this one puzzles me; it reminds me of *cementerio*, cemetery.) It is around now, I think, that Michael tells me that the house is going to be "rather larger" than we had originally envisioned, but I still can't visualize it and I am too busy with other things to stop and consider.

By Thursday, big dump trucks labor down our potholed road to deliver load after load of large river rocks to fill the foundation trenches, plus gravel to go on top of the river rocks, and then sand and gravel to fill in the muddy entrance to the building site so heavy trucks can keep coming in.

One night, as Michael sits at the table studying the plans, he says, "Hmmm, it looks like Lourdes has cramped the bathrooms too tight." He finds his calculator and does some measurements. "Yes, there's no way we can get a shower in there. I'll just move the bedroom wall over a half meter." Michael, master plumber, loves bathrooms. We have three in our modest-sized Portland house, plus a tiny WC secreted in a bedroom closet. In our Cañar house, we will have a full bath in each bedroom and a smaller *baño social* off the courtyard for visitors. This is a total luxury here, where some country houses have a simple outhouse or latrine, and many still have none, as the custom is to use the surrounding woods and fields, a practice that makes hygienic sense when one has no running water.

In Lourdes's original plans, the doorways were narrow, the ceilings low, and the rooms relatively small. This reflected not only her diminutive size, but also a general penchant of Ecuadorians for cozy rooms and spaces. Maybe it's the climate. In colonial Cuenca and through the nineteenth century, upper-class sitting rooms had small cupboard-like alcoves with doors to give privacy and warmth to courting couples and old arthritic aunts. Or maybe it's simply a matter of scale: if one is four feet ten, as is Lourdes, the American standard of an eight-foot ceiling feels way too high.

I read somewhere that the architect Frank Lloyd Wright designed his buildings to fit "normal" height and body dimensions, based on himself. "I took the human being, at five feet eight and a half inches tall, like myself, as the human scale," he reportedly told his students. "If I had been taller, the scale might have been different." This attitude did not sit well with many of Wright's contemporaries, one who referred to his "sadistically low ceilings." Another said to him, "Whenever I walk into one of your buildings, the doorways are so low my hat gets knocked off," to which Wright calmly replied, "Take off your hat when you come into a house."

Michael's height is just that of Wright, but having grown up in cramped fifties and sixties houses, he says he has always preferred spaces proportionally larger than his body. He loves the extravagance of the ten-foot ceilings in our Victorian house in Portland, even though the rooms themselves are not large.

I'm five feet six inches, and having grown up in small postwar houses in small-town Colorado, I didn't even know ten-foot ceilings existed—anywhere! But I too am drawn to open interior spaces. One of my favorite homes was a spacious turn-of-the-century duplex in Toronto where my son and I lived for ten years. With storefronts at street level and two story apartments above, the rooms were in a row, opening off a long hallway, but large with high ceilings and fine finish details.

In the end, Lourdes agrees to make the bathrooms larger, the ceilings higher, and every doorway the American standard of two feet wide and eighty inches high. But a future friendly squabble will be over the countertops in the kitchen. Michael will argue they must be his standard of thirty-six inches, but Lourdes can't conceive of such height that, for her, would make the work surface at chest-level. Of course, Michael will win that one too: the long granite countertops of both sides of the kitchen will be the American standard of thirty-six inches.

~

On Friday, the first payday, Michael is the paymaster. In preparation, he notes the figures in a notebook and makes little cash envelopes for each worker. The crew is coming to our house after work, and by five o'clock we are ready. Michael has asked me to be present to add both formality and friendliness to the occasion. The workers come shyly through the door, apologize for their muddy boots, and sit down on our wooden chairs and benches, hands between their knees. Michael hands out the money packets and makes a short speech, saying that because they had done such a good job this first week he is raising everyone's pay beginning next week. In turn, he requests that they arrive promptly at eight in the morning. Nods all around.

He asks if anyone had *quejas*—complaints—or suggestions. One young worker, Pablo, Belesario's son, speaks up to say that he too is a *maestro* and therefore should receive more in his pay packet. I see Michael's eyebrows rise, but Belesario confirms with a nod that his son is more skilled than the other three youths. Michael looks puzzled at suddenly having another *maestro*, but he hands over the extra money and says jokingly, "The first *queja*." Nobody laughs. Finally, we stand up and formally shake hands all around, each of us saying in turn, "*Hasta lunes*," until Monday.

Our Cañar house is under way at last.

~

JOURNAL, JANUARY 21

I've been asked for the first time to photograph the Fiesta de San Antonio by the village leaders of Junducuchu, high on a mountain above Cañar, and I'm thrilled. Junducuchu is a conservative, traditional community, and I could never take photos of the annual three-day folk/religious fiesta without a special invitation. Pedro Solano, a teacher and one of the leaders, told me to come to the church on the town square on Saturday *medio día*, midday, but beyond that I know nothing.

Come Saturday, I find a few men and boys sitting on the steps of the church. Scattered and resting on the ground around them is a collection of giant mask-like affairs called *"vacas locas"* (literally, mad cows), constructed from wood and leather, with papier-mâché heads and horns and tails made of horse hair. I know the men and boys will carry them over their heads and dance as they lead the procession up the mountain

At the church entrance, an old man with a small *tambor*, a drum, and another man holding a *dulcena*, a small reed flute that sounds a bit like an oboe, begin to play. Immediately, the *vacas locas* get up and dance in the plaza in front of the church, swinging their masks this way and that, sometimes grunting and snorting and chasing bystanders. The older men especially enjoy playing the role of pursuer. One in particular has taken notice of me and grabs me roughly from behind as I take a photo. He appears to be already a little *pegado*, the local term for inebriated, and I remind myself to stay out of his way.

Then, incredibly, I see an entire brass band gathering on the other side of the church entrance: three trumpets, three trombones, a bass drum, and a snare drum. People gather around, and as the band begins to play, there's a flurry at the church entrance and two young women emerge, swinging charcoal burners with incense, followed by two older women, one carrying a tiny statue of San Antonio in a wooden box with a glass window. She has a white shawl wrapped around her shoulders and tied at the bottom of the box. The procession starts around the square at a fast march, and I run to keep up. I know we're headed up the mountain and I have a long day ahead.

CHAPTER 5

"You're Going to Live *Here*?"

~

Cañar center

"YOU'RE GOING TO LIVE *here*, in *Cañar*?" the young woman behind glass at the Empresa Eléctrica asks, her white-painted eyelids emphasizing her incredulous look. To answer, I have to bend down to speak through the tiny half-moon window at my waist level. "Yes, we're building a house here. That's why we need an electrical meter."

As she pushes some documents through the opening, she turns to her friend at the next window and says, *sotto voce*, "These gringos are coming to live in Cañar!"

She might have added, "Can you believe it?"

I think it's safe to assume that no one not tied to Cañar by birth, a job, or other special circumstances would choose to settle in this homely, chilly high-land town of southern Ecuador. Michael and I are the only foreigners in town, by choice, and an enigma to all. Many Ecuadorian acquaintances from other places ask, "*Why?*" And even after we cite our history here, my interesting work with the indigenous community, a landscape we love, long-standing friends, and a simpler lifestyle that suits us, we usually get a stunned moment of silence followed by, "But do you really *like* Cañar?"

Although if you were passing through this place today, with the clear blue sky, warm air, lush fields rippling with ripening grain, and the fantastic view of the mountains rising up all around, you would think, as I do at this moment, leaving the Empresa Eléctrica, "What a beautiful place to live!"

~

When Michael and I arrived a month ago to begin our first Cañar "half life," we moved back into the same small house we had rented last year and where we will live while we build the new house. During the six months we were gone, two American anthropologists, Jason Pribilsky and Suzanne Morrissey, and their four-year-old son, Jacob, lived here while they did research in Cañar. They left just before Christmas, and we came back in January to find everything neatly in place: the unpainted tables, benches, and chairs; the heavy wooden beds that Michael made last year; the dishes and pots and pans; and the fridge, gas cooker, and countertop oven. Dust everywhere, for it has been the dry season, but otherwise it is a sweet comfortable house to come back to. A "soft landing," I called it, remembering other times we've arrived in Cañar and had to stay in local hostels with miniature rooms, stone-hard beds, head-knocking doorways, and bathrooms down the hall.

Our little house sits smack against a hillside at the rear of a narrow walled-in lot, facing a rough cobblestone street in a twenty-year-old neighborhood on the edge of town called, strangely enough, Ñucanchi Wasi, Quichua for "our house," the same name as the indigenous center in town. Of course, no Quichua-speaking families live here, for this is a mestizo community, as is every residential area within town. Indigenous people have always lived in the countryside, with their land, crops, and animals, and I'm sure most still prefer it that way. But since the town of Cañar was established, systemic racism and de facto exclusion has meant that practically no indigenous person—obviously indigenous by appearance, I should say—has lived inside the town. (Of course, given that mestizo means "mixed race," many, if not all, townspeople have indigenous ancestors.)

In our house, one long room downstairs serves as kitchen, dining, and living room, with a bank of east-facing windows that provides plenty of morning light and welcome solar heat. Everything important takes place in this *sala*. When Michael is not cooking or at the construction site, he sits at an oilcloth-covered table with his chessboard, Sudoku book, house plans, or the plumbing parts he has brought from Portland. He studies these parts as he would a puzzle and imagines how they'll fit under the floors and inside walls to connect to sinks and toilets and showers.

I usually work at an adjacent table, which looks like a mini-office with two laptops, notebooks, books, pens, clips, colored pencils, CDs, address book, cameras, and cell phone. The *sala* is also home to a prized asset in Cañar: a working telephone that came with the house. A ridiculous, flimsy, bright turquoise thing, it hangs precariously on the wall, is often out of service, and rarely rings, but there it hangs, just in case.

When Paiwa, our ten-year-old goddaughter, drops by after school, she crowds in with me to do her homework, or she'll sit at Michael's table and he'll show her how to play chess. When she's studying geography in school, he explains continental drift with the help of the map of the world on the wall. ("You mean Africa was connected to South America?" she asks, eyes wide.

Paiwa and Michael playing chess

"*No es posible!*") It's a cozy space, and a pot of potatoes boiling on the stove or a pan of lasagna in Michael's countertop oven is enough to keep us warm when the sun goes down. At mealtime, we have to clear one or the other of the tables.

Step out the door into the patio and on your right, against one wall, you'll see a two-part concrete sink, common to almost every household around here. One side is a deep well for storing water, the other a shallow basin for hand-washing clothes, with a built-in washboard to scrape your knuckles. Across the patio sits a freestanding tiny structure—the bathroom, with baby blue toilet and sink and a homemade tile shower. An executioner's switch with dangling cords inside the shower provides hot water. Mild shocks are common. Next to the bathroom, a half-spiral stairway runs up to a second-floor balcony, which gives access to two small bedrooms. Think motel. Total size of the house: about five hundred square feet.

On the flat roof of the bathroom sits a blue plastic water storage tank, affectionately called a "*chancho*," pig, because it is squat and round. Anyone who can afford it has a *chancho* because otherwise you are dependent on the city's limited water supply, erratic service, and the seasonal weather cycles (dry season = severely rationed water). During the night, city water lines open and fill the overhead tank. In the morning, the water is shut off. Gravity provides the water until the tank is empty. I was reminded of this the other morning when I foolishly washed clothes, watered the flowers, filled the patio sink, and then discovered we were out of water until the next day.

Taken at a glance from the street, the place looks like half a house or, as Michael says, as though someone started building and decided to finish it off quickly without adding the front half. Two ugly columns left standing alone, topped by rusting strands of rebar, attest to something having happened! Our landlady, Doña Hilda, later tells us the house belongs to her son, Telmo, and he did indeed leave, mid-construction, to work on other projects, intending to come back, add other rooms and move in. Lucky for us he didn't, because rental houses are not easy to find in Cañar.

Nonetheless, Cañar is experiencing a construction boom like it's never seen before. All around us we hear hammers, drills, and chisels against stone, usually accompanied by radios at full volume to keep workers entertained.

In my daily walks into town, I see old adobe houses being flattened and hauled away in a day, and new buildings of brick or concrete block begun immediately. I step around piles of sand and gravel—workers even use the streets to mix mounds of fresh concrete, forcing cars to drive around.

Three or four months later, most buildings are complete with metal roofs and blue opaque glass windows, an architectural touch that's all the rage at the moment. Other structures take years of stop-and-go work to finish, with boarded-up doors and windows and rusting lines of rebar swinging above.

This construction fever is almost entirely a consequence of money sent home by migrants in the United States, Spain, Italy, Venezuela, and Chile. The 1960s and 70s saw a trickle of emigration from southern Ecuador, mostly to the eastern United States. The great wave that affected Cañar province and the indigenous communities took off around the year 2000, when a perfect storm of uncontrollable inflation, soaring unemployment and poverty rates, and a devastating El Niño caused Ecuador's economy to collapse, banks to fail, the government to default on its foreign debt, and the president to resign, but not before switching the country's currency to the U.S. dollar.

It is estimated that nearly a million Ecuadorians left the country in the next five years, 10-15 percent of the population, and dollars sent home to parents, children, and spouses have utterly transformed the national and local economy. In 2006, the Inter-American Development Bank estimated these funds at two billion dollars, behind oil exports but ahead of tourism and bananas.

On Sundays in Cañar, when country people come to town for market, the bright yellow Western Union office just off the square has lines of people out the door and up the street. The famous telegraph company, established in the United States in 1855, has found a new mission in Latin America as a "financial services and communications company." SEND MONEY is the first item on their website; RECEIVE MONEY, the second. Local banks, seeing an opportunity, have also started offering money transfer services, treating indigenous clients with respect for the first time, and even hiring a Quichua-speaking clerk. The other day, as I stood in line at one bank, I witnessed a scene I've seen many times before: a Cañari man, with his wife and two young children standing by, withdrew what must have been thousands of dollars. They stepped aside and the man counted every bill before the bulky packet disappeared into the depths of the woman's wool skirts.

~

Yesterday, when I stopped by the healing center of my old friend, Mama Michi, I gave her and her assistant Beatriz an update on our house construction. They listened raptly, then had a short discussion between them in Quichua before Mama Michi turned to me: "Beatriz wants to know if you are preparing a meal for the workers every day?"

"Are you kidding?" I answered, or the equivalent in Spanish, *¿Estás en serio?* "Of course not!"

"Yes, it's a big sacrifice," Mama Michi sighed, "and a big expense. But that is the custom here. When one is building a house, the woman is required to fix lunch for the laborers as long as the construction lasts—three, four, five months." Later, when I mentioned this to Michael he said that's why he gave everyone a raise last week, so that they can buy their own lunches or have their wives bring them to the worksite.

I may not fix lunches, but I do have my uses. When we needed a water meter on the house site, I followed instructions from the secretary at the water company and camped out on the office steps one morning before eight o'clock to grab "*Ingeniero* Sergio." I brought him down to the site for an inspection and he told us exactly what we had to do before we could have a water meter: dig a trench to the "matrix" at the top of the hill, lay in half-inch flexible pipe, build a wall to hang a water meter, buy and mount the box for the meter. "Then we'll come and hook up the water," said *Ingeniero* Sergio. That was a good day's work.

And I was certainly a critical player in the electrical meter affair. I went back to the Empresa Electrica again and again with money and documents, as requested by the young woman with the white-painted eyelids. This included a certificate from the municipality declaring that our property is free of debt, an advance payment of our property taxes ($18.42), copies of the deed, a copy of Michael's passport, and payment of nine dollars for an electrical inspection. After another inspection next week, I'll go back to pay for the meter and—the gods willing and no more documents required—someone will come to install an electrical box on the tool shed.

Electricity and water service taken care of, next I get to tackle the complicated issue of a telephone for the new house. According to Doña Valvina, my contact at the telephone company, there have been no new residential phone lines available in Cañar for about five years. Until last week, that is, when I missed getting in on a lottery for new lines. I was in Cuenca and simply forgot. Someone who didn't forget later described it: "The forms were available for only a few hours, and it was like fighting for tickets to a rock concert."

"Too bad you didn't come," Doña Valvina said in the tone of a stern teacher. "Now you'll have to go to the main office in Azogues, before eight o'clock, and wait for *Ingeniero* Filipe. Maybe he can help you get on the list."

But, then again, maybe I won't go. Do we really need a telephone this year, or next? We are often without service for our silly little turquoise phone hanging on the wall in our rental house, and anyway I rather enjoy the peaceful life without it.

~

JOURNAL, FEBRUARY 6

Another wet, chilly, foggy day in a stretch of erratic weather.

Late morning, I get a phone call from Hollywood—yes, Hollywood, California! It was not totally unexpected, however, as a producer named Bob Fitzgerald had been in touch by e-mail, having found me on the web by searching "Cañar." He is developing a screenplay that involves some Cañari history (or maybe myth) and had arranged to call me today with questions.

"Think Indiana Jones," he says as an opener. According to legend, in 1533, when the conquistador Francisco Pizarro was holding the Inca leader Atahualpa prisoner in Cajamarca, Peru, a group of Cañaris was called upon to bring a cargo of gold to help pay the ransom.

The story goes that when the Cañaris heard that Pizarro had broken the agreement by executing Atahualpa (after first baptizing him as a Christian), they dumped the gold into Lake Ayllón, on the Inca Trail about a day's walk from present-day Cañar, and went home.

Later, gold-hungry conquistadors heard of the treasure and even tried to dig a canal to drain the lake, but no gold was ever found. The myth persists today that the gold is still in the lake, and some say it carries a curse against those who would try to find it.

So much for the backstory. Fitzgerald says his script will spin a tale—half truth, half fiction—around an ill-fated 1997 French-American expedition, led by Cañari guides, to look for the gold. The leader of the expedition had a heart attack and was airlifted out, leaving behind the other members of the group. The weather turned nasty, the left-behind folks got word that an angry group of locals was coming to cause trouble, and they called the helicopter back to save them. The helicopter came, but fell into the lake, and the Cañari guides helped to save everyone.

An improbable narrative for a film? Yes, but I liked this guy. He asked intelligent questions, and at least he's trying to get some history of the Cañari right. I said I would go visit the village of Sigsig, nearest to the lake, and take some photos for him.

Otherwise, a quiet, productive day. Evening alone with Michael, who made a delicious spinach/egg pie for dinner, and I recorded the recipe while it was fresh in his mind.

CHAPTER 6

The Lives of the Workers

~

Belesario, Santos, and Rosa

EARLY ONE AFTERNOON, I walk down to the construction site with garden-ing tools, intending to spend a pleasant couple of hours watering and doing battle with the weeds in my little patch of struggling bushes. It's a futile exercise, with so many workers tromping around, but it helps me feel a part of the pro-cess. And I like to take photographs of the work in progress.

Rosa, Maestro Belesario's wife, is there. She's brought her husband's lunch, as she does most days, and probably helped out a bit on the site, as she likes to do. Now she sits on a pile of sand, enjoying the sun and looking very pretty in her bright skirts, multiple sweaters, and white hat. She greets me with a shy smile and offers to help when she sees what I'm up to. As we work, we chat, as women do, and I gather all sorts of interesting information. She tells me that Francisco, a quiet young worker who has not shown up for work this week, is her brother. We'd known he was a relative of one of the *maestros*, as are all the workers, but we didn't know how he fit into the family constellations.

"Francisco won't be coming anymore," Rosa says matter-of-factly. "He left for the *Yonny* today."

It takes me a moment get it. At first I think she is saying that Francisco has gone to visit someone named Johnny. Then I remember that "the *Yonny*" is local jargon for New York, easier to say in Spanish than "Nuevo York." Rosa is telling me that her young brother has embarked on the long and dangerous trip north as an illegal migrant. He is seventeen.

Rosa points to another teenage worker and says he's her son, Pablo. I recognize the pleasant kid who always smiles at me, the same one who spoke up on the first payday to say he was also a *maestro*. A couple of weeks ago, Michael told me that Pablo had asked for a day off to take an exam. "That's good, he's finishing up his high school courses," I thought. The next week when Pablo didn't show up for work, his father, Belesario, said his son had gone to the hospital to be with his wife while she had a Caesarean. This seemed impossible, but it turned out to be true. Pablo, also seventeen, is married and a father. When I ask Rosa about Pablo's exam, she tells me it was to finish sixth-grade primary school, the end-point of education for many poor young people.

Our third teenage worker, Manuel, is so quiet and shy I know nothing about him except that his father is José María's brother, Santos, a passive, sad-looking man of about forty-five who almost never speaks. He and his wife Mercedes have six children, and some afternoons Santos brings his five-year-old son Juanito to the construction site. Juanito plays in the sand and Michael sometimes lets him be his "assistant" and carry plastic pipe. I try to imagine an American five-year-old—such as our grandson Cosmo—being allowed to play on a construction site. But then I'm reminded how children here, from an early age, are eager to participate in adult labors. Boys of three or four play at harvesting wheat with their own little scythes and little girls of four or five carry dolls on their backs and help cook on a wood fire.

While we weed, Rosa tells me that her family owns no land other than where their house sits, somewhere below us in the *comuna* of Chaglaban. "We are only *partidarios*," she says.

"You mean you plant on other people's land and share the harvest?" I ask, guessing at the meaning of the word.

"*Sí, somos muy pobres,*" she says with a rueful smile, her missing front teeth emphasizing that fact.

~

"There would be *no* economy in this area without illegal migration," Arturo shouted over the noise of his delivery truck as we rattled along a rough mountain road. He had picked us up in Ingapirca, a village several miles from Cañar, where we'd gone for an outing and where he found us standing by the road waiting for a bus.

Arturo owns a large store in Cañar that sells all manner of household goods, furniture, and *electro-domésticos*—fridges, stoves, blenders, washing machines—and he told us he'd just delivered a large sound system to an indigenous family high in the mountains near the Inca Trail.

There are several reasons why Arturo is so successful as a businessman in Cañar. In addition to coming from a long-established "white" mercantile family, he has fair prices, delivers to customers no matter how far away they live, and, according to our Cañari friends, he treats the indigenous people with respect. Of course, cash-in-hand, freely spent, tends to buy respect, but I think Arturo is a basically decent man. Most of the appliances in our house have come from his store, and we have watched his business grow exponentially as the country has recovered from the financial collapse in 1999.

Michael and I lived in Cañar the year right after the crisis, when the economic heart of the province seemed moribund. Highland villages were literally emptying out as men and boys left weekly for the *Yonny*, leaving behind women, children, and old folks with almost no source of income. Women tried to take on the agricultural chores of the men, but there was no way they could keep up with the physical demands of raising children, plowing, planting, weeding, and harvesting, along with caring for the old folks. It was a time of extreme hardship and suffering for nearly everyone.

We returned to Cañar in 2005 to find the place transformed. Money was flowing, seemingly to every family we knew. New shops were opening, the weekly market was again full of life, colorful houses were going up in the countryside and in town, everyone—including old grandmothers—carried new cell phones, and small white Toyota pickup trucks seemed to be a new species that had hatched while we were gone.

One Sunday market day, I walked around the streets and made notes, amazed at the changes:

- At a street stall, a young woman ponders a bead necklace that costs two dollars. She decides she wants it and pulls a fifty-dollar bill out of the inner pocket of her skirt. The vendor begs for smaller change.

- An old Cañari woman stands in front of a hardware store, shouting in Quichua into a cell phone, no doubt talking to a son in New York or New Jersey. "They're asking twenty-five dollars!" she is probably yelling over the racket of the street vendors. "Shall I pay it?"

- An elaborate wooden dining table and eight fancy chairs are set up in the street in front of Arturo's store. At five hundred dollars, this is something no poor Cañar family would have dreamed of owning a few years ago. When I walk home later, it is being loaded into a truck, sold.

- Miguel, an indigenous man we've known for many years, used to sell pirated CDs from a makeshift stall on the street. Now his business is so brisk he has moved his operation to a small storefront. When we stop in to say hello, we watch as he makes a sale and pulls a wad of rolled bills out of his pocket: hundreds, fifties, and twenties. He later passes us in the street, driving a new truck, tooting his horn to get our attention. (We later heard some gossip that he has a new business as a *chulquero*, a moneylender.)

~

It's taken me years to understand how the complicated, secretive, and risky business of illegal migration works. And there is still much I don't know. But I've heard many anecdotes, some directly from friends, others from secondhand accounts and newspaper articles—as well as plenty of *chismes*, or gossip—so I can stitch together a pretty good picture.

The clandestine trip always begins with local intermediaries, perhaps a neighbor in an isolated highland hamlet, a mestizo contact in a nearby town, or a "professional" señora in Cuenca with an office and waiting room. All are called "coyotes," the first link in a complex chain of illegal immigrant traffickers who arrange every detail of the trip from the Andean highlands to the final destination in the United States—commonly New York, New Jersey, Connecticut, Chicago, or Minneapolis. In general, at least at the local level, it's a network run by the poor (or recently poor) for the poor, built on trust within the communities and on word-of-mouth accounts.

It's the job of the local coyote to facilitate arrangements among the potential migrant, family members, and *chulqueros*, who are also often local folks. *Chulqueros* can be relations, neighbors, or, often, family members already in the United States. Most moneylenders charge terribly high interest, which is accepted as part of the engine that keeps the system running. For collateral, the borrowers most often use the family land, their traditional source of survival. Risky though that is, families figure it's worth it to get their relative to the *Yonny*

Countryside with migrant houses

so they can start sending dollars home. There are so few men left to work the land anyway.

In 2010, the cost of the trip to the United States was about twelve thousand dollars, a huge debt for a poor family. That amount is paid in increments as the *migrante* moves north, but it doesn't cover extra costs if an unlucky man or woman ends up in jail in Guatemala or Mexico. The Ecuadorian government sometimes pays for the return trip of citizens captured in these countries, but other *migrantes* languish in jails or safe houses until a family can pay bail (or ransom, as it were).

Initial arrangements made, the migrant will simply disappear one day, having informed no one but close family (such as Rosa's brother Francisco, who didn't show up for work this week). A neighbor might see a young man climbing the road to town, carrying a duffel, and say, "There he goes—off to the *Yonny*," but more common is a middle-of-the-night departure on a local bus, witnessed by no one.

Most *migrantes* from Cañar, like my acquaintance Delia, start out from the coast near Guayaquil in dangerously overloaded fishing boats that have been converted for human smuggling along the Pacific coast. She described a voyage of six days to reach Guatemala. "It was a small ship—maybe forty feet and we were about a hundred people—but we were comfortable enough. Everything was well planned. There was sufficient food and a good variety: one day it was beef, the next day chicken. There were crewmen preparing the food and that was the first time I had seen a man cooking." (Her experience was much better than most I've heard.)

Once off the coast of Guatemala, the migrants are ferried ashore in small boats to begin their journeys through Central America and Mexico with the guidance, at every point, of coyotes. Along the way, the travelers rest in safe houses or remote ranches that are clandestine cogs of the underground route. As the migrant moves north, the family at home is squeezed to pay for the next stage. A phone call or message comes to the family: "Jorge has made it to Guatemala. Pay the señora in Cuenca five hundred dollars so he can move on to Mexico." Another call comes from the U.S.-Mexico border: a thousand dollars more before the migrant can cross. The final payment is due once the migrants reach Phoenix or Los Angeles, where they are kept virtually prisoners in horribly overcrowded apartments or houses until the last payment is made. The contract is completed with a clean set of clothes, an airline ticket to the final destination, and an escorted trip to the nearest airport. If a migrant is picked out of a line at the airport and taken into custody, the contract is still considered ended. But if the migrant "falls" in Guatemala or Mexico and returns to Ecuador, he or she is guaranteed another try—usually three tries total.

The lucky ones make it to the U.S. border in three weeks. For the unlucky ones, it can take much longer, or never. The newspapers are full of the calamities that befall *migrantes*. An overloaded boat goes down off the coast of Guatemala and all on board are lost; an American Coast Guard ship intercepts a boat and escorts it back to Ecuador; migrants are jailed in Guatemala, fall under the wheels of the "train of death" through Mexico, succumb to thirst and heat in the deserts of Arizona, or die violently in the crash of an overloaded van in Texas. Some even die for lack of medical attention while in detention in the United States.

Migrants are instructed by the coyotes not to carry identification, so if something happens, it is often months before the families back home get word. Sometimes migrants simply disappear without a trace and families never know what happened.

Since the majority of the migrants are young men in their twenties, once in the United States, they crowd in with brothers, fathers, or cousins in small apartments and immediately set to work to pay off the coyote debt. From the stories I've heard, it generally takes a migrant about year to pay off the debt, if he can find a job, which means the family in Ecuador has to wait that long before the dollars start coming back to begin building a house or to send a *novia* (girlfriend or fiancée) or the wife. "Preserving the marriage," which translates as: "If I don't go, he'll find someone else," is the common explanation given by women who leave their children behind with relatives to join their husbands. These children left behind are raised by grandparents or older aunts and uncles, many of whom are semi-literate or speak only Quichua. (One Cañari organization, TUCAYTA, an umbrella group of agricultural cooperatives, reports that 40 percent of the children among their twenty-six member communities are affected by illegal migration, an entire generation.)

The stories of the women are the hardest to hear. One I knew slightly, María, left her village to join her husband and didn't tell her five-year-old daughter that she was leaving. Once in the United States, María reestablished contact by phone, but her daughter was so angry and hurt, she refused to talk to her mother for a year. Her younger daughter, who was two, barely remembers her mother. Each girl lives with a different grandmother, further fracturing the family.

Living in the United States does not necessarily lead to enlightenment when it comes to education, at least when it comes to girls. I know of one father who refused to help his oldest daughter, Beatriz, a good student, go on to university, even though the tuition was nominal, but he offered to pay the enormous cost to bring her to the United States where she would be a factory worker or a cleaner in a hotel. She won a scholarship and stayed in Ecuador, getting a degree at the technical university in dairy management.

Another friend, Verónica, who was caught in Arizona, described her detention and repatriation as an experience worthy of Kafka. She was held for three months in a private prison, in rooms without windows. "The day after they told us we were returning to Ecuador," she said, "we were taken to a holding cell and kept all night without a place to lie down or anything to eat. The following day, they took us in a bus to an airfield where a large unmarked plane waited. Inside it was completely bare except for seats. On the flight we were given no food, only water. The plane landed in two or three countries, in El Salvador and maybe Honduras, before we arrived in Ecuador. By then I was faint with hunger."

Verónica stayed in Ecuador a year and then returned to the United States in two attempts. She now lives somewhere in New Jersey with her boyfriend, and I hear she has a new baby.

~

Back at the construction site, Rosa and I are still pulling weeds and chatting. Rosa doesn't know it yet, but she, too, will soon be one of these grandmothers taking care of a grandchild. Within a few months, her son Pablo will be on his way to the *Yonny,* followed shortly by his young wife, the one who gave birth by Caesarean. Whenever I run into Rosa after that, she will have a baby on her back, but she will look quite proud and happy to have this new role in her life. I will understand. As a grandmother who rarely got to see her grandsons as babies and toddlers, I will even feel a touch of envy.

～

JOURNAL, FEBRUARY 28

Paiwa comes by after school and spends the afternoon with us. When it gets late we invite her to stay for dinner and spend the night and she calls her mother at the photo studio. María Esthela says she'll come by early in the morning with Paiwa's school clothes and to braid her hair. (Paiwa, like all little Cañari girls, almost never cuts her hair and it is now down to her waist.)

When it's bedtime Paiwa doesn't want me to read one of her books for our usual bedtime story, but asks me to tell her the story of the book I am reading, *The Constant Gardener,* by John le Carré. "This is the kind of book I want to read," she sighs, gazing at the cover—a romantic photo of Ralph Fiennes and Rachel Weisz from the movie version.

I protest that the story is too long and complicated, but she begs me to tell it. So I start, "Well, the story is set in Africa, and it begins with the violent death of this man's beloved wife. . . ." Paiwa's eyes grow large and she continues to study the book cover. "A large drug company is testing its medicines on poor Africans, and the wife is a lawyer researching these crimes, because the Africans are dying from the experiments. . . . The black doctor she is working with—who everyone thinks is her lover—only loves men, but in this country it's illegal. He's homosexual—do you know what 'homosexual' means?" I stop to ask Paiwa. She nods gravely.

I go on, condensing the narrative, hitting the high spots. "At the end, the husband has uncovered the scheme of the drug company, and he is waiting to die at the same spot where his wife was murdered, sitting on the side of the lake."

I open the book and read the last line: "He heard a sound of feet sliding down the white rock."

Paiwa shivers with delight and says she is ready for bed.

CHAPTER 7

Carnival

Sins and Repentance, Abundance and Reciprocity

~

Women carrying cuyñaña *in Carnival procession*

BOOM! BOOM! BOOM! In the days leading up to Carnival, one of the most important festivals in Catholic Latin America, we are awakened every dawn with what sounds like cannon fire. Several *bombas* in a row, then silence until the next day.

I've learned not to bolt out of bed, but I'm always left wide awake and wondering what those early morning fireworks mean. Did sixteenth-century Spanish priests establish the practice to remind the locals they were newly made Christians? Or maybe to frighten them into getting to the church for an early mass? Or maybe the faithful are to be brought abruptly awake to consider their sins before the excesses of Carnival and the forty days of Lenten austerity? And these days, who on earth gets up at the crack of dawn to let off pyrotechnics? Adolescent altar boys, I imagine; I tend to blame all loud noises and public disturbances on adolescent boys.

Carnival in Cañar is the most colorful, complex, and boisterous of holidays, a great mash of indigenous traditions, Catholic customs, social interactions of mysterious origin (kids and teens throwing water or cornstarch on one another), and vacation getaways. Carnival always falls in February or early March, a "moveable feast" dependent on the day of Easter. As a photographer, it is my favorite Cañari event because it is one of the few times I can freely take photos without asking permission.

The unofficial festival starts the weekend before Ash Wednesday, the first day of Lent. *Carnaval lunes* and *Carnaval martes* (Monday and Tuesday) are national holidays, and Ash Wednesday is a religious holiday when Catholics go to mass to have a cross of ashes marked on their forehead as a sign of repentance to God. After Ash Wednesday, most folks, having settled into holiday mode, simply take off Thursday and Friday. Then it's the weekend again, making it a glorious ten-day holiday.

In Ecuador, wherever people live, they want to be somewhere else for Carnival, seeking a change of climate, a place where they think they'll have more fun, or—most common—joining family at opposite ends of the country. Those who live in the chilly mountains want to be at the warm beach; those from the hot and humid coast migrate to the refreshing mountains. Those from the noisy city yearn for the tranquil countryside; those who live in the boring countryside hanker for a few days of action-packed city life.

Michael and I always stay right here. We learned years ago that to try to travel during Carnival is to invite a trip from hell. Also, for the past few years, TUCAYTA, the indigenous group of agricultural cooperatives, has invited me to document their cultural event, *Pawkar Raymi*, a Quichua term meaning a fiesta of flowering or first fruits.

"This was our own Andean festival that was appropriated by the Church," my friend Pedro Solano told me. "Its original purpose was to celebrate the spring equinox and the maturing of our crops, to give thanks to *Pachamama* for her abundance." When I look around, I see the timing is certainly right. In late February, Mother Nature is in her full glory, with potato fields a sea of purple blooms, tall corn shamelessly waving its silk—looking for a partner to pollinate—and the beans, peas, and squash in bounteous flower.

Each year a different cooperative community plays host for *Pawkar Raymi*, preparing an outdoor space large enough to accommodate a few thousand people, building a stage for music and dance performances, and providing enough

Tayta Fidel Guamán with family

food and drink to all who come. For the host community, it's all about abundance and reciprocity and bringing honor to the *comuna*, but since it's such an expensive affair, some poorer communities ask to be passed over for lack of resources when it comes their turn.

The central figure of the festival is *Tayta Carnaval*, (loosely, Father Carnival), who, according to Cañari legend, represents the god or spirit of the mountains. The night before *Carnaval*, he makes symbolic rounds of village families, where he expects to be offered food and drink. He can bring good luck or bad depending on the generosity of those visited. (Sounds familiar, a bit like Father Christmas coming down the chimney and expecting milk and cookies.)

The most striking element of the *Tayta Carnaval* costume is the flat, round, cowhide sombrero edged with long bright strings of yarn, ribbons, or balloons hanging down to cover the face. On top of these homemade sombreros, which can weigh up to ten pounds, Cañaris attach everything from fresh fruits, sheaves of grain, and small bouquets of flowers to entire cooked guinea pigs, with little red chiles stuck in their mouths, and desiccated deer heads.

The most famous sombrero, belonging to Pedro Solano, features a preserved condor on top. A few years ago, some thieving reveler stole its feet, and each time I see this national symbol of the Andean world, it seems to be getting smaller and more ragged, but no *Pawkar Raymi* fiesta would be complete without its appearance.

Pawkar Raymi begins with a colorful and noisy procession that lasts hours as it weaves through the countryside and town, led by the president of the host *comuna*. He or she carries a gorgeous rooster with a twenty-dollar bill attached to its comb that will be passed on to the next year's host president. Men and boys dress in elaborate *Tayta Carnaval* costumes—wooly chaps called "*zamorras*," large sombreros, and sometimes masks. As they walk, they play small homemade drums or bamboo flutes, called "*pingullos*." Some women and girls also dress in costume. One group of women from the host community carry the *cuyñaña*, a platform with a cornucopia of fruits, vegetables, and flowers, cooked chickens, and live guinea pigs in a cage attached to the bottom of the platform.

At each community the *carnavaleros* pass through on the procession—which can cover as much as ten kilometers and take up to six hours—local folks wait in temporarily built *chozas*, thatched huts, to offer specially prepared food and drink so that everyone has the strength (and incentive) to move on to the next *comuna*. Once at the host community, the revels last well into the night and, for some, the next day.

~

On a brilliant Saturday morning after days of rain, I decide to walk down to this year's host community, La Posta, and see how the preparations are going. I don't know the people of La Posta, and I want to introduce myself, or at least let them see me with my cameras, before Monday. I invite Michael, but he says dryly that he has no interest in watching an animal being sacrificed. He is remembering a few years ago when I documented the ritual killing of a cow in Mama Michi's community when it played host. After hours of photographing and filming, with liberal shots of Zhumir all around, I was accidentally slapped on the head with a bloody piece of meat when a tipsy man danced around with it on *his* head. (I was never sure if that was a traditional part of the ritual or not—his dancing with the meat, not my slap.)

Michael also recalls a moment of the same day when he was offered a cocktail of fresh blood mixed with Zhumir. He had demurred, but was embarrassed because he prides himself on full participation in any rituals we're invited to be a part of.

I say I don't care to see *that* again, but other interesting things might be happening. So I pack my cameras and rain gear and take off walking downhill toward the Cañar River, maybe five kilometers away.

Once on the road, I'm reminded that Michael and I made this walk about seven years ago, just before the economic crisis that sparked mass migrations out of this province. Then, I was charmed by the old adobe houses, the fields of barley, the old woman with her sheep, the huge cacti I remember seeing beside an old corral—a traditional rural scene. Today, I am struck by the changes. Many of those old adobes are falling down and abandoned, and in their place brightly painted new houses dot the landscape, looking from a distance like perfect dollhouses.

So it is a refreshing sight to come across a group of old folks building a crude *choza* alongside the road. From this thatched-roof hut they will be serving food and drink on Monday to the *carnavaleros* in the procession. The eight or ten men and women, dressed mostly in well-worn, hand-loomed clothes, have taken a break for a communal lunch. I see wooden platters and pots of food laid on a cloth on the ground.

With friendly gestures one of the women motions for me to step inside the hut, and, as my eyes adjust to the darkness, a quick glance around tells me I don't know a soul here. The woman gestures that I should eat, and I take some warm potatoes from a wooden platter and dip them into a hot sauce in a small bowl. The assembled folks look me over with appraising eyes and make amused comments to one another in Quichua.

An old man offers me a small glass of Zhumir with a look that says, "Let's see what the little gringa does with this!" I shoot it down, hand it back with the standard "*Dios le page*" (May God repay you), and make small talk to let them know I am not a total stranger to these parts. I'm not sure they understand my Spanish because in response I only get nods and smiles and what sounds like more friendly jokes in Quichua.

Hoisting my pack to take my leave, I explain that I am getting to know the route the *carnavaleros* will take on Monday. "*Pues, váyase*," someone says in friendly Spanish. (Roughly, "Well then, get on with you!")

Thirty minutes later, as I come down the hill approaching the school and community center of La Posta, I see women crouched along the edge of an irrigation ditch, washing tripe, long tubes of intestines. Good, I think, the killing of the cow is over. Then as I walk into the schoolyard I see a bull standing tethered to a post by a ring through his nose, obviously waiting to be a second "sacrifice" of the day. Off to one side, in front of a makeshift open shed, I see a man chopping raw meat on a large wooden block that sits on the ground. Inside, women are gathered around pots on a wood fire, cooking for the throngs they expect on Monday.

Twenty or so men are at work erecting a stage. Judging by the yelling and gesturing, it's not going very well. As soon as I sit down on the steps of the school to watch the proceedings, a youngish man with short hair, who appears to be in charge of the stage construction, staggers over. His white button-down shirt and new pants clearly announce he's recently come from the *Yonny*. He is very drunk. Leaning over me, his face uncomfortably close, he begins speaking in Quichua, then switches to Spanish. Through his slurring words, I understand he is saying how unjust it is that gringos can travel back and forth to the United States at will, while Ecuadorians have to travel "like dogs, hidden and groveling, at great risk and expense, maybe ending up in jail in Guatemala or Mexico before being returned to Ecuador." That last bit came out very clear.

"It *is* unjust," I say, sliding away. "I'm not in agreement with the U.S. government policies nor with the president. I really hope things change with the 2008 elections."

The young man continues to hover over me in a slightly menacing way, eyes swiveling, breath strong with drink. He doesn't seem to register what I have just said, but after an uncomfortable pause, he puts out his hand with, "I want to be friends. Welcome!" Relief. We shake. He goes back to helping the men build the stage. I wait a few minutes before I get up, so as not to appear to be fleeing.

But as I walk out of the schoolyard, the older man who was chopping meat approaches me with a plate. "Eat," he commands. "Eat before you go." I immediately recognize his offering as cooked curdled blood. It resembles purplish-brown cottage cheese. At this point, I lose all my cultural sensitivity and usual concern for protocol and say abruptly, "I can't. I'm sorry! Thank you anyway." I walk on. This day is not turning out as I'd hoped.

I make it to the river in another hour or so. After staring at the broken bridge swept away recently by the flooding Cañar River, I start back up the mountain, knowing it will be a hard two- to three-hour climb home. A soft mist is falling and the sky looks like serious rain. As I approach the La Posta school, I can hear preparations for the fiesta still in progress. I will have to walk by again, and I'm afraid I'll be offered more curdled blood, or worse, fried tripe, the logical next course.

Suddenly I am in front of the school again, but this time no one notices me because everyone is busy butchering the bull. I sit on the grassy bank across the road to catch my breath, realizing that, despite all my encounters today, I haven't taken a single photo. I knew the old folks building the *choza* wouldn't want to be photographed in their old clothes, and the young man just returned from New York scared me a little with his drunken tirade.

I get up to walk on when—incredibly—a yellow taxi appears, coming up from the direction of the river. A yellow taxi in Cañar? That's a strange sight I've never seen before. It must be that some visitor joining family for the holidays— maybe another returned migrant with cash in his pocket—has hired the taxi and paid handsomely to travel in style from Quito, Riobamba, or Cuenca.

I don't hesitate. I jump into the road and raise my arm to hail the taxi as though I were on the streets of Manhattan instead of a rutted, muddy road in the *comuna* of La Posta, Province of Cañar, Republic of Ecuador. The taxi slows and stops, I climb into the back seat, and the startled driver asks, "Where to?"

~

JOURNAL, MARCH 4

Late afternoon, Michael and I take a walk down to the house site, and because it's a nice day and feels like a holiday, we keep walking into the countryside below. It's the day after Carnival. Following the paths alongside irrigation canals, we reach the new road to Cuchucún, then cross back on a path to Chaglaban, our own little *comuna*.

I've brought my camera and take some photos of old abandoned adobe houses. We see a woman in a field cutting tall grass for her cows, moving rhythmically as she bends, swings, and straightens, her bright red skirt contrasting with the vivid green around her. It is a perfect scene, but I know better than to take a photo; she's aware of me, even fifty meters away, and would resent my photographing her while she's working.

Approaching Chaglaban, we come across three teenage boys resting in a field, still dressed in their Carnival outfits. They'd obviously spent the night outdoors, a sort of rite-of-passage for young Cañari men during Carnival. I recognize one from the procession the day before, when he'd lifted the fringe on his hat and asked me to take his photo, then stood very still and stared into the camera. But right now these boys are not interested in us because their attention is riveted on two young women walking by them toward the village. But when I ask if I can take a photo, they agree. Three boys resting in a field, still in their Tayta Carnaval costumes. It's one of my favorite photos.

CHAPTER 8

Sticks and Stones, Mud and Horse Manure

~

Building the foundation wall

IT'S THE FIRST WEEK OF MARCH, following the long bacchanalia of Carnival. Three workers managed to return to the construction project on Wednesday, three others on Thursday, and by Friday one of those had disappeared again. *Chuchaki*, hungover, was repeatedly offered as the reason. Belesario, our main *maestro*, stayed away all week.

We are now more than two months into our house construction, and as a daily visitor to the site, I think things are moving along beautifully. I've watched as the chalk outline became the stone foundation walls, as tamped-down earth became subfloors, and as eucalyptus timbers from the Sunday wood market became the post-and-beam framework, going up this week. Every time I make the five-minute walk down the hill to visit the construction site, I exclaim over each new development and take photographs, like a tourist visiting an endlessly changing roadside attraction.

Talk to Michael, however, who works on the site every day, and you'll have a different picture. "Things aren't moving nearly fast enough," he says unhappily the other day as I stood beside him watching the workers. "The *maestros* insist on doing things their own ways, but if they'd followed the architect's instructions we would be two weeks further on." He says that the workers' greatest fear is not to have work, so they simply forge ahead with whatever materials are available, not wanting to stop or ask questions that might mean a delay.

"A couple of weeks ago, Lourdes instructed Belesario to buy twenty-five eucalyptus beams as floor joists," he goes on. "She specified they should be twenty feet in length and of an exact thickness. On Sunday morning Belesario went to the market to buy the wood, but when he discovered there was none available that met Lourdes's specifications, he simply bought what was on hand. This week the workers laid down the floor joists. When Lourdes showed up, she took one look and said they were too thin; the wooden flooring laid on top would be springy."

"Now to compensate, the workers are building these stone columns to reinforce the floor joists, taking an extra week." Michael gestures to the space below where a hen and her chicks are scratching around in the soil.

"But look how beautiful they are," I say, bending down to examine the perfect stonework of the columns. "Too bad they'll be covered up."

He harrumphs and turns away to his work.

Michael has said before that the construction boom generated by migrant dollars has brought traditional farmers, such as Santos and José María, into the workforce because so many young men have left. Some, like Belesario, call themselves *maestros*, even though there seem to be no requirements other than previous experience, or watching more skilled men.

From the beginning, Michael's suspected that Belesario might be semi-literate or even illiterate. He pretends to understand the plans when Lourdes and Michael discuss them, but Michael has noticed that he never brings plans to work or refers to them when talking to the workers. On top of that, Michael is beginning to suspect that Belesario has a drinking problem. He often doesn't show up on Mondays or for a couple of days after fiestas. *Chuchaki* is the freely given excuse. Still, we're wary of jumping to conclusions, and with Michael on the site every day and Lourdes visiting a few times a week, no major mistakes have been made. So far.

José María, who can obviously read and never misses work, covers for and defers to Belesario, which we assume means he has less experience in construction. He certainly has less confidence. We are trying to treat this relationship delicately and not look to José María as the more capable and dependable *maestro*, but it's becoming clearer every day that he is the one who should be in charge.

Later on, we will discover another kind of *maestro*—those who come from the city to look at the job and give a bid: the tile guy, floor finisher, glazier, and painting contractor. These guys arrive in big trucks, are well dressed, knowledgeable, and client-friendly. They exude confidence and convince us their price is reasonable and the job will be well done. An agreement is made with a handshake. But then low-paid young workers are sent from Cuenca to do the work, often with no supervision and left on their own to make ill-considered decisions. We won't see the *maestro* again until time for the bill.

~

Meanwhile, I continue to marvel at how much of our house is, simply, hand crafted. Six workers dug the foundation trenches with picks and shovels. They built the foundation walls by hand with river rocks, quarried stones, and mortar. To make subfloors, they tamped down a mix of sand and gravel with a sort of crude ramming tool. This week Santos and a helper are hand carving pegs on

Mercedes and Rosa digging the waterline channel

both ends of the eucalyptus posts to fit into hand-bored holes in the foundation and overhead beams. From my perspective, it's the Tinkertoy school of construction with a few Lincoln Log touches thrown in.

And it's not just the men who work on the site. When we need a long trench for a waterline from the main road down to the house, José María declares, "That's a job for women!" He suggests his brother's wife, Mercedes, and Belesario's wife, Rosa. The next day, the two women show up in their embroidered wool skirts and take up picks and shovels. They work as hard and as steadily as the men for two and a half days, digging a three-hundred-foot-long trench a foot deep to bury the half-inch water line. They earn the same wage, too.

Only a few machines have intervened in the construction process, other than that of the blade man who leveled the site in the first days. When the time comes to pour concrete into the foundation forms, Michael and José María go to the nearby town of Tambo and rent an old gasoline-powered concrete mixer, the kind that looks like an early space capsule on wheels. With the help of a hired driver and truck, they haul it back to the house site. Michael calls me to come down to take a look. "José María says he'll sleep in the tool shed to guard the mixer."

"Someone would steal *that* thing?" I say, looking over the battered contraption.

"José María says a concrete mixer would allow someone to make a living, so who wouldn't want to steal it? Besides, it has wheels and would be easy to roll away." José María sleeps in the shed the next three nights.

Watching the workers make and pour the concrete is like observing a beautiful synchronized dance. As José María dumps a sack of dry cement into the hopper he yells, "*Agua!*" Santos comes running with a bucket of water while another helper dumps in buckets of sand and gravel. The machine spins around and around as José María stands holding a big wheel, like a captain steering a boat. After a few minutes, he cranks the wheel to dump the mix into a waiting wheelbarrow, manned by another worker who runs along a pathway of wooden planks to tip the load into a trench. Belesario waits with a bamboo pole that he plunges into the wet concrete to vibrate out air bubbles.

~

Of course, the Andean peoples have been building their own shelters for thousands of years and it's no mystery to them how to make a house without machines. They simply used the materials and tools at hand to build houses adapted to the climate, landscape, and local conditions. For the Cañaris, it was the clay-like soil they found beneath their feet that could be mixed with water and straw, formed into adobe blocks, baked by the sun and stacked to make the walls of a house. *Páramo* grass that grows high in the mountains provided the thatch for the roof. If the roof was renewed every few years to prevent water damage, these houses could last a hundred years.

But twenty-first-century tools do have their allure. When I walk down to the site a few days later I find it abuzz—literally, in the case of Michael, who is at work with his new chainsaw. He is thrilled to have had an excuse to buy this new tool. "The large timbers for post and beams, rafters and joists require something more than a handsaw," he said the other day, as he prepared to go shopping in Cuenca. "We can also use it for firewood," he added almost apologetically, needing one more excuse for his new toy.

The massive tree trunks that will be columns at the front and back entrances have arrived on a truck from Cuenca. The tree trunk idea came from Lourdes, who said the columns would offset the "massiveness" of the mud walls. This detail would never have occurred to Michael or me, yet we immediately see that it is a great idea, one in a series of changes that have made this house much larger and more complex than we had ever imagined, but also much more beautiful. We've given up asking Lourdes how much it will all cost, but simply hand over sums of money when she requests them.

The full contingent of Cañari workers are here today, along with Javier, an experienced carpenter Lourdes has brought from Cuenca. She says she must work carefully now with Javier and the *maestros* so that no mistakes are made in the positioning of the beams for the ceilings. I watch and listen as Lourdes talks with the workers. As always, she is patient in correcting their mistakes and guiding them to the next phase. "Stone columns can compensate for shaky floors," I hear her say, "but nothing can strengthen a sagging ceiling."

Lourdes has a quiet, persuasive manner that is always reassuring when we fear that the *maestros* might have screwed up. Whether they have or not, she always says evenly: "We'll do this (or that), and then it will be alright." Despite her gentle nature, Lourdes is steely serious with the workers, and they seem to respect and like her. It didn't take them long to figure out that she knows more than they do (though there have been a few instances when they have convinced her their way would work better). The workers always address her respectfully as *arquitecta*, or *Arquitecta Abad*, in keeping with the Latin custom of calling an educated or skilled person by their title. She, in turn, always refers to Belesario and José María as *maestro*.

Later, when Lourdes is ready to leave and the three of us stand talking beside her little truck, she mentions some problems, none of them new. She says the *maestros* won't tell her when materials are not available or won't call her when they have questions. "Also," she says, "I'm now certain that Belesario cannot read the plans." (Sadly, Michael had to fire Belesario the next month for drinking. He had missed too many days of work, and Lourdes told Michael she could smell liquor on his breath while on the job.)

But given all that, she is still optimistic that everything will go well and we'll have a quality house in the end. Her enthusiasm infects Michael, which makes me happy. I hate it when he has doubts or regrets, and this would be a terrible project to start regretting.

At next payday, when the workers come to the house, Michael serves some liquid refreshment for the first time—small shots of Zhumir—and gives a little lecture about communication, quality of work, and correcting mistakes. No one says a word, nor changes expression, but I think the message was well received, along with the Zhumir.

The great American architect Louis Kahn once said that bricks and other building materials *wanted* to be certain kinds of structures. Well, I don't know if eucalyptus wood, river rocks, quarried stone, mud, straw, bamboo, and horse manure really *want* to be an earthen house in this remote corner of Ecuador, but I'd like to think Mr. Kahn would approve.

~

JOURNAL, MARCH 8

International Women's Day. I load my photo gear in my backpack and walk up to the indigenous center in town, once a beautiful, rambling hospital run by nuns. I've recently done a photography workshop here with the women's group sponsoring the march today, and I've brought extra cameras, hoping some of my alums will help me document the event.

The march is scheduled to start at nine o'clock, but by eleven o'clock, we are just a few women lining up in the courtyard. Then, as we start up the street, trucks and buses arrive, full of women, and they join us with banners and hand-painted signs. We march to the town square, around the park, and up to Avenida San Antonio, down Guayaquil Street, and, two hours later, back to the center for the day's program and lunch.

There, I'm amazed to see how many others have shown up—there must be five hundred women, children, and a scattering of men. We gather around the big courtyard, sitting on the grass and steps and on the volley-ball court in front of a loudspeaker system and speakers' table.

And then, just as the program is about to begin—bad luck!—the skies open. Not just drizzle or sprinkle, but a downpour. The event cannot continue outdoors, and when I hear, "*Compañeras,* let's move inside," I decide I'm tired and hungry and I want to go home and eat and rest. I'll come back, knowing from experience that the program will go on for hours.

I walk the short distance home under my umbrella—for once I've remembered to bring it—and have lunch with Michael, who has come up from the construction site. An hour or so later, I return to find the auditorium packed and the last speaker wrapping up. The crowd sits politely and quietly, even the children, although it's past two o'clock and no one has eaten lunch.

I go into the kitchen in a far part of the compound to see what's happening. A few women and a couple of men are trying to figure out how to serve the vast amounts of food they've been preparing all morning. Without a plan, kitchen helpers begin ferrying huge pots of food to a patio near the auditorium. I follow with my camera.

There, I watch with amazement as several women form an assembly line to fill plastic plates with rice, potatoes, a chunk of meat, a piece of lettuce, and hominy, while runners—mostly young men—grab the plates and dash down the hall and into the auditorium, serving first the speakers at the table, then working their way through the seated crowd. I finally put down my camera and help, grabbing the full plates and handing them off to runners. In about fifteen minutes, everyone has been served a hot plate of food. Now it's time for the music and dancing.

CHAPTER 9

We Become *Padrinos* . . . Again

Michael with Nuncito and family

"CATHOLIC! CHRISTIAN! ADULT!" Padre Enrique fairly shouts, his finger jabbing each word on the blackboard. "These are the requirements for being godparents!"

It's a Saturday afternoon in early March, and Michael and I sit in a catechism classroom next to the big church on the square, crammed in a school desk designed for two small children. Around us sit other pairs of parents and godparents, all of us here for a "lesson" on our baptism ceremony tomorrow. Huddled in the desk in front of us sits Andrés, the father of our future godchild, Nuncito, and Andrés's widowed mother, Mama Rosita. Andrés turns to speak to me, and I can smell drink on his breath. His uncommonly white skin is red and raw from years working in the burning sun, his lips cracked and a little bloody, his upper front teeth missing from a fall or accident.

Padre Enrique gestures to the crucifix hanging above the blackboard and says in a softer voice: "*¿Somos Católicos, cierto o no cierto?*" We are Catholics, right or wrong? No one answers, and the priest laughs in a friendly fake way, hoping to release the tension perhaps.

Out of the corner of my eye, I catch Michael nodding slightly. I can feel how tense he is, hoping this priest won't look directly at him next and ask, "Are *you* a Catholic? Are *you* a Christian?" (With his cap in his lap, doubled-up knees, and size twelve boots crowded under the desk, there is no question that Michael qualifies as an adult.) I too am praying that Padre Enrique won't turn his gaze on me. Sitting in this classroom, at a tiny desk, with a tough teacher at the head of the room, I feel a little like a schoolgirl who has not done her homework.

Despite his stern gaze and loud voice, Father Enrique has a kindly face, with big ears, a bald pate, and large brown eyes. He is dressed in a button-down shirt, a crewneck sweater, and a dark blue jacket that picks up the dust of the blackboard each time he strikes it with his finger. I've heard he is from Spain, as are so many of the priests who have served Cañar over the years. Maybe his outsider status gives him extra weight with his audience today because everyone sits quietly and respectfully. But then this is a Catholic town and priests and nuns have always commanded respect. Outside, I hear the murmur of folks walking by as they leave afternoon mass.

~

Against our better judgment, Michael and I have agreed to become godparents again, making this the fourth time we have stood up in the church, allowed a priest to think we are Catholics (or at least Christians), and promised to take on partial responsibility for the religious and moral education of a Cañari child. Our first godchild was Paiwa, daughter of my photography students, José Miguel and María Esthela. After Paiwa, we became godparents to Plinio's younger daughter, Adelita, and then to Mama Michi's grandson, Rantin, middle child of her daughter Zoila, whom we've known since she was a teenager. In both cases, the fathers were in the United States, and a surrogate stood in for the baptism ceremony.

It was Paiwa's baptism that brought us back to Cañar in 1998, after more than four years in Portland. We thought we'd left Ecuador behind for good when we received a letter from José Miguel announcing Paiwa's birth, two years before, and asking us to come be her godparents. We were touched and tempted. I remembered they had lost their first baby years ago, an unexplained death at five months, and this new little child must represent great hope for their future. In the same letter, José Miguel wrote that he and his wife had become "real photographers" and ran a professional photo studio in town. That cinched it. We missed Cañar, and the baptism invitation and the prospect of seeing my students as professional photographers gave us two good reasons to return.

During our six-week visit, the ethnographic museum in Cuenca, Museo del Banco Central, invited me to return the following year for an exhibit of the Cañar portraits I'd done in 1991–93, and the U.S. embassy in Quito offered to sponsor the trip if I taught a weeklong photography workshop at the museum for indigenous participants. Thus began a chain of events that, these many years later, brings Michael and me to this catechism classroom, seated in the child-sized desks, on this Saturday afternoon.

Padre Enrique is reminding us that becoming godparents is the beginning of a lifetime commitment, and we rehearse a series of questions/answers for tomorrow's baptism. "Do you agree to provide books and supplies for your godchild if the parents are not able to do so?"

We *padrinos* answer on cue, in unison: "*Sí, asumimos la responsabilidad.*"

Then, "Do you agree to assure a Catholic education for your godchild?"

After each response, when everyone else in the room makes the sign of the cross, touching forehead, chest, and right and left shoulder, Michael raises a feeble hand to his chest and I adjust my glasses.

Our newest godchild is Nuncito, the last of four children born to Andrés, another of my first photography students. He and his beautiful young wife, Luz, had been among our earliest friends in Cañar, and we loved their two darling girls, Toa and Sisa, miniature versions of their mother.

Years later, during another of our visits to Cañar, Luz died a sad death. Andrés first told us that his wife had died of head injuries several days after an old aunt hit her with a piece of firewood during a fight. They had been drinking. Later, Andrés changed the story to a "heart condition," and we didn't ask questions.

Of all our original Cañari friends, this sweet gentle man has made the biggest mess of his life. We've watched as his promise as a high school graduate (rare for his generation) evaporated into an early marriage with too many children too fast, and the crushing drudgery of being a poor farmer with little land. (In contrast, his sisters and brother have made use of their hard-won educations and created stable professional lives, as agronomist, teacher, and lawyer.) By the time of Luz's death, she and Andrés had both been drinking heavily, if episodically, for several years, and reduced to living in a two-room hovel on the edge of her family's land. By then, they had two other children—the youngest Nuncito, barely a year old when his mother died.

Andrés was in no condition to care for his children. He gave Nuncito to Luz's sweet old grandmother, Mama Juliana, who had asked to care for the baby "until she died." He left the other children, three girls from about three to eight years, with his own widowed mother, the valiant Mama Rosita. Several years later, when Mama Juliana died, Nuncito also came to live with Mama Rosita. By then, years of malnutrition and inadequate care had left the boy seriously undersized for his age, with possible developmental problems. I remember photographing him years ago at Mama Juliana's hut, right before she died: a tiny boy dressed up like a Cañari man by his proud great-grandmother.

We didn't see Andrés again until in 2000, when he showed up at our house one day with some important news. He had decided to "*ajuntar con una vecina*," as he put it—informally marry a neighbor. Manuela was a single mother who had worked many years as a maid in Cuenca, and she'd recently come home to live with her mother and daughter. (Pregnancy before a marriage is completely acceptable within the Cañari culture, but a young woman having a baby on her own, without a *novio*, or betrothed, is severely sanctioned. Unmarried young mothers often leave the community, while their own mothers take on responsibility for the illegitimate child. Manuela's was such a case; her daughter Marisa, five, had lived with her grandmother all her life.)

Andrés had come to invite us to a wedding—not his, but that of Manuela's sister, Benita. He said this occasion would serve as his and Manuela's "coming out" in the community. (That story is the chapter, "A Wedding in Cañar" in *Cañar: A Year in the Highlands of Ecuador*.)

During that year, and in the years since, we've watched with great sadness as Andrés's life has spiraled downhill as he continues to drink heavily, with frequent injuries and collapses. An accidental overdose after spraying with herbicide landed him in the hospital, and he's had several stays in a Cuenca clinic for alcoholism. Meanwhile, as his four children moved back and forth between grandmothers, he and Manuela had two of their own. Counting Manuela's first little daughter, Marisa, this makes Andrés the head of a fractured family of seven children.

Nuncito is nearly ten years old, and he could not be baptized before now because his father never registered his son's birth with the church. Andrés's sister, Mercedes, a good friend of ours, has hinted over the years that Michael and I would make good *padrinos*; I'm sure she was thinking we might provide her nephew a measure of protection and opportunity. This year, after Mercedes finally forced her brother to register his son's birth, she formally asked us to be Nuncito's *padrinos*. We agreed, wanting to offer Mercedes a sign of solidarity and friendship, though wary of tying ourselves to Andrés and his troubled family.

"As Catholics we should all be named after saints," Padre Enrique is saying. He frowns when no one answers. "*¿Cierto or no cierto?*"

"So," he continues in his loud voice, "which of these are saint's names: Michelle? Erica? Brian? Edwin?" Looking around the room with mock, wide-eyed disbelief, he gives a good-natured but again slightly fake chuckle and says, "Edwin?! ED-WEEN?!" The Spanish pronunciation with the emphasis on the "ween" gives it a wicked twist.

"These are North American names," he goes on, "influenced by the effects of migration to a capitalist, consumerist culture! *¿Cierto or no cierto?*"

Stunned silence fills the room. Surely every person sitting here has a relative living in that "capitalist, consumerist culture" to the north and is grateful for the dollars coming back from it.

"So tell me," Padre Enrique goes on after a beat, his dark eyes boring into us. "What are some proper names for Catholics?"

You could have heard a pin drop.

"María!" he bursts out impatiently. "Now there's a good Catholic name." I groan inwardly, recalling the endless confusion that arises from every woman of earlier generations being named María and every man José.

Michael with Nuncito after the baptism

"And here are some other saints we should be naming our children after." The priest glances down at a list on the table. "San José, San Pedro, Santa Cecilia, San Jorge, San Andrés, Santa Dolores, Santa Mónica . . ."

Then he looks up in triumph for his zinger conclusion: "There has NEVER, EVER been a Saint Edween."

After admonishing us to be at the church the next day promptly at two o'clock, Padre Enrique releases us. I feel a collective sigh in the room as we struggle to get out of the small desks. As we stand, I lean over to Michael and whisper, "If he asks you your name tomorrow, tell him that it's Edwin."

~

JOURNAL, MARCH 30

Michael told me this morning that he has burned off fifteen pounds since January and gained two belt loops. While he's not unhappy to be back to his college weight, he joked that he's having a hard time keeping his pants up.

We go down to the house site with the video camera to do a little tour for Scott and Susanne, our son and daughter-in-law in San Francisco. Michael soon leaves to go to the market, while I stay to separate some trees that I've planted too close on the east side of the house.

Juan, our neighbor who sold us the lot, comes over to the fence, curious to see what I've planted and to chat. I take particular care to be loquacious and newsy as I want to be on good terms with Juan and his wife, Rosa, and I know giving personal information generates a certain amount of trust, or at least a sense of familiarity.

I tell him that while we're in the United States, Michael and I both work to make enough money so we can live here without looking for paid jobs (underlying message: we are not rich, retired Americans). And I tell him our plans to live here six months. Finally, although this had not been my intention at the outset, I say how happy we are to have this property and add, "If you ever decide to sell that triangular piece of land below us, please allow us to have first chance to buy it."

His face reveals nothing, but I can see he's pleased with the direction of the conversation. We parted as friendly neighbors.

CHAPTER 10

Strike!

Blocking the Pan-American

WE ARE UP AT SIX O'CLOCK on a Wednesday morning and standing beside the Pan-Am Highway by six thirty, waiting for a bus to Cuenca. I didn't have time for breakfast, so I stuck a couple of Michael's bagels in my pack. On Monday, when we tried to go to Cuenca and found the roads blocked by a strike, Michael came home and worked out his frustration by making bagels. Today, we are trying again because we need to get to Cuenca to extend our visas. Plus, Michael reminds me, he must buy some lox and cream cheese before the bagels are gone.

Last January, we came into the country with the usual tourist visas, which gave us ninety days. These will soon expire, but we're not worried because in past years we've extended our visas without any problem. We simply went to the *Ministerio de Relaciones Exteriores,* paid about five dollars apiece, and a young official stamped our passports—whack! whack!—and we were good for another ninety days. We expect to do this again to make us legal until we leave at the end of June.

At the highway, the few people hanging around tell us, *no hay paso,* can't get through. But Michael and I have lived through many strikes in our years in Ecuador, and we know from experience that while everyone has an opinion, and rumors circulate like crazy, no one really knows anything for sure. Plus, the real situation tends to change from hour to hour.

I look up and down the Pan-Am, the only north-south transportation artery through Ecuador that is usually roaring with heavy long-haul trucks and buses, and see that it is virtually empty and eerily quiet. A few local taxis ferry people to work and parents drive their children to school.

But it is early, so we decide to stick around and try our luck.

This strike—or *mobilización,* as it's more accurately known here—was called a week ago by the national indigenous organization, CONAIE (Confederation of Indigenous Nationalities of Ecuador), to protest the government's signing of a free trade agreement with Colombia, Peru, and the United States. The government says the purpose of the agreement—known as the *Tratado de Libre Comercio,* or TLC—is economic integration among the countries in the Western Hemisphere. But CONAIE argues that the TLC favors the U.S. economy by ensuring access to Ecuadorian markets and natural resources, which threatens rural economies and the environment and, by extension, the economic and cultural survival of the indigenous people.

CONAIE called for a coordinated national *acción,* by the usual method of blocking the Pan-Am Highway, to send a message to the government. Indigenous communities in each province were directed to build and maintain roadblocks in their area, an effort coordinated in Cañar by the UPCCC, the local CONAIE political affiliate.

In the days leading up to the *acción,* trucks with speakers drove through indigenous communities calling on men and women to come build the barricades and maintain the strike, and I heard announcements on the local radio station, Radio Ingapirca. But until now the *bloqueo* seems to have been an uncoordinated, hit-or-miss affair. During the day, protestors drag trees, branches, and big rocks onto the highway to create barriers, although a few cars and small trucks get through by swerving around rocks and brush strewn along the road. At night, local police or military clear away the barricades and big transport trucks and a few buses get though. The routine seems to be nonconfrontational and nonviolent, with protesters and police taking pains to avoid one another.

On the first day of the strike, I rode up the mountain with a group of protestors, hoping to get some photos. Men and women from several villages— maybe one hundred in total—had gathered to build a barrier at a high point on the Pan-Am, between Cañar and Cuenca. When we arrived, a few large rocks had already been rolled down the hillside onto the highway, partially blocking it, but someone told me that the real *acción* was to be the delivery of two dump truckloads of gravel that would completely close the road.

We waited a couple of hours for the trucks, but the day was so sunny and warm and the mood so festive that the gathering felt more like a Sunday outing than a political action. Women in bright skirts sat on the grassy hillside above the road and enjoyed themselves, gossiping and knitting. Young people milled around, flirting and giggling, excited to have a day off from whatever they would otherwise be doing. The men showed off their prowess every now and then by rolling a few more big rocks onto the road, but without a serious effort to stop the few cars and trucks that ventured to run the obstacle course. And I enjoyed watching it all and taking a few photos.

Finally, two matching yellow dump trucks appeared down the road about the same time as the local police. Four or five transit officers dressed in military fatigues left their car fifty meters away and walked slowly into the crowd. The trucks, meanwhile, had slowed to a stop and sat waiting. I watched as older Cañari men, community leaders, moved toward the policemen to shake hands and speak. When I got close enough to get a photo, I could hear one of the men say "*colabore*" to a policeman. Collaborate. This is standard Cañari protocol during a *bloqueo*: asking the police to support the strike. The policemen continued to slowly maneuver through the crowd in a friendly way while the two trucks slowly approached, turned around, and got into position to dump their loads. It was almost comical, watching the crowd, the police, and the trucks engage in this slow "dance."

The drivers raised their truck beds, opened the tailgates, dumped the gravel, and took off at full speed while the police continued to stand around and the protestors began walking back to town. The *acción* seemed to be over. I joined the walkers, tired and ready to go home. Tonight the military men would remove enough gravel to allow some trucks and buses through; tomorrow another village would be called upon to maintain the barricade by whatever creative means they might come up with.

～

On this morning a week later, Michael and I still wait for a bus beside the Pan-Am, but now we are chilled to the bone. We consider hiring a truck to try to get us to Cuenca, so Michael crosses the road to talk to Rene, one of our regular drivers, who sits in his truck waiting for business. Rene tells him the strike has "hardened" and no one can get through. But he offers to take us as far as the first *bloqueo*, where, he says, we can walk eight kilometers or so of "no-man's land" to another blockade farther south. From there, we can get a truck or taxi to take us to Cuenca.

"No way," I say when Michael comes back to propose this. I simply can't walk that far today. As I was planning to spend a couple of days in Cuenca, my backpack weighs about fifteen pounds with laptop, books, camera, and a change of clothes. "And besides," I end with a groan, "It's really cold today and it will be even colder on top."

We wait at the bus stop another few minutes, and just as we are about to go home, a yellow Transportes Cañaris bus appears. "Cuenca! Cuenca!" the driver's helper hangs out the door and yells, as though everything were normal.

Ah, warm bus. We find our seats, and I take off my hat and scarf and open my book. Michael leans over and says, "This driver must know something others don't know. I think we'll actually get to Cuenca today." We settle in for the two-hour ride.

Buses in Cañar are privately owned, but their proprietors belong to cooperatives that include a complex network of relatives, drivers, mechanics, and helpers who aspire to be drivers. Two bus lines run between Cañar and Cuenca, alternating every fifteen minutes under normal circumstances. The system is usually efficient and dependable, and in times of strikes and *bloqueos*, owners and drivers will do just about anything to keep the buses running. They communicate with cell phones about when and where roads are open or closed and if any alternative routes exist.

At the crest of the mountain outside Cañar, we run into the first barricade of trees and rocks. The road is completely blocked. At this early hour, there are no protesters maintaining the blockade, but there's no way we can get through. Hardly missing a beat, the driver backs up fifty meters and takes off on a dirt road running east, in the direction of the old San Pedro hacienda. "Here's what the driver knew," Michael says, looking well pleased. "This road will take us around to the other side of the *bloqueo*."

Although we've walked this area many times, I've never seen the country from the high vantage point of a bus. I stop reading, sit back, and enjoy the detour, with spectacular views of mountains to the east that mark the frontier with the Amazon, and intriguing little settlements in the lush green valley below. "Let's walk this valley one day when the house is done," I say to Michael. "When the house is done . . ." is preface to any reference these days to our future lives in Cañar.

The young driver's assistant starts down the aisle collecting fares, and as he comes near us I can hear he is trying to get everyone to pay fifty cents extra. We are only eight or ten passengers, but folks are arguing back in a friendly way. "The strike is not our fault," says one man. "Why should we pay more?"

"It's taking us even longer than usual to get to Cuenca," points out another passenger.

The young assistant, who can't be more than sixteen, pleads in return, "Look how far out of our way we are going. Think of the gas . . . and you're getting extra service. Almost no one can get through these days." Seeing the logic of his argument, touched by his youthful earnestness, and grateful to be on our way, we all pay the extra fifty cents.

An hour later, we bump back onto the Pan-Am and continue without incident to Cuenca.

~

Two days later, we are on our way home on another Transportes Cañaris bus. The strike continues, but I read in the Cuenca paper that the Cañari leaders and the provincial government agreed to open the Pan-Am four hours a day. No mention of *which* four hours, however.

An hour north of Cuenca, we come to the first blockade, an enormous pile of earth dumped into the roadway from a steep hillside, looking almost like a landslide. But it doesn't quite cover the two lanes, so the driver tells us to get off while he inches the bus over the mound, tipping precariously to one side. We climb back on the bus, but forty minutes later, we come to the second blockade on the mountain above Cañar. Here the road is completely blocked with trees, rocks, and old tires. Apparently, we have missed the four-hour window. We sit for ten minutes while the driver chats on his cell phone, before his helper yells back at us: "*No hay paso.* You'll have to get off and walk."

Michael staggers down the highway under the weight of two boxes of groceries and plumbing materials, while I follow, carrying his heavy shopping bag along with a bag of my own and the overloaded backpack. A few other passengers, less burdened, march ahead of us on the highway, while some take off running on trails or dirt roads into the country; no doubt they know shortcuts to their homes.

We've gone about a hundred meters before two friendly young men catch up

Bus service interruptus

with us and offer us a ride. They say they've parked their car below and climbed the hill to examine the blockade. They say they want to get to Cuenca, but they don't sound too urgent and I think the whole thing was a lark for them. They help us carry our things to their car, give us a ride to our front gate, and refuse to take anything for their good deed.

~

A series of rainy, cold days follow, with lots of complications at the house site. The strike has pretty well stopped all deliveries, so trucks can't get through with the gravel, sand, and rock we need. Also, the special load of wood that Lourdes has bought in Cuenca can't be delivered. Michael frets that the crew will soon run out of materials and thus work.

Then one night we hear on the radio that, although negotiations to end the strike continue, the Pan-Am will be open the next morning from five to eight o'clock. Michael calls Lourdes, who says she will send a truck with the wood along with Javier, the carpenter. Michael gets up at five fifteen and shoots down two espressos while waiting for José María. They walk to the highway to meet the truck at a quarter to six and guide the driver to the house site. There, he backs over Michael's new waterline, breaking it, but Michael later says it was worth it to keep the crew working. Lourdes arrives soon after in her little pick-up. She talks to the workers and explains that Javier will spend several days on the site to direct the framing of doors and windows. Then she jumps back into her truck and heads back to Cuenca before the roads close again at eight o'clock.

~

JOURNAL, APRIL 10

Paiwa comes after school, at one-thirty, and effectively ends my workday. As delightful as she is to have around, her time eats my time. After lunch, as I sit in the sun on the patio reading, and Paiwa sits nearby playing with a doll, she asks me out of the blue if I could live without Michael. I say I could, but I wouldn't want to. Then she asks me if I would "die" without books, and I say yes.

For school tomorrow, she has an assignment to research trees and she wants to do it on the Internet. Will I help? She's never been on the Internet. So we walk into town to one of the new "cyber cafes" that have sprung up lately and I introduce her to Google and show her how to search for "parts of trees." Paiwa catches on immediately, although when I explain that certain websites have commercial interests (one tree site is sponsored by a paper company), her eyes glaze over. It's not time for that lesson yet.

On the way home, we stop at one of the street stalls selling pirated CDs and DVDs. Paiwa wants to find *Selena, The Movie*, with Jennifer Lopez. She is obsessed with the story of Selena, the Tejano singer-songwriter who was shot and killed a few years ago by the president of her fan club. We find it, for one dollar, and Paiwa goes home happy.

CHAPTER 11

Putting Out Fires

~

The house fully framed

OUR TIME IS GOING TOO FAST! It's the first of April, three months into our house construction and three months before we leave at the end of June. Michael has been in a terrible funk these past couple of weeks as he attempts to install his American-standards electrical and plumbing systems in this ad hoc world. He says the project is now so far behind schedule that he'll have to come back this fall to finish his work.

This house has no basement—Michael's usual plumbing domain—so he has to lay many of the pipes now, and correctly, as they will soon be buried beneath concrete slabs in some rooms, wooden floors in others, and earth in the case of the courtyard. This week, he's laying large plastic pipes, drilled with holes for drainage, under the courtyard. Other pipes will crisscross beneath the house to bring cold and hot water to the kitchen and bathrooms, carry waste to the new septic tank, and send gray water (from bathroom sinks, showers, and laundry) to irrigate the field below. Michael wakes in the night and puzzles over the complications, then scribbles notes and diagrams in his notebook in the morning.

"Putting out fires, that's all I do," he grumbled this morning. "I'm nothing but a troubleshooter, runner for materials, buyer of tools, and on-site dogsbody, all while I'm trying to solve my own problems."

Yesterday he went down to the construction site ready to work, only to be told by the *maestros* that they were nearly out of lumber. With the framing going up fast, the house seems to eat an endless amount of wood. So Michael ran to the local lumberyard and placed an order. Hours later, the wood was delivered and unloaded before it was discovered that it was another customer's order. While the workers reloaded the wood, Michael ran to the lumberyard again—none of our phones are working—and straightened out the order with the owner, Don Pepe. But when Michael tried to pay for the wood with a hundred-dollar bill, Don Pepe looked it over carefully and wouldn't take it because it carries the series number of counterfeit bills that Colombians are circulating through this area. All this happened before lunch.

After lunch, he went back to the site to find that one of the *maestros* had used Michael's special coil of ground wire to patch together a makeshift extension cord to run the sander. (Michael is very particular about using a ground wire, which protects appliances and computers against damaging errant electrical currents, but no one understands its purpose here.) Meanwhile, another worker had driven a pick through some plastic piping that Michael had just buried in one of the bathrooms. Then, the final straw, he found that yet another worker had borrowed his drill and left it in the sawdust.

"See what I mean?" he says bitterly later that afternoon. "I just haven't learned to accept that construction workers here don't come with their own tools. That means I provide everything—hammers, tape measures, drills, picks, shovels, files, grinders, saws, and wheelbarrows . . . . The men use 'em, abuse 'em, break 'em, lose 'em. Remember when our main *maestro* came to work the first day with only a metal tape, with the first meter of numbers unreadable? That should have been a clue."

"But it's completely understandable," I argue back. "These are not professional construction workers, but *campesinos*, some barely out of school. They're not used to handling tools with care, and as poorly paid manual workers, there's no way they can afford to buy their own tools."

Despite the grousing, it's clear Michael thrives on it all. He charges out the door every morning before eight o'clock to be on site when the workers arrive, usually stays all day, and sometimes can't resist getting in on the hard physical labor. During the foundation work, he described (rather immodestly) how he helped break an enormous rock with a sledgehammer and chisels. Then the other day he came home bloody after wrestling with a giant *penco*, a spiny cactus-like century plant that he saved from the construction chaos and transplanted in what one day might be our yard. At this stage, every time I visit the site, he's up in the air crawling on the ceiling joists, installing electrical wire. I beg him to be careful. A few months ago, a *maestro* fell from an overhead roof beam on a construction project in town and died.

~

Now it's time for *our* roof. Michael went down to the site a couple of weeks ago to find Santos working with an adze, carving the end of each wooden rafter in a large pile on the ground. "Jaguars," Santos said simply when Michael asked him what he was doing. "For the roof." He is indeed a man of few words, so we never learned where the idea came from to carve animal heads on the ends of roof rafters. I wouldn't have thought "jaguars" once I saw the rafters lined up to create the roof eaves, but the result is certainly beautiful. (Later, I read that the jaguar, like the serpent, condor, and macaw, is a common figure in Andean cosmology and art . . . but in architecture?)

Roof beam jaguar details

A week later, a motley crew of roofers arrived with tools (yes!), sleeping mats, blankets, clothes, and cooking gear. Contracted in Cuenca by Lourdes, six men and teenage boys came first, and other helpers followed, until one day I counted twelve men up in the air. They tread the beams fearlessly like tightrope walkers, and I tremble at the thought that one might fall. So far we've not had one accident on the project.

The roofers live on site during the week, sleeping in a "nest" they've created in an attic space above a bedroom ceiling, accessible only by ladder. It's the only protected place in the house as all the other rooms are open-beamed and open-walled.

We've never met their boss, the roofing contractor, but Lourdes—the ultimate boss—told the workers they couldn't cook on the site; the wooden framework is a delicate set of matchsticks that would go up in a fiery instant. Also, I mentioned the obvious to Michael, that there are no sanitary facilities on the site, and I hated to think what the workers are doing, and where, when nature calls— the neighbor's cornfields? Michael said only that he had suggested the workers keep a shovel handy. I'm sure genteel Lourdes was too delicate to say anything.

One Saturday morning, with the roofers gone to Cuenca for the weekend, I walk down to take a look around. I peek into the space where my darkroom will be and see a hotplate set up on the brick floor, with dirty dishes scattered around. So the workers *have* been cooking here. It looks safe enough, however, so I won't tell Lourdes. I climb to the top rung of the ladder and peer into the dark den where the roofers sleep, see a tangle of clothes and blankets, and quickly retreat.

Flying around in the sawdust of the courtyard, I find a page from ¡EXTRA! a supermarket tabloid with a photo of a bare-bottomed woman with a miniature soccer ball over her groin. ("Sexy! Discover Rebecca!" the headline screams.) Incredibly, little Ecuador has made it to the World Cup this month; the team will beat Poland and Costa Rica before being trounced by Germany. Sex and soccer make an unbeatable combo to sell newspapers to bored young men stuck in backwater Cañar.

~

Roof tiles made with unglazed terra-cotta (Latin for "baked earth") were brought to the New World by the Spanish in the sixteenth century, but they've probably been used for shelters as long as clay has been fired. Tile roofs can last up to one hundred years or longer, but the tiles themselves are delicate and can easily break; they are also heavy and require more structural support than other roof types. In Cañar, clay tiles or thatch were the only roofing materials on country houses until recently, when cheaper and faster cement asbestos and metal materials such as corrugated iron began to be used. As I walk around, I see lots of old adobe houses with walls crumbling, but their lichen-covered roofs are still intact.

Our roof will be a combination of the old and the new. We'll use traditional half-barrel-shaped, unglazed tiles, but they will be attached with a thin wire to a network of notched wooden strips laid over plywood sheets and thick asphalt. A labor-intensive and expensive system, but, according to Lourdes and the roofing contractor, guaranteed to be windproof and waterproof "forever."

As the roofers work, they toss broken tiles, asphalt strips, wire, nails, and bits of wood into the patio or onto the ground below. One of my only contributions to the house construction these days, other than recording it with photos, is picking up debris. (And I will be finding those bits of the roof in the garden for many years to come.)

Since the beginning, we've understood that cleaning up on the job is not part of the workers' responsibility. It is ours. There's no regular garbage collection here, so Michael and I create piles of rubble and rubbish and hire a driver with a truck to take them away. We don't ask where.

Today, Saturday, ill-humored and frustrated that he's not been able to get much done with so many roofers in his way, Michael goes down to the construction site to work alone with José María. He comes back in the afternoon, elated that they've strung nearly a "half-kilometer" of electrical cable. This accomplishment returns him to his old self: happy, expansive, affectionate, and praising the dedication and skill of his workers and even the roofers. Tools? Of course, he's happy to provide them. Why not?

~

Despite the fact that our small rented house has become an extension of the construction site—filled with plumbing parts, electrical supplies, and bathroom fixtures—I've managed to carve out one small working space for myself. My laptop and cameras occupy one table, where we also eat and where Paiwa sometimes crowds in to do her homework or set up her electronic keyboard and play us the latest "canned" tune she's learned at her music lessons (percussion and background musicians provided, Paiwa picks out the melody with one finger). We praise her extravagantly.

My work: I'm presently finishing up audiovisual archives for local organizations, delivering photo CDs, videos, and sound recordings of everything I've documented since I came in January—Carnival, Fiesta de San Antonio, International Women's Day, Primero de Mayo—plus a written register of dates, event, content, etc. When I have the time, I spend a few extra hours making attractive covers for the CDs and videos with color photocopies of the images that match the events.

This archive was my brilliant idea for a project this year. Of all the groups I've worked with in the last fifteen years, not one has an audiovisual record of its activities. Most operate as cooperatives that change leadership every few years, and the outgoing team often takes home what few photos or videos were created during their watch, or the materials get loaned out, or simply lost. For years I've been hearing, "We *had* a collection of photos, but they seem to be lost," or "The video camera just vanished."

So several months ago I proposed to the president of each organization that I would develop an archive of their activities, volunteering my labor as a photographer/videographer, if they would reimburse me for the materials. The idea met with great enthusiasm, with an additional request. Each organization wanted the photos and videos of *other* groups. Although TUCAYTA sponsors Carnival, UPCCC wanted those photos, and TUCAYTA requested photos of Inti Raymi, a fiesta put on by UPCCC. Even within organizations, work groups such as the health committee want their own photos. No one trusts anyone else to keep track of documentary materials. I agreed to everything.

I also requested that someone from each group work with me as a sort of apprentice, documenting events, workshops, or meetings, so that I could pass on the technology and skills and they could do their own documentation. Everyone loved that idea, too.

But after several months, when I deliver the CDs, videos, and written inventory, after I accept the praise and thanks, folks are rather puzzled when I mention the cost—usually under twenty dollars. "We don't have petty cash," I hear from one secretary, and from another, "Can you make us a discount?" One started digging into her purse to pay me. "I'll come back later," I always end up saying, but then I don't.

Nor have I had much success passing on the technology. Everyone is busy, and equipment is scarce, doesn't work, or gets lost. I try loaning my camera for an event if someone will work with me, and that has helped, but I think, at least for now, this archive will be my personal initiative. I don't mind. The cost is minimal and I enjoy being the Cañari community documentarian. (It was, after all, my original dream when I first came to Cañar years ago.)

To stay calm and patient, I carry a novel to appointments and meetings— which can start up to two hours late, be put off until the next day, or simply be canceled. I've had so much reading time lately that I just finished the eight-hundred-page *Anna Karenina* in two weeks. At this rate, I'll soon run out of books. Then it *will* be time to go home.

JOURNAL, MAY 5

We've been without our house phone for two weeks, and today I'm determined to get to the bottom of the problem. Friends of friends are arriving this afternoon from Guayaquil, and the only way they can find us is to call once they get off the bus.

I climb the steep hill into town and then up a side street to the telephone office. There, I'm sent straight upstairs to the office of the *técnico*, where other complaining customers are already crowded around a beleaguered man sitting at his desk. With a phone at each ear, he looks up at us hopelessly, his eyes red and irritated behind thick glasses. One customer is saying he's been without a phone for a month, another says three weeks. All are begging to have service turned back on, using the particular wheedling tone that Ecuadorians employ when asking a favor.

When it's my turn to speak, before I can even open my mouth, the *técnico* asks my number and the name of the landlord and writes out a repair order. The desk is littered with such orders. "I can live without a telephone," I say (I rehearsed this while waiting), "but friends are coming to Cañar today by bus and their only way to contact us is by phone. They don't speak Spanish and don't know where we live."

The poor man barely listens. I'm sure he's sick of hearing about everyone's urgent reason to have their phones reconnected—"sick kid" seems an especially popular cause. He explains that Cañar is expanding its phone service, and work on the new lines has damaged the old lines. The contract is with a local contractor.

"So that's private business for you!" he says, standing now. "If it was up to us, we could do something, but with a contractor, we're helpless!"

Then he speaks directly to me. "In your country, you have good services, and complaints get action, but here . . . " he finishes the thought with a shrug.

Now I feel a little ashamed and sorry for him. "I understand," I say, as kindly as possible and leave the office.

CHAPTER 12

Personae non Gratae in Ecuador

(or) Why We Went to Peru Last Week

~

Carlos and Michael crossing the bridge to Peru

THE YOUNG IMMIGRATION police officer behind the desk flips quickly through Michael's stamp-filled passport, turning it this way and that before looking more carefully, page by page. "Here it is!" Michael says, leaning a little too quickly across the desk and pointing to his Ecuador tourist visa. "Stamped when we came into the country on January 11, and good for ninety days!" The officer does not blink or look up.

It is April 10, one day before our visas expire, and we are in Cuenca, at the Ministry of Foreign Relations, to request an additional ninety days to stay in the country. Weeks ago, when we checked in with this very office, we were told—erroneously I now suspect—that we could only apply for an extension *one* day before our present visas expired. That seemed crazy to me then, but we were busy with the strike and construction snafus and didn't check with anyone else. Now we have dutifully shown up on the appointed day, as instructed, even though I feel terrible, with a fever and cough, symptoms of *la gripe*, the flu.

After an hour sitting in a line of chairs in the hallway, we are finally escorted into a small office marked *Migración*. Two desks sit side by side, each manned by a young uniformed man, average age about twenty-two. Earlier, while waiting our turn, I had watched this pair through a glass partition as they fooled around—poking one another, making jokes, giggling. I was reminded of my own adolescent son and his friends, years ago, half attracted, half repelled by the sheer physical and sexual energy they suddenly possessed. In the case of these two young men, I suppose their energy is also fed by the frisson of absolute power they feel over supplicants like us, two gringos—"probably rich ones"— asking for visa extensions.

"Hmm," the one who attends us says, "I see you have changed visas."

"Yes, but . . ." Michael and I answer in unison, an annoying habit we have. I let him go on: "We were in Ecuador last year with a special cultural visa for my wife's grant. It was good for one year. We left in July and came back this January as tourists. As you can plainly see, these are two different visas."

"But you already *had* a visa last year," the officer says stubbornly, his eyes narrowing. "That means you can't extend this one."

The logic of this completely stumps us. What did one visa have to do with the other? Michael and I take turns arguing. The first visa was for *last* year; this one is for *this* year. We are entirely legal, and we have the right to an extension, like any other tourist.

"Besides," I say finally, "if there was a problem, surely the immigration officers at the Quito airport would have noticed when we came into the country." (An unwise comment, in retrospect.)

The young officer just shakes his head, unmoved. But Michael and I persist, saying in unison several times, "*No es justo.*" This is not right! Finally, the officer looks up and around and yells to his partner, "*Ven acá!*" Come here! The second young man has been leaning on a filing cabinet nearby, cleaning his fingernails and obviously listening. With heads together, they study our passports like schoolboys trying to figure out a math problem. After a minute, the second officer shakes his head as if the situation is hopeless.

"I'll call the office in Quito," our guy says, stepping to the next desk and picking up the phone. I watch as he makes a highly suspicious one-minute phone call in a country where no official phone is answered in fewer than many rings and several tries. Even tense and distracted with a fever, I am sure it is a fake call.

He puts the phone down and hands back our passports. "You must go to Quito or Guayaquil to take care of this," he says in a stern voice.

"But we can't go on such short notice," I say, my voice rising several tones. "Our visas expire tomorrow, I have *la gripe*, and we are in the midst of building a house. It's not possible to travel right now to Quito or Guayaquil. . . ."

Stony silence. Michael asks what would happen if we didn't do anything, if we let our tourist visas expire and simply stay in the country.

"Then you'll be illegal," the officer says flatly, "and that means you can be arrested or fined two hundred dollars each when you do leave the country." Seeming to lose interest in us, he steps away to the other desk where his partner sits.

Michael and I stay put in our chairs, stunned at what amounts to a mini-disaster and unsure what to do next. As we sit there, a bizarre scene begins to play out at the desk next to us. The two young officers are elaborately counting out bills: five, ten, eleven, twelve, thirteen—and so on, up to nineteen. They discuss at some length that one dollar is missing; there should be twenty. Then they recount, slowly fingering each bill.

Michael and I sit and watch, incredulous. What on earth is going on?

The men tuck the money away and continue to ignore us. Finally, there is nothing left for us to do but get up and leave. In the taxi, Michael and I realize at the same moment that the little performance counting the money was a signal that these two young upholders of the law wanted a *propina*, a bribe. But of course! How stupid of us to forget we are in a country that regularly ranks among the most corrupt in Latin America. A measly twenty dollar bill would surely have resolved things.

We spend the night in Cuenca, as I am in no condition to travel. Next day, we visit our old friend, Isabel León, a travel agent we've known since we lived in Cuenca in the early 1990s and who has helped us with visa matters in the past. She too doesn't understand why we can't have an extension of a perfectly good tourist visa, but she thinks it might not be too late to try the *propina* strategy. She suggests we leave our passports and twenty dollars with her, and she will send her office boy back to the immigration office the next morning and try to get our passports stamped.

It doesn't work. Bribes, like soccer goals, depend on timing, and we have missed our chance. Next day, Isabel proposes one last strategy. She will call her special contact in Guayaquil. "He can get anything done for a price," she assures us. So our passports go to Guayaquil on the morning plane. The special contact calls Isabel to say that for two hundred and fifty dollars he can get our visas extended, but for only thirty days. We would still have to pay a two hundred-dollar fine each when we leave the country. We tell Isabel we won't do it. The passports come back on the evening plane.

There is another serious complication. We have initiated the process to become residents of Ecuador, and all the paperwork is being handled in Quito by an unseen immigration lawyer, Dr. Jiménez (all lawyers are called "doctor" here). He has told us the process will take a few weeks and that the final step will be to send our passports to the Ministry of Foreign Relations in Quito to have new residency visas entered and signed. But, of course, this can only happen it we are in the country legally. As of now we are *ilegales*, illegals, *personae non gratae en Ecuador*.

One option, and the only one now, is to pay the fine, leave Ecuador, and return again as tourists. This will give us an additional sixty days—we've already lost the extra thirty days by overstaying our visas—but we'll have enough time before our scheduled departure for Portland at the end of June. Hopefully, this will also allow us time to acquire our residency visas; otherwise, we'll have to come again next year as tourists.

But by now I am too sick to travel, having neglected to go to a doctor until my flu has become a full-blown bronchial infection. So I visit a pneumonologist in Cuenca, who sends me for a chest x-ray, lectures me on "chronic bronchitis," and writes a prescription for antibiotics. We slink back home to Cañar. Could things get any more complicated?

~

A month later, when I am finally cured, we return to *Relaciones Exteriores* in Cuenca, pay the four-hundred-dollar fine, have our passports stamped to show we're legal (and thus allowed to leave the country), and buy bus tickets for Peru for the next day.

Early the next morning, we take the so-called luxury bus from Cuenca to Huaquillas, the border town with Peru about five hours away. "Luxury" in this case means a big TV mounted behind the driver with nonstop movies blasting. Three Jean-Claude van Damme features later, we have dropped eight thousand feet through a series of mountains to the coastal plain of banana plantations, cacao, barefoot children, energy-sapping heat, and men in hammocks. Why is it I rarely see a woman in a hammock in the middle of day?

The bus lets us off at the Ecuadorian immigration post a few kilometers outside of town. Michael and I are nervous as we join the line at the small concrete building, along with an assorted group of backpackers and other bus travelers. We needn't have worried. When our turn comes, our passports get nothing more than a quick glance by the immigration officer and a good whack of the stamp on the appropriate page, allowing us to leave Ecuador.

We hire one of the taxis lined up outside the immigration post to take us into

Huaquillas, a chaotic border town that is a mishmash of street stalls, sidewalk vendors, pushcarts, moneychangers, taxi drivers, and scammers of all sorts, according to the guidebook. To cross the actual border into Peru, we must walk across the short "international bridge" that spans the Zarumilla River.

Once on the bridge, the level of activity, potential thievery, and importuning by bag carriers and drivers accelerates to a frantic level. We have barely gone a few steps before a man jingling car keys waylays us. "Hello, my friends . . . *muy peligroso acá,*" he says. Very dangerous here. "*Mucho robo.* Let me take you safe in my taxi . . ."

I march ahead, clutching my backpack to my front, but Michael slows to talk. Within about a minute, he has hired the man, whose name is Carlos, to drive us to the Peruvian *migración.* I can't believe it, but Michael later tells me he remembered when we'd come across this border five years ago that the Peruvian immigration post is a few kilometers away. It would indeed be dangerous, if not impossible, to walk that far. "Besides, I just liked his face," Michael says.

Carlos, neatly dressed, does have a kindly expression—perhaps practiced— that conveys we should trust him. We follow him a short distance beyond the bridge to a dusty street where his newish, whitish sedan sits parked alongside a long shed where a line of men squat, filling greasy five-gallon containers with gasoline. "*Mucho contrabando,*" Carlos says in the tone of a friendly tourist guide. Lots of contraband. "In Peru, the official price of gasoline is five dollars a gallon, so these guys bring the stuff in from Ecuador and sell it along the roads for much less."

Once on our way, Carlos begins his pitch, driving slowly and turning his head to talk only to "Señor Michael," somehow sensing that I still don't trust him. He says this short taxi ride is only the beginning of how he might be of service to us. Once we have our entry visas, where would we like to go? To the beach? He can take us to some beautiful beaches, only sixty kilometers away, for a short vacation. Or to Tumbes, the first town, only forty kilometers away? He knows a good hotel there, *muy bello, muy barato,* very nice, very cheap.

Michael finally tells him that what we really want is to get our entry visas to Peru stamped and go right back into Ecuador.

Carlos sees his opening. "Ah, Señor Michael. For that you will have to stay forty-eight hours in Peru. Very inconvenient! Very expensive! Sixty, one hundred dollars for a hotel in Tumbes. Dinner, too," he adds with relish, changing his story about the cheap hotel.

"But maybe I can fix it for you with the immigration police. They are my friends. Only twenty dollars for each passport and I will get them stamped. You'll be in and out! *Así!*" Like that!

In the back seat, Michael and I speak to one another in English, *sotto voce*. "I don't know if I trust this guy," I say.

"What else can we do?" Michael answers. "We don't want to spend two nights in Peru. And I think he's OK. Let's do it."

As Carlos pulls into the parking area in front of Peruvian Border Control, Michael sticks a twenty-dollar bill into each passport and hands them over. "Stay in the car . . ." Carlos orders as he gets out and disappears into one of the squat buildings. Michael and I sit silent with our separate thoughts. I am reminded that, although we are experienced travelers, fluent in Spanish, and careful not to be scammed, situations like this can quickly make us feel vulnerable.

"That man has just gone off with our passports," Michael says finally, staring with furrowed forehead in the direction where Carlos disappeared.

"Yes, but *we* have his car," I reply lightly, beginning to enjoy myself. I take photos out the window of the Border Control before seeing a sign that says "*Prohibido tomar fotografías*." I turn to see Michael looking glum and photograph him.

"Yeah, but *he* has the keys," he mutters.

We needn't have worried. Carlos comes back in fewer than ten minutes and proudly shows us our passports stamped with a Peruvian entry and exit stamp. He drives slowly back toward the bridge, looking over his shoulder and pointing at the stamps as Michael and I examine our passports to make sure the dates are right. Everything looks good.

"Now," Carlos says solemnly as he pulls his car into his dusty parking spot. He turns off the ignition and twists around to face us. "We will settle on something for me, eh? While we stay here in the car here, just us, very safe, no thieves."

Yeah, I think fleetingly, just very trapped.

"How about thirty dollars?" Carlos says. He reminds us that he has given forty dollars to the border police, and thirty seems appropriate compensation for him.

"I was thinking another twenty would be fair," Michael says politely, pulling out his wallet.

"Noooooooo, Señor Michael. I fix your passports. You can go back to Ecuador right away. Excellent service. You didn't have to stay twenty-four—I mean forty-eight—hours in Peru, in expensive hotel, and dinner, too. Thirty dollars is very good."

Carlos accepts twenty-five. Then, as a friendly gesture, he escorts us back to the international bridge, "so you won't be robbed," he adds pointedly. We shake hands and he gives us his cell number in case we want to get in touch. You never know.

It is now about three o'clock in the afternoon, and although we have been traveling since we left Cuenca early this morning, and are hot, tired, and thirsty,

Welcome to Ecuador

we know what we have to do: grab another taxi, go back to the Ecuadorian border post, and pray they will let us reenter the country, fewer than two hours after we have left it.

It works! With barely a glance at our increasingly busy passports, and another whack of the stamp, the immigration officer gives us tourist visas for sixty days, well beyond the date we're due to leave Cañar.

We feel fantastic, like kids who've just gotten away with something. We walk to the little store next to the immigration building, order two cold beers to celebrate, and sit at the table outside to wait for the bus to Machala, the hot coastal city two hours away where we plan to spend the night before heading back to Cañar tomorrow.

"We did it," Michael says triumphantly as we click beer bottles. "Legal again!"

~

JOURNAL, MAY 15

I have promised Paiwa that I would come down to her house and visit her grandmother today. I want to record Mama Paula telling the same stories that I recorded with Paiwa a few weeks ago, which she'd said she learned from her grandmother. Almost as an afterthought, I take the video camera and tripod.

As I come down the rough path to their house, I see Paiwa out in the field, dressed in work clothes—pants and old sweater, with her long hair loose. She yells that she's cutting feed for the cow and will come soon.

I find Mama Paula sitting by the woodpile outside her house, stooped and old but with the same sweet smile. I've brought her a bag of mandarins, and within a few minutes, she's peeled one and is chewing it with the few teeth she has left. Her hands are horribly affected by osteoarthritis, and when I touch her hand, she points to her feet and says they are the same, "almost good for nothing."

Mama Paula goes on to recite the work she was capable of doing in the past: "I could do everything—haul adobes, work in the fields, help build a house . . ." Paiwa, who has joined us, looked at her grandmother with such affection it is heartbreaking. "You never told me that," she said.

"Now, I'm good for nothing," Mama Paula says, "I can't do anything . . ." She begins to cry. "No, no, but you're here for Paiwa, and for María Esthela," I say, referring to Paiwa's mother. "That's important work." She isn't fooled, but her tears quickly pass.

I set up the tripod, video camera, and recorder on a stump near where Mama Paula is sitting. With the sun and the shade of the tree behind her, I can see it is a perfect place to film. Paiwa sits on an overturned bucket in front of her, off-camera, and I sit on another overturned bucket between the tripod and the recorder.

Mama Paula tells three or four stories, with a little prompting from Paiwa to get started. But once launched into a tale, Mama Paula is totally involved, animated, focused. In her jumbled mix of Quichua and Spanish, I understand almost nothing and have a hard time knowing when the story is over. After one, she says clearly in Spanish, "And that's the story I heard from my grandmother." Later, I ask if she knows any songs, but she says no. I can see it is time to finish up, but Mama Paula is obviously gratified at the attention, and I am delighted with the results.

As Mama Paula prepares to go feed her cow, and as I continue to film, she wraps a eucalyptus leaf tightly around a swollen finger. "She does that every day, for the pain," says Paiwa.

CHAPTER 13

On Becoming Residents of a Foreign Country

(or) "Just Go Get Married Again!"

~

House with roofers

WE ARE DOWN TO OUR LAST two weeks in Ecuador, with reservations home to Portland where we have dentist appointments, concert tickets, scheduled visits with family in Santa Fe and San Francisco, and an important anniversary celebration with friends. The tenants renting our house are scheduled to leave. Our Portland life is poised to go into motion, which means everything must run like clockwork *here*, so we can go *there*.

Trouble is, nothing runs like clockwork in Ecuador.

We suspected getting residency visas might be complicated, but we had no idea how byzantine the process would turn out to be. Back in April, our Quito immigration lawyer, Dr. Jiménez, assured us it would take a mere couple of months of *tramites*—paperwork—to navigate the process. According to him, we had only to submit the right documents to qualify as *inversionistas*, investors, pay the hefty legal and government fees, and voila! Done. *Visas indefinidas* that would allow us to go and come and stay as long as we like. I guess "right documents" were the key words that failed to warn us of what was to come.

Since then, Michael has made three trips to Quito, an eight-hour, nighttime bus ride from Cañar. Arriving in Quito at six in the morning, he would go to the Hilton Hotel for coffee and a crossword, take care of business during the day, fly back to Cuenca in the afternoon, and catch a bus back to Cañar by night. It was exhausting and expensive.

The first trip, Michael delivered notarized copies of our passports, photos, police reports, and *escritura*, the deed to prove we own land. But then, for complicated reasons, we didn't meet the financial requirements to qualify as investors because we couldn't prove a value of at least twenty-five thousand dollars for the land and house. Although we had paid more than that for the land alone, the sale had been recorded at the municipality at a much smaller amount, according to our lawyer Vicente Tenesaca, so we would avoid the high taxes. "Everyone does it," he said with a shrug. Underreporting the amount of a land purchase is apparently routine and not even illegal in the eyes of the municipality, though certainly this practice works counter to its own interests.

So after the first trip to Quito, when Michael came back with the bad news, Vicente called the municipality and asked for a *tasador*, or appraiser, hoping the unfinished house would help to add enough value to qualify. But then the roof became the issue. Since it was not yet done, the appraiser said he could not count the house as finished or give it a value.

More bad news. Vicente came to the house to tell us. We sat silent for a while; then Vicente suggested that he and Michael go talk to the city engineer. Michael changed out of work clothes, shaved, and went off with Vicente, coming back thirty minutes later to say the engineer had agreed to come on Monday to take another look at the house and give it a value.

And that's what happened, at least on the surface. The engineer came, took a look, and agreed the house would be worth so much once the roof was on. He signed some papers that Vicente had prepared, maybe with a little *propina* snuck in, and we squeaked above the minimum amount to qualify as *inversionistas*. Michael went back to Quito with more documents.

Finally, Dr. Jiménez called to say the moment had come to send our passports to the Ministry of Foreign Relations for the final prize: signed, sealed, and stamped *visas indefinidas*.

"Let's just send the passports by courier," I suggested to Michael when we got the call. "It's safe and fast and cheaper." But no, Michael would sooner send his right hand with a courier than his passport. So he made a second trip to Quito to personally hand our passports to Evita, Dr. Jiménez's secretary.

As the end of June approached and we'd heard nothing, we got nervous. When Michael called the office and got Evita, she said in an offhand manner, "Oh yes, everything's ready. Come to Quito on Monday to pick up your passports."

Relief. Our plane reservations for Portland were for seven days off. Sunday night Michael got on the bus at eleven o'clock, claiming, as he always does, that he sleeps just fine. In Quito, after his usual stop for coffee, newspapers, and a crossword, he arrived at the lawyer's office just as it opened. But Michael was in for an unpleasant shock: Dr. Jiménez told him that the passports were not in his office, but at the *Ministerio*. But, "*no problema*," he would send his runner, José, with Michael to pick up the passports. (Paper chase employees like José deliver and pick up documents and wait in lines.)

At the *Ministerio*, Michael's worst Kafkaesque fears were realized. José found the proper office, where he and Michael joined a long snaking line in front of a window. Their turn came just before the office closed for lunch. José engaged in a short discussion with the person behind the window, took a proffered document, and turned to Michael: "Now, just go back to Cañar and get this paper signed and you'll be done!"

At that point, as Michael describes it to me in a call from the Quito airport later, "I totally lost it. I ranted and raved at José, and my only regret was that I wasn't able to rant and rave at that duplicitous Dr. Jiménez and his careless secretary, Evita."

Poor Michael. We are stuck in a paperwork purgatory known as the point of no return. Or is it Dante's eighth circle of hell, which I believe is fraud? We do not trust this Dr. Jiménez and feel that from the beginning he led us in the wrong direction, or—most likely—he simply wasn't paying attention. Evita too, when she casually told Michael everything was ready. But now it is too late to start over with another lawyer, and we can't leave the country with our passports lying indefinitely in some dark corner of the *Ministerio de Relaciones Exteriores* in Quito.

After that phone call, I know what I have to do. I call our travel agent in Cuenca, Isabel, cancel our flights to Portland, and buy new tickets for the first week of July. This is expensive, as our economy tickets were nonrefundable, but it does give us new return tickets for September (when we've discussed Michael coming back). Then I walk to the Internet place and send e-mails to everyone who needs to know that we will not be back in Portland until a week after we'd planned.

Michael comes through the gate at eight o'clock that night. I'd expected to see a broken man, but he is surprisingly cheerful. Over drinks, he gleefully describes his adventure, right down to the weather, his fellow bus passengers, and what people were wearing in the waiting room at the *Ministerio* (he knows how I love these details). He insists he will go back to Quito in a couple of days to deliver the last official form that José handed him. But I convince Michael we can fax this one, reminding him he will still have to make another trip to Quito to pick up the passports. He agrees, for once, but asks that I take charge of running down the document, whatever it is, and getting it to Quito. "And now I get to go back to the construction," he says with a contented sigh, conveying that the complexities of building a house are nothing compared to those involved in becoming residents of Ecuador.

The next day, I visit our lawyer Vicente, who looks over the "critical" document and tells me that it is related to a kind of rural property tax, called an "*impuesto predial.*" I've never heard of this tax, but apparently, in order to get residency, we have to prove that we have paid it. Sounds simple. Vicente sends me to a depressing office above the old market, where I am met by a tired middle-aged clerk in a shabby suit behind a beat-up desk. When I tell him what I need, he bends his head over a thick ledger for a few minutes before announcing that we owe eight dollars and four cents. I lay a ten dollar bill on top of the desk. The clerk opens a top drawer with his right hand, and, with a quick little slap, his left hand neatly makes the bill disappear. I sit surprised for a moment before I realize that I've just unwittingly paid a *propina*. But the clerk looks so tired and beat down I don't begrudge him a penny of that one dollar and ninety-six cent bribe.

"Now just go to the notary for a signature and make a copy and you'll be done," he says, echoing José, the Quito paper chaser.

The next day, I call Dr. Jiménez to tell him that I have faxed the last document.

"*Excelente, excelente!*" he says loudly, but then, after a short pause, he adds that he's just realized that *un documento último* is required: our marriage certificate. I laugh out loud and say, "No way! We certainly don't carry around our marriage certificate."

"In that case," he says, "You'll just have to go get married again at the civil registry office in Cañar. Send me the notarized certificate." There's a moment's silence on my end before I say, "*Que locura!*" What craziness. "But we'll give it a try."

When Michael comes home that afternoon, I tell him, without preamble, that he has to marry me again. He looks uncomprehending for a moment before I add, "for the visas." He bursts out laughing, then sweetly drops to one knee and asks if I will be his bride. To celebrate, he makes a special cocktail of rum, lemon juice, and sparkling water. Then we have a second one.

A little tipsy, we talk about the crazy, particular path our lives have taken since we met twenty years ago in that little hostel full of bird-watchers in Monteverde, Costa Rica. If I hadn't convinced him to stay a few extra weeks for a planned climb of Mt. Chirripo, and if the climb hadn't been so difficult and we hadn't behaved so well and impressed one another so favorably, he might not have stayed on for the next five years. We wouldn't have gone to Ecuador for two years after that, then Oregon, then back to Ecuador where we are building a house and planning to live part of every year for the rest of our lives.

The next morning, sober and serious, we go to the *registro civil* and read the list of requirements posted on the wall for nonresident foreigners to marry. It's immediately clear that Dr. Jiménez's suggestion will not work. The first requirement is proof that the applicants are not already married to someone else, a *coup de grace* for that plan in that we are, strictly speaking, each legally married to someone else.

So we go on to Plan B and walk over to the office of Dr. Bermejo, the notary who handled the legal documents for our land purchase. He's always been friendly, and when we tell him our dilemma he looks at us with mock solemnity and says, "Señora Judy and Señor Michael, are you married to one another?" We answer, "Si, Doctor Bermejo." He tells his secretary to type up a document, which he signs and stamps.

I call Dr. Jiménez to tell him a "sort of" marriage certificate is on the way. "*Excelente, excelente!* Tell Michael to be at the *Ministerio* in Quito at 8:30 on Monday morning. He can pick up the passports himself."

So Michael makes his third overnight bus trip to Quito. He spends all Monday morning at the *Ministerio* waiting for some official called "*Señor Director General*" to arrive and sign the visas that have supposedly already been stamped into our passports. The clerk tells Michael that *Señor Director General* had to make an "urgent trip" to Guayaquil over the weekend, and he was not yet "upstairs." (We both read this as an extended weekend at the beach.)

While he is waiting, Michael makes several increasingly desperate calls to Dr. Jiménez's office, convinced he is once again on a wild goose chase.

Finally, near noon, Dr. Jiménez himself shows up at the *Ministerio* "to assist." He tells Michael to stay in the waiting room while he disappears through a doorway to an inner office. Perhaps the lawyer talked to someone who has clout, called in a favor, or paid a bribe, or maybe all three, because he comes out in about ten minutes with two passports in his hands.

Michael calls to tell me the news. He says his experience with Dr. Jiménez and his minions, and with the Ministry, has been so excruciatingly slow and humiliating that he can't believe it is over. He sounds low-key, almost depressed. (Postpartum, I think to myself.) He is taking the afternoon flight to Cuenca, but he can't face the bus ride to Cañar. Will I come to meet him? He wants to have a special dinner somewhere and spend the night at our favorite little hotel, La Orquidea.

That evening, with friends joining us for dinner, Michael comes around to a jubilant mood as he recounts the details of the last three weeks. He makes it all sound funny, casting himself as a kind of Quixote knight-errant, jousting with the powers that be in Quito. I tell my story about the "re-marriage" fiasco. We laugh at every new twist and I can see the story of how we became residents of Ecuador is already becoming legend.

~

JOURNAL, JUNE 20

My friend Segundo Palchisaca, the cultural officer of UPCCC and a fellow photographer, has asked me to film and photograph the election of the *ñusta*, or queen, for Inti Raymi, the big fiesta that falls around the summer solstice. All fiestas in Cañar have queens, but the Inti Raymi queen is the most important one for indigenous Cañaris. Each community or organization puts forth a candidate, who must dance in costume and give a speech in Quichua, and her reign lasts for a year—sort of like Miss America. Segundo tells me election night will begin with a procession through the country before ending up at Ñucanchi Wasi, the indigenous center in town.

I walk into town about eight o'clock, dressed too warmly in a heavy sweater, a down vest, and a fleece jacket, but I know how late these events can go and how cold it will get. I finally find the procession winding its way around a big hill just outside town, called Cerro Narrio.

The small crowd—maybe one hundred people—is led by a ten-man brass and drum band, and four or five *vacas locas*, men carrying large "masks" of cows. Every few minutes, someone sets off *bombas*, fireworks. One man plays a *pingullo*, a small flute that sounds, with its high reedy tones, like a snake charmer's flute.

I'm immediately struck by the sight of a man and woman dancing in the road at the head of the procession. This is very odd, as Cañari women

Vaca loca

are modest and reticent, and I can't imagine one making a spectacle like that. Then I realize that the "woman" is a man. He and his partner are *rucuyayas*—festival clowns—and their role is to interact with one another and the *fiesteros* to make us laugh. At one point, the "woman" goes to the side of the road, flips up the back of her skirt, and squats down as if urinating. The crowd loves it.

We walk on around Cerro Narrio, cross the Pan-American, climb into town, and go around the square before heading back to the UPCCC. I look at my watch; it's now nine thirty, and judging by the crowd milling around the center, the election was scheduled to begin hours ago. The leaders of the procession, wanting to make a big entrance into the auditorium, find the doors padlocked on the outside. Someone runs for the caretakers, an older couple who live nearby. The old woman comes with a ring of keys and slowly tries each one. I hear her mumble "wrong key, wrong key," and she goes to look for second set. None of those keys work either. While she's gone for the third bunch, I find another entrance, go inside, and sit down to join the others waiting.

CHAPTER 14

Leaving Cañar

Lourdes and Michael with his list

"I WAS AWAKE FOR HOURS in the night, making lists," Michael said early this morning. "I just don't think I can do it all before we leave." He looked tired and worried, scribbling on one of the many notebooks and pads scattered around our cluttered living quarters, putting it down and picking up another without remembering where the latest one is. Same with his pens; some of his lists are in red ink, others in black.

We are down to our last week in Cañar, and our leaving seems to be all about making lists. In the case of Michael, the lists are tasks to finish before he leaves, especially related to the plumbing and electrical systems. In my case, it's a list of future things to bring back in January for the new house. Mine is rather tentative

because the project is now so far behind I don't know if we'll even be moving into the house next year. But optimistically I write down things we'll need:
sheets, pillowcases, towels, comforters, curtains, nightlights . . .

Later, when I walk down to the site, I find Michael going over one of his lists
with Lourdes. Clutching a notebook covered with his scribbly handwriting, he
is urgent and tense. Lourdes stands beside him, looking calm, patient, and reassuring, even a little amused. She still doesn't understand why Michael needs to
do all the plumbing and electrical work now; in her experience, these installa-
tions are done after the walls are finished.

"Why don't you just *stay*?" I hear her ask, as though this idea has suddenly
occurred to her. "There are so many things to decide—windows, doors, floors,
tile for the bathrooms, countertops for the kitchen. I need you here," she says.
Lourdes is only half serious, but Michael doesn't get her light tone and only
shakes his head and looks even more worried. I know he wants to go home with
me and not stay here alone, even if it means coming back in September. This
building a house and making a life in a faraway place is a two-person enterprise,
not at all fun by oneself.

Lourdes then presents her own list, mostly immediate things for Michael
and me to decide: Where do we want Javier to build bookcases? Where do we
want niches in the adobe walls? She has an idea for some Cañari-motif reliefs
around the patio. Could Judy come up with these designs before we leave? I can
see by Michael's expression that he views her list as frivolous.

I decide not to get into this discussion and instead take a walk around the
house. The roof is finally finished—a beautiful job—and the roofing crew is
gone, along with their pots and pans, sleeping blankets, and extra clothes. The
last piles of broken tile, bits of wire, nails, and strips of asphalt-impregnated
chova (heavy tarpaper) have been roughly raked up and stacked into little
mountains around the house and in the courtyard. It's a big mess, but I'm
beyond worrying about acting as debris collector now that we are so close to
leaving; surely someone will clean it up before we come back next January.

In the courtyard, I look up to see the steel supports for the glass roof that
workers from Cuenca installed last week. The structure is beautiful, presently a
deep raw-steel red, but Michael says it will have to be painted. What color do I
want? Another decision to be made.

This central patio was our first design requirement, going back to the days
when we thought our "second life" would be in Mexico. And our original
vision that all rooms open into the patio has been realized. But a glass roof?
That brilliant idea came later. We still can't decide who first suggested it, so
Michael, Lourdes, and I have agreed to share the credit. I know I was inspired

by glass-covered patios in museums and hotels in Cuenca, converted from colo-nial-style homes. Lourdes might well have been an architect on some of those projects, so maybe it was she who first proposed a glass roof. And Michael—well, he just recognizes a good idea when he hears it, and I love to hear him say, "Yeah, let's do it!"

In Portland, our kitchen opens onto a deck with double French doors. In warm summer months, it becomes a natural extension of the house, an outdoor room filled with plants where we have drinks and dinner on warm summer nights. But in chilly Cañar, of course, rare is the day when we can sit comfort-ably in the open air. So by covering the courtyard with glass, building the house around it, and planting an interior garden, we're hoping to create a similar space, but one that also acts as a solar collector that will help warm the other rooms. Our only other heat source will be a fireplace.

Javier, the carpenter, is in the living room, measuring for the windows and doors he will make in his Cuenca workshop. He's framed in the big windows that look north toward the mountains and west toward the coast. I already know this room will be the heart of the house, where Michael will commune with his chess machine—we'll put a little table right there in the corner where the two windows meet—and where we'll watch the sunset every evening and have din-ner in front of the fire.

My reverie is broken when I glance down between the floor joists and see, amidst the chaos of construction, a mother hen and five or six chicks who have made a little nest next to the stone foundation wall. I imagine they belong to our next-door neighbor, Magdalena; I hope they find their way home before the floor covering is laid down.

In the kitchen, José María and two helpers are laying large smooth river stones over the tamped-down earthen subfloor, to be covered with a concrete slab and later topped with tile. The stones seem way too beautiful to be covered—how about a tempered glass floor? Again, I am amazed that the basic building blocks of this house are, well, so elemental. So old. Stones that were under water for eons will now be under our kitchen floor, maybe for eons more. Topsoil that has been here for a few hundred years will be mixed with water and straw to make our walls. A eucalyptus tree that grew in the countryside around here a few years ago is now a beam in our living room, where it might last for a hundred years.

I walk on around the courtyard into my studio. This is my domain, and I get a thrill imagining working here, even standing in the midst of the construction mess. The room is large—about twenty by twenty feet—and will serve as office, studio, meeting room, and overflow guest room. When the roofing crew made spaces for two small skylights, I argued with Lourdes that they should be twice

José María laying rocks for the kitchen floor

the size, and the result is a room flooded with light. The little room at the east end, which was the roofers' "kitchen," will eventually be my darkroom.

Outside, beside the house, Santos is working with an adze to shave strips off giant bamboo, called "*guadua.*" He has been doing this for days; as the most patient and passive worker, Santos always gets the repetitive and boring jobs. Lourdes tells us that tomorrow the workers will begin nailing these thin "furring" strips, or lath, every four or five inches on both sides of the framed walls. Then, she says, she'll hire extra workers and bring friends from Cuenca for a *minga,* a cooperative work day, to fill the wall spaces with a mixture of thick mud and fine straw, resulting in walls about twelve inches thick. After that, she says, the house will have to "rest"—harden and dry—for about a month.

I can't believe I won't be here for the phase of our house construction that interests me most, the one I most want to document. Lourdes has told us that in the old days the mud and straw were mixed by tethered horses walking in a circle around a central pole, but in our case it will be the workers and volunteers treading barefoot on the mixture in the courtyard. I'll miss that! Finally, after the walls have dried, a special *maestro* will come from Cuenca to apply a finish of plaster, called "*empeñete*" made of horse manure, mud, and a binder of either a chemical glue or a natural one made of the viscous liquid from the flat-leaved cactus that grows around here.

A couple of weeks ago, Michael went with Lourdes to visit the horse farm near Cuenca where she'll buy the manure mixture (to be delivered to the construction site in barrels), and he learned some arcane facts about this finishing touch. Horse manure was probably first added to stucco by accident, when tethered draft animals were used. As the horses' hooves mixed the mud, the manure was a free additive. At some point, builders discovered that the mud mixed with manure made a stronger finish, with reduced cracking and erosion. For good *empeñete*, the manure must be aged and fermented so it won't rot on the wall or cause mildew. The fermentation process also makes it completely odorless.

Finally, according to José María, who apparently knows about these things, the manure can't come from just any old horse, but only those that are pasture-fed so the manure will have high fiber content. The final result, inside and out, Lourdes tells us, will look like any finished adobe surface, although it will have to be painted to preserve the finish and prevent water erosion.

Meanwhile, stacked and waiting in one corner of the courtyard sit beautiful sheaves of *paja*, the fine straw that grows in the *páramo* above twelve thousand feet. Our old friend, Juanito Tenesaca, cut the sheaves in a highland pasture and sold it to us by the *mula*—a traditional system of measuring by the load a mule can carry. Juanito no longer owns a mule, or a pasture (I suspect he paid someone to cut their straw), but he remembers well when his father worked on the local hacienda, delivering *mulas* of grain or wood, and he still knows how much *paja* a mule could carry.

~

Our last day in Cañar dawns cold and gray, but we've both had a good sleep and are awake by six o'clock. The wind has blown all night in fitful gusts, suddenly opening or closing the ill-fitting doors in our little house. Michael goes down to the kitchen to start the coffee while I stay in bed and think of all I must do today. When I go down, I see he is concentrating on piles of keys. Michael collects keys like a packrat and he often doesn't know where they belong. He shows me a ring of keys with an attached bottle opener that says Bridgeport, a Portland brewery.

"What are these for?" he asks. Who knows? Brought from one of his jobs? Brought by a visitor? He shrugs and puts them back on the shelf.

"And don't forget to take that key back to the hotel in Quito that you carried away in your pocket in January," I remind him.

Back upstairs, I sort out my photo gear and try not to forget anything that I will need in Portland. With our new return tickets, we could both come back in September, but I suspect it will be only Michael. One of us needs to earn some income, and I'm hoping to have editing and writing work in Portland.

By nine o'clock, we've packed our bags, put the house in order, and are standing on the side of the Pan-American, waiting for the bus to Cuenca, where we'll
catch a flight to Quito. We'd hoped to sneak out of town without advertising the
fact that we're leaving a house full of things, and a construction project unfinished, but that's impossible. As we stand with our suitcases, a steady stream of
friends and acquaintances walk or drive by, waving and calling out, "*Buen viaje.*"
"*Vuelven pronto.*" Come back soon.

By eleven o'clock, we're in the Cuenca airport, drinking beers and watching
the World Cup game between England and Portugal. During lunch, we hear
a big noise on the tarmac and go over to the windows to see supporters with
placards cheering a presidential candidate who has just flown in for a campaign
stop. Cynthia Viteri, a youngish, blond, very attractive, conservative member of
Congress, dressed in her signature open-necked white shirt.

"Do you think she could be the next president of Ecuador?" Michael asks as
we stand looking down.

"A woman president of Ecuador?" I say. "No way!"

But I was wrong. Eight months later, in a bizarre turn of events, newly elected
Ecuadorian president Abdalá Bucarám, known as "El Loco," was declared men-
tally unfit to govern by the National Congress after five months and "dismissed."
(In one moment of madness, widely reported in the press, at a political rally, he
lifted the skirt of his vice president, Rosalía Arteaga, to show off her "fine legs.")

After being charged with corruption, Bucarám fled to Panama, where he
remains today. Vice President Arteaga should have become president, but the
constitution was vague on succession and the Congress swore in its congressio-
nal leader, Fabián Alarcón, as acting president. But the vice president successfully argued that she should be president, so three days later she was sworn in.
But two days after that, with support from the Congress and the army—always
a critical player in national political disputes—the Congress reinstated Alarcón,
and Rosalía Arteaga was forced to resign.

So much for Ecuador's two-day (first) woman president!

~

JOURNAL, JULY 6

At about seven o'clock on the morning we are leaving Cañar, Mariana,
Mama Michi's youngest daughter, knocks on the gate. She has brought
some things for us to take to family members in the United States. Over the
years, we have carried in our luggage everything from cooked *cuyes* (guinea

pigs) and *máchica* (toasted barley flour) to kilos of *mote* (dried corn). It is not unusual for Cañar families to send these things, since private courier services in town advertise two-day delivery to New York or Spain of everything from eggs to chicarrones. But in the past few years, Michael and I have come to insist that we cannot carry anything but cards and letters when we travel to the United States.

However, "cards and letters" can be loosely interpreted, as everyone knows, and this morning Mariana arrives with videos, music CDs, and *remedios*, herbal medicines from Mama Michi. But since Mariana is the only one so far who has come to send things, and we're at the point of leaving, we say we will be happy to take them.

After she leaves, staring down at the offerings on the table, Michael says, "Wouldn't it be interesting to study how the objects people send to relatives in the United States have changed over the years?" We are remembering a young man who came to work as a volunteer in a neighboring village. He traveled back to the States with ten cooked guinea pigs wrapped in foil for a Cañari family's relatives. This was pre–9/11.

PART TWO

~

CHAPTER 15

The Return

~

President Rafael Correa placard in Cañar

JANUARY 14, 2007. We arrived in Cañar yesterday after a long trip that began three days ago in Portland with a mix-up in our airline tickets. Though booked on the same flights out of Portland and Atlanta, we had different destinations in Ecuador. I was headed to Quito, while Michael would continue on to Guayaquil, a thirty-minute flight farther to the south coast. Because he'd returned to Cañar in the fall to work on the house, we'd bought our tickets at different times and hadn't noticed the mistake until we got to the airport in Portland. I argued with the Delta agent, sure it would be a simple matter to change Michael's ticket to Quito. Sorry, not possible in this post-9/11 world. Mr. Jenkins was welcome to leave the plane in Quito, the agent said, but his luggage must go on to Guayaquil. Buying a new ticket, for a mere eight hundred dollars, would solve that problem, of course.

Once on our way, we resigned ourselves to this arrangement, but I was worried. Not only would I have to wrestle two enormous suitcases by myself through customs, into a cab, and to the hotel in Quito late at night, but I was also carrying almost ten thousand dollars in a money belt around my waist (the legal limit allowed). Michael was carrying an equal amount, and he would be landing even later in Guayaquil, long considered the "Naples" of Ecuador with its high crime rates and street violence. (Over the years, Michael and I have gone back and forth on how to get dollars to Ecuador. I believe in electronic bank transfers; Michael, in cash-around-the-waist transfers. This time he won out, arguing that we will need ready cash for the construction.)

But all goes well. By eleven o'clock that night, I am safely checked into a small familiar hotel in Quito, La Casa Sol, and I have called Guayaquil to reserve a room for Michael at the guesthouse he discovered last year, Hostal Tangara. Then I pour a glass of wine from the half-bottle I'd bought at the reception desk and get into bed with my book. I have traveled this day from near-sea-level Portland to more than nine thousand-feet Quito, the second highest capital city in the world, and I know from experience I will have insomnia tonight and a headache tomorrow. I also know it is not a good idea to drink alcohol, but relief makes me reckless.

My inconveniences and small discomforts pale next to those in the story I start reading: *The River of Doubt: Theodore Roosevelt's Darkest Journey* about Roosevelt's 1914 trip down an unexplored tributary of the Amazon with his son, Kermit. The ill-prepared expedition cost several lives and nearly killed the former president when he contracted malaria and suffered a leg injury that became infected with flesh-eating bacteria. At his lowest point, he told Kermit to leave him to die in the rainforest. Wine finished and the hour late, I close the book and turn off the light, thinking about men and their follies.

The next day, after a short restless sleep, breakfast at the hotel, and an early-morning talk with Michael about our respective flights to Cuenca that afternoon, I have time to kill. My flight isn't until five o'clock. I take a brisk walk through the Amazonas district, called the "new" Quito as opposed to the historic colonial center, where we stayed on our first arrival in Ecuador in 1991. There, we were promptly robbed in the street by a team of thieves, one a tiny woman who butted Michael in the chest while her male partner sliced his pants and extracted his wallet. (I hear from my friend Marta that the old city is much safer these days.)

Quito's name comes from its original inhabitants, the Quitu tribe, which occupied the area nearly two thousand years ago. In 1462, the Incas invaded and incorporated the region, along with southern Colombia, as the northern part of the largest empire in pre-Columbian America. In 1534, Spanish conquistadors swept into the region and captured and executed Rumiñahui, the Inca warrior who led the resistance against the invasion. Declared a city by the Spanish in 1541, Quito has grown into a sprawling urban area of more than two million people.

On this Sunday morning, however, the streets are nearly empty and no stores are open. A once-prosperous residential area, Amazonas has in recent years turned into a warren of small hotels and hostels, restaurants, boutiques, and bars, and the neighborhood is beginning to look a bit derelict. Even the city's best bookstore, Libri Mundi, on Juan Leon Mera Street, and the adjacent Galería Latina, where the best quality handcrafts are found, look tacky and sad, with peeling paint and dusty awnings. Farther on, I pass by the same ugly, unfinished high-rise of cast concrete and naked rebar that Michael and I saw the first time we landed in Quito, sixteen years ago. It sits behind a chain-link fence, completely unchanged. I recall a similar abandoned high-rise overlooking San José, Costa Rica; cast concrete towers with reinforced steel must be complicated to tear down.

At Parque El Ejido, the large green space that divides the new and old city, I run the gauntlet of cheap souvenir stands and makeshift art galleries. It is early still, and the vendors are leisurely setting up their stalls. I walk to one end of the park and came back around, and it's still early. As I cross the street toward the Hilton Hotel, thinking of a second coffee, I notice a large contingent of police, soldiers, and black SUVs around the entrance. I step through the entrance to take a look, and see—amidst a gaggle of European tourists gathered in the lobby for a day's outing—a flurry of preparations for something, or someone, important. A number of security men stand over a line of workers on their knees, carefully straightening a red carpet that has been rolled from the hotel entrance, around the front desk, and down a long hall. I follow the red carpet to its end at the elevators, where I encounter a man in a suit with a receiver in his ear and a list in his hand.

"Who's coming?" I ask boldly. He looks at me, uncomprehending for a moment, and when I repeat the question, he pauses before answering very carefully, "*No sabemos.*" We don't know.

That's a carefully rehearsed lie, I think as I walk back to the street. In front of the hotel, I see some men from *la prensa* hanging around, and I know they will talk. I ask the closest photographer what all the fuss is about and he says the new president of Ecuador, Rafael Correa, is to be inaugurated tomorrow, January 15. *Diplomáticos* are arriving from everywhere, he says: Hugo Chávez from Venezuela, Evo Morales from Bolivia, Mahmoud Ahmadinejad from Iran, and Daniel

Ortega from Nicaragua. "This is one of three hotels where they will be staying, but for security reasons no one knows who will be where . . . ." So the security guy by the elevator was telling the truth, I think.

I buy a paper on the way back to my hotel, curious to learn more about this new president. Before the constitution was reformed in 2008, presidents in Ecuador's volatile democracy" could only serve one four-year term, and most were ousted before that, forced to resign or to flee the country because of corruption, or the debt crisis, or economic collapse, or political maneuvering. One, the only woman, lasted only two days. In sixteen years, Ecuador has had eight presidents, so a new one doesn't generate a lot of excitement among the electorate.

Presidential campaigns in areas as remote as Cañar are always interesting, however, in their creative efforts to gain the votes of the poor, illiterate, and uninformed. I saw an example in Cañar a few years ago when one political party built outhouses all over the countryside, equipped them with tiny porcelain toilets, and painted the exterior walls the party color, an unfortunate baby blue. The idea being, I suppose, that folks would vote according to color. But in the last few years, I've adopted the resigned attitude of our indigenous neighbors— who quickly discovered that their toilets were useless without running water— that one political party is pretty much like another. All are jostling to get to a place where they can benefit the rich and powerful, and themselves, of course. The urgent concerns, such as health and education, of the rest of the country are largely forgotten the minute the election is over.

Today, however, I read that the soon-to-be president, Rafael Correa, is unique among politicians in that he is not from the Quito elite, the Guayaquil wealthy, or the military, but from a mestizo, working-class family. Born in 1963 in Guayaquil, he was educated on scholarships in Ecuador, Belgium, and the United States, where he received a PhD in economics from the University of Illinois at Urbana Champaign in 2001.

A political dark horse until he served briefly in the previous government as finance minister, Correa was forced to resign after he advocated poverty reduction, expressed skepticism of a free trade deal with the United States (the *Tratado de Libre Comercio*, the cause of last year's strike), and argued to close the U.S. military base in Manta on Ecuador's coast. I remember his joke, widely reported in the press: the United States could keep its air force base at Manta as long as Ecuador could have a similar base in Miami. He lost his job soon after.

A self-described "humanist" and "leftist Christian," Correa won the November 2006 elections with 57.2 percent of the vote in a run-off with Ecuador's richest man, the banana magnate Álvaro Noboa. In his campaign, Correa promised to put an end to political corruption (Ecuador regularly ranks among the fifty most corrupt nations, according to Transparency International) and reform the abysmal education and health system.

I was impressed to read that his new cabinet is made up of 40 percent women, including the minister of defense, and the first African-Ecuadorian as culture minister. His vice president, lawyer and politician Lenín Moreno, is wheelchair-bound since being shot in a 1998 robbery attempt.

~

Reading all this about the new president gives me hope, and I am in a good mood when I arrive in Cuenca that evening and meet Michael's flight from Guayaquil an hour later. It is late, we are tired, and so we decide to stay over at Hostal La Orquidea and spend an extra day in Cuenca taking care of business before going on to Cañar.

The next morning, our first battle is with the Banco de Guayaquil over a money transfer to Lourdes's account that appears to be in limbo—or, according to pessimist Michael, "probably lost forever!" I'd sent the wire from Portland more than three weeks ago, but Lourdes had neglected to tell us she hadn't received it until just before we left home. Our bank in Portland confirmed that everything was in order there; the problem had to be at the receiving end. "It will be found," I'd said to reassure Michael. "Money just doesn't get lost in the ether." "Yeah, sure!" he'd replied sardonically. "Banks never lose money."

In the lobby we run into Lourdes, who breathlessly says, "The funds were found just this morning!" But because we want to know what had gone wrong, and to avoid this happening again, the three of us troop upstairs and crowd into the tiny office of Lucy, a bank manager we'd dealt with last year.

As I pull papers out of my file folders, and Michael and I talk over one another, Lourdes gets in her comments in rapid-fire Spanish. Lucy tries to respond to all of us at once, but it is confusing. I mention that I have transferred money several times in the past six months using the same forms, filled out the same way, with no problem. Lourdes confirms that she has always received the funds. Lucy, in turn, points out that I have always neglected to put in one bit of information. I reply that, even so, it hadn't seemed to matter with all the other transfers. But then Mediator Michael jumps in to say, "Yes, I'm sure that must have been the problem, that Judy missed putting in some info," and discussion stops. Shrugs all around, except for me. I am glaring at Michael.

But I do recognize the moment as my cue to stop asking questions, such as, "Then, how did it happen that the funds were found this very morning?" So we leave the bank with no clear answer as to what had gone wrong, but with Michael further armed to argue we should carry cash and not rely on banks.

We walk over to Lourdes's office a few blocks away to have a talk about the house construction. "Things have gone slower than I expected," she says matter-of-factly. "The windows and doors are going in this week, but the tile floors still have to be laid, the wood floors sanded and finished, the kitchen counters resolved, and Michael has to install all the bathroom and kitchen fixtures." We sit silent for a moment, absorbing this discouraging news, before I say, politely, "Well, at least some things are happening." We've been in Latin America long enough to know that no project—construction or otherwise—moves smoothly on schedule. Michael only says he is anxious to get to Cañar and back to work.

But in fact we are both deeply disappointed at how far behind the house is, and we don't even ask when we might move in. As with last year, we have only six months before returning to Portland.

Afterward, it's time to go shopping. Lourdes has told us that we need to buy toilets, faucets, light fixtures, and countertop materials, so Michael and I grab a cab and take off for Avenida Remigio Crespo, where all the new kitchen and bathroom fixtures stores are clustered.

Between Michael and me, nothing highlights how differently our brains work than shopping. I like a slow approach, cruising, perusing all possibilities, cataloging information for the future, not buying but looking . . . and looking and looking. A right-brained approach, you could say. Michael, a left-brained shopper, charges directly to the first object on his list, looking neither right nor left, buys it, and gets the hell out of the store.

In the enormous showroom of bathroom fixtures, I wander from display to display in a sort of daze, trying to absorb everything before focusing on what we need. That's how I find myself staring at a sit-down shower stall with foot and back massage, aromatherapy, telephone, FM radio, ozone sterilization, steam generator, tropical monsoon showerhead, and 12V ceiling lighting. I am wondering where on earth a product like this came from when Michael calls me over to the other side of the room. "Hey, what do you think about this faucet set? Like it? OK, let's buy it! Now, let's go look at toilets! Come on! Over here!"

Toilets are easy; we only need three and there is not much variety. Although I prefer the lowboy commodes, Michael the plumber argues that they don't work that well, so I easily give in. But then I feel faint at the thought of our next task: choosing light fixtures. I suddenly remember a famously stressful day years ago when, for our rebuilt house in Portland, I had to choose twenty-one light fixtures in one day! That put me in bed with a fever afterward. Now,

I beg off looking at lights for another day, and Michael kindly agrees; it will be months before we need them.

Then we are off to another showroom to look at slabs of marble and granite for the countertops. But because the kitchen is Michael's domain, the decision is his, and I am only minimally involved in giving my abbreviated opinions: "That one's too dark, that one too busy, that one too pink."

Also, I am distracted, riveted by the television in the corner of the showroom, broadcasting President Correa's inaugural address. When I see he is wearing an embroidered shirt, indigenous style, and speaking in Quichua, I have a sudden lump in my throat. At that moment, I remember something else I'd read about Correa in the Quito newspaper: In his youth, he had spent a missionary year with Salesian priests at a school in a poor highland town, where he acquired some knowledge of Quichua. Surely no president of Ecuador has ever given an inauguration speech in the native language of the country's original peoples.

~

JOURNAL, JANUARY 15

Reading a newspaper later, I learn another tidbit about Correa, revealed by a rival politician during the campaign, that makes Ecuador's new president seem even more "of the people." During a difficult period in Correa's childhood, his father (now dead) agreed to carry illegal drugs aboard a flight to the United States, where he was arrested and spent several years in jail. "I don't condemn my father," Correa said in a statement for the press. "I think he was a victim of the system, like so many others; my father wasn't a criminal, he was unemployed and desperately seeking to feed his family."

CHAPTER 16

On This Day a Year Ago

~

House with paja

WE ARE ON THE BUS TO CAÑAR by nine o'clock the next morning, with four big bags stashed below in the cargo hold and my heavy backpack with two laptops, several cameras, and other photo equipment balanced on my knees like a precious baby. Another carry-on with more gear rests on the floor securely between my feet. Michael sits beside me with his own backpack and carry-on, but neither are as heavy or as full as mine. Michael considers me too "soft" about bringing things for others. Inevitably, as we get close to leaving Portland, a few calls and e-mails come from our Cañari friends, asking us to bring items they believe to be less expensive and better quality if they come from *el norte*. I bring what I can, especially for friends who are professionals and who can repay me—a camera and flash for Segundo, a photographer, and a laptop computer for Ranti, an engineer.

Then there's the large amount of money I have strapped around my waist to worry about. Once in Cañar, we have only to hire a truck and driver and within minutes we and all our gear and cash will be safely in our little house, and I can finally relax.

In fact, the motion of the bus and the sun coming through the window have already made me so relaxed that I doze for most of the two-hour climb up and over the Continental Divide. As we round the last mountaintop, I rouse to look out and feel that familiar thrill when I first see our town scattered across the valley below. The day is brilliant, cloudless, and the long view of the valley and the mountains in the distance is breathtaking. Michael, doing Sudoku beside me, barely glances up; his two months spent here last fall have inured him to Cañar's special magic.

When our hired truck pulls up in front of our house, we find the street nearly blocked with a bulldozer and dump truck. Our landlord's son, Telmo, stands by, and through the dust and noise he yells that he has bought the lot next to our house to build a garage for his father's bus—one of the Transportes Cañaris that runs back and forth to Cuenca. He says he'll be expanding our house and moving into it once we leave. This means we have to be out and into our own house in the next six months.

Michael has warned me that our living space is crowded with things he bought when he was here in September, but I am not quite prepared for what I see. In the big room downstairs, a kitchen range, two shower stalls, a bathroom sink, a kitchen sink, and a big blue pump are jammed in amidst tools and plumbing parts. I can barely thread my way from the door to the one table left free, but I don't say a word, remembering Michael's sacrifice of the weeks spent here alone this past fall. Everything is covered with a fine layer of the gravelly grime that shakes through the roof and ceilings. The house sits against a hillside, with its flat roof level with the vacant lot behind.

We leave everything as is and head straight down to the construction site; Michael is anxious to show me what's been done since I left last July. As we walk, I remind him that it was exactly one year ago when we came back to Cañar for a first look at the scrubby cornfield we had impulsively bought six months before, fearing that the site would look smaller than we remembered, the view not as fine, or the neighbor's piglets not so charming.

When we reach the road above the house, Michael rushes on down to the site to greet the workers, but I stay and take a moment to look. I'm pleased to see that the house looks harmonious with its environment: a one-story, earthen-colored structure with a red tile roof sitting low on the hillside, looking over the valley with the mountains beyond. The exterior adobe walls, warm in the sunlight, are patchy and not yet given their final finish, but I like them just like that.

A massive eucalyptus column supports the front entrance *portal*, or porch, one of Lourdes's ideas that we thought a bit over the top, but now that it is in place I see it counterbalances the thick adobe walls and looks just right. Wide eaves below the roofline remind me that Lourdes said good overhangs are essential with an "earthen" house to protect walls against dampness and rain. Our brilliant architect has also attached a brick walkway to three sides of the house, another practical touch in this muddy climate.

I decide to follow that brick walkway and take a tour outside the house before going in. At the back, facing the mountains, another porch is supported by two smaller eucalyptus columns, with railings on two sides. This little portico was also an afterthought of Lourdes's, but a wonderful idea, as it gives us a 180-degree view of the valley and mountains. My only issue is the two-foot-wide stairway that connects the porch to the yard. It feels like a ship's ladder— too narrow, too steep. Standing there, I decide to propose that we should tear out these steps and remake them about three times as wide. We'll sit on those steps when the weather is warm, to watch the sunset or visiting children playing on the future grassy area below that I've imagined. Between the two builders, Michael and Lourdes, I don't get much chance to come up with original ideas.

I step through the open doorway into the living/dining/kitchen area. Javier, the carpenter, is here with a crew of three men putting in windows and doors made with a native reddish-brown wood, called *seique*, that resembles mahogany.

The living and dining area is, to my eye, perfectly proportioned—one long room with double doors leading in from the courtyard and other double doors out to the porch, with windows along the north and west sides. The open-beam vaulted ceiling reminds me of the ski lodges of my Colorado youth—again, not exactly what we had in mind when we first conceived of a "simple adobe house," but I couldn't be happier with the result.

The kiva-style fireplace, under construction in one corner of the living room, has given Michael a few sleepless nights lately. The question is: Will it work? Months ago, when I sent Lourdes a photo of a corner fireplace from a "Santa Fe style" magazine, Michael also sent drawings and instructions for the construction, inspired by a booklet he found in our local Powell's Books. *The Forgotten Art of Building a Good Fireplace* recounts the story of eighteenth-century

Fireplace in process

inventor Count Rumford, who created a sensation in London when he introduced the idea of restricting the chimney opening so that smoke would go up into the chimney rather than into the room, choking the homeowners. Apparently, the principles of the Rumford fireplace have not been improved upon for two hundred years. Lourdes says she's directed the workers to use those plans—constructing a smoke shelf behind the damper to prevent downdrafts—but we are still half expecting the room to fill with smoke the first time we light a fire.

For such a chilly climate, you would think fireplaces would be common in Cañar, but firewood is expensive and our indigenous neighbors use wood only for cooking, considering it wasteful to build a fire simply to be warm. I've seen fireplaces in some middle-class homes, but generally they are for decoration only—a place to stick an artificial flower arrangement or a piece of sculpture. Middle class or not, no one has heating systems in Cañar. Another sweater, a heavier jacket, a brisk walk into town—that's how people stay warm.

I step into the kitchen, where José María has just poured the concrete supports and undersurface for the countertops. I greet him formally and ask about his young daughter, Lourdes, who has kidney disease and started dialysis recently; we agree to talk at length later with his wife, Narcisa. I think the countertop supports look a bit out of plumb, but I decide not to say anything on my first day back. Yesterday in Cuenca, Michael and I looked at a large piece of granite that I suspect he cannot resist buying for the long countertops along the south and north sides. He's in here now, taking measurements.

Michael's kitchen is larger than I remembered. Too large for my tastes, certainly—I count nine steps between stove and sink—but this is Michael's workspace and "food art studio" (my words, not his), and it's just as he wants it: big and open. I had suggested a butcher-block table in the center, where everyone could gather and be a part of the cooking action as in our Portland kitchen, but he says he doesn't want anyone in his way. We'll see. I look up and wish we'd put a skylight in the kitchen when the roofers were here. Why hadn't we thought of it?

Double windows over the sink look out toward the mountains. That's where I'll be spending a lot of time washing dishes, I suppose. Ecuadorian appliances might be advanced enough to offer multi-function showers, but dishwashers are still rare and terribly expensive.

Back through the living room, I step directly into the courtyard, the heart of the house. This was our first design requirement and certainly one of our best ideas. In Spanish-influenced architecture, all domestic traffic passes through the courtyard—or patio—from entrance to exit, from room to room. And so it will be with our house. Years ago, when we lived in Cuenca, I never missed an opportunity to peer into the open doorways of old houses and admire interior courtyards filled with plants, flowers, and fountains. Behind what I could see from the street, there was usually another, more private patio, and finally a walled garden. I had fantasized about living in such a place one day. Many of these typical Cuenca townhouses with three patios are now converted to hotels and restaurants, one, in fact, called Tres Patios.

The curving brick walk around the courtyard looks to have just enough space in one corner for a small table and chairs. This is where I hope we'll have lunch each day, warmed by the sun. The tempered glass panels have been installed over the steel beams, now painted dark forest green, and the space is flooded with light and warmth. A twelve-inch gap between the tile roof and glass cover will allow air circulation and prevent our courtyard from becoming a steamy hothouse. The center will, I hope, eventually be filled with plants and maybe even a fountain if Michael gets inspired.

I step in my studio and find the spot where I hope to make portraits. The large room is nearly square, which I love because it evokes the square format of my Hasselblad camera, and the two large skylights fill the room with diffused light. The brick floor is just as I imagined it—a deep red, though at the moment an unfinished, dusty red—and the walls will be painted a warm white. The little room in one corner of the studio will be my darkroom and good for storage when we're not here.

The two bedrooms, mirrored spaces facing across the courtyard, are also nearly square. (Symmetry might be a good thing in feng shui, but when my 87-year-old mother comes to visit later this year, the identical interior spaces will continually confuse her and she often ends up in our bedroom when she thinks she's in hers.)

I end my tour where I started—standing on the back portico overlooking the mountains. The field below me, a waving sea of tasseled green corn, now belongs to us, in name anyway. We had intended to buy this property as part of the original sale, but Juan and Rosa had so vacillated, time got so short, and we got so nervous that we settled for the smaller piece. Last fall, when Michael was back for six weeks, Juan, in a chat over the fence one day, had mentioned casually that he might want to sell the extra piece of land. He mentioned a price, and Michael countered with a lower figure, but they never talked again. When Michael left for Portland, he told Vicente that if Juan should renew his offer, Vicente had permission to bargain for, and buy, the land.

Just a couple of weeks ago, Vicente called us in Portland to tell us that we were now the owners of another odd-shaped cornfield, smaller than our original lot but critical to our privacy and view. It was a great relief. Had anyone else bought the land in this country of no-zoning, they could have built a house or a barn—or a wall, for that matter—directly in front of our living room windows. Now I look out over the field of tasseled corn and am thankful we will always be able to see the mountains.

Juan and Rosa had planted the corn before the sale and, I suppose, like last year with our first property, we will have to wait for the harvest before we can claim the land. It doesn't matter, as we have no plans for it other than to invite José María to plant it for himself and his family in return for being our caretakers during the months we're away.

Back home that afternoon, Michael unpacks the supplies he has brought from Portland, including some particular screws for the new kitchen range, sitting right now in the middle of the room. When he bought the stove last year, he'd noticed that the burner knobs had rusty screws in the middle, and he has brought stainless steel ones from Portland. He goes into town to buy a special tool and carefully installs the new screws. Privately, I marvel that with all the big jobs that need to be done on the new house, Michael's first priority is this miniscule task. But when he stands back and exclaims how happy he is with the result, I have to be, too. Sometimes it's easier to concentrate on small details than the overwhelming big picture.

~

Paiwa at twelve, with author

JOURNAL, JANUARY 16

Our second day in Cañar, I come home from town to find Paiwa waiting for me on a bench in the patio. At first glance, I see she has changed since I last saw her; her face is more mature and she is taller. But that impression fades as she jumps up and gives me a hug; then she is simply Paiwa.

"There is so much to tell you!" she says, excited. She has formed a Cañari dance group with five other girls from her community (including José María's daughters, Lourdes and Sara), and they won first prize in two competitions around Christmastime. She believes her group won, in part, because she gave an introduction in Quichua. She recited it for me in Quichua, then in Spanish. "Quite impressive!" I say, "Did you write that yourself?"

"No, of course not! My Papi wrote it."

Paiwa turned twelve in December and she is in her first year of *colegio*, which is the equivalent of seventh grade here, and I can so clearly see her developing a conscious pride in being indigenous. I remember when she was in first grade, becoming aware of the larger culture, asking a million questions, and trying to negotiate her way in this complicated white-mestizo-indigenous world. Why were "town kids" sometimes treated differently by the teachers? Why was her hair so black, and mine so light? She wanted light hair. And last year when she lost an art contest prize that she was confident she would win to a boy "from town," it broke my heart when she said she thought it was because she was indigenous.

But I think she's been figuring it out, quietly; at least she no longer asks questions. And now she is winning prizes for speaking Quichua and creating "traditional" dances (she says she comes up with the routines herself). "And my two new girlfriends in *colegio* wear *polleras* and sombreros with their uniforms, just like me," she adds eagerly. (Uniform rules at Paiwa's school allow indigenous girls to wear *polleras* and hats.)

CHAPTER 17

Reality Sets In

~

The glass-covered courtyard

IT'S A BRILLIANT SATURDAY MORNING, and for the first time since our return we've slept through the night. Fitful sleep is one of the realities of coming back to high-altitude Cañar, and it feels wonderful to wake at seven o'clock to see the sun coming through the bedroom curtains and feeling completely rested.

Yesterday Michael spent the day shopping in Cuenca, and he arrived home last night elated with the results: three toilets, two pedestal sinks, faucets, hardware, and several light fixtures. But he was especially excited about one light fixture. Simple and well-designed fixtures are almost impossible to find in this country, where little exists between a single bulb (the choice of many country folks) and elaborate chandeliers (the choice of many wealthier folks). This

morning Michael asks me to walk down to the house with him and try the fixture out in various rooms.

As we step through the front doorway, I feel like a kid about to open a present because we are alone in the house for the first time without the workers. We
stand in the courtyard a few minutes looking around with held breath, but all
I can see is the complete chaos of wood curls and sawdust, paint and concrete
splashes, bent nails, broken tile pieces, and other debris.

A lot happened while we were gone, great interesting stuff that Michael and
I could only reconstruct through the photos that Lourdes sent, and through her
later descriptions. As best I can tell, here's the sequence:

1. Once the workers had covered the framed walls with thousands of bamboo
lath strips (which Santos was still splitting when I left last July), two *albañiles*
(masonry *maestros*) directed the preparation of the mixture for the walls, which
included different kinds of earth and clay, sand, fine gravel, and fine thatch cut
into four- to six-inch lengths. This preparation took about week, as the material
needed to be well mixed—the workers walked through it with rubber boots—
and turned over several times.

2. Lourdes told the regular *maestros* to round up as many relatives as they could
for a weekend *minga*—a volunteer work exchange (but, in this case, paid) that
is a tradition in the Andes; she also invited her architect friends from Cuenca
who were interested. About fifteen people gathered on a Saturday morning at the
house site to stuff the mixture between the slats to fill the wall spaces. Very messy
work. As each framed wall had two sets of laths, with a twelve-inch space between,
people worked from both sides to create solid walls. Once the weekend *minga* was
over, Lourdes hired extra workers for another week to finish filling the walls.

3. The house "rested" for three or four weeks to dry the walls, the length of
time depending on the degree of sun and wind. Lourdes took small core samples
to determine when the walls were dry enough for the next stage.

4. A second mixture of finely sifted earth, water, and fine thatch formed the
finish plaster, which was applied to walls inside and out. (The thatch serves as a
binder, much like the horsehair in the old lime-based plaster we took out of our
Portland house.)

~

Although the mud walls look great, we walk around the house in a gloomy
mood. In the kitchen, Michael is shocked at the mess of the new concrete pour
to raise the floor level. The floor was originally to be brick, but Michael changed
his mind and now wants to use a much thinner tile. But how on earth can tile

Filling the walls with mud and straw mixture

be laid over those great swirls and wavelets of hard concrete? Rubble is piled everywhere. Michael wonders if the workers were drunk. He had a problem this past Friday when two young helpers from Cuenca tippled from a bottle from noon on, until they had to be sent home on the bus, very drunk. We'll have to wait until Monday to see what Lourdes and the tile guy say, if they plan to send the young workers back.

The brick floor in my studio will be beautiful once the sawdust and construction debris is swept away, and the grinder does its work to make it smooth. Then, I suppose, a sealer will be applied and we'll have to wait for that to dry. The tile floors have yet to be laid in the bathrooms, but I see the boxes of tile stacked in the little construction shed, a promising sign that the tile crew will come next week. Michael holds up the fixture here and there, but the rooms are so messy and unfinished, it's a futile exercise. He leaves it in its box in one corner of the bedroom, saying we'll decide later.

Since it's a gorgeous day, we take a walk down the valley toward the river, then back through the fields toward Chaglaban, our own little *comuna*. We see many people out in the fields, plowing and planting, and women and girls washing clothing in an irrigation canal or natural spring. Everyone greets us with a nod or a wave, the gringos with the new house in Chaglaban, and we are pleased to know most by name, or face.

Earlier, I'd noticed a bulldozer at work in the big field below us, to the west, and we end our walk here to check out what is happening. We are appalled, but not completely surprised, to see that the bulldozer has carved straight lines in the field that look suspiciously like streets and flattened areas that look like house lots. Sure enough, as we reach the juncture of our *calle sin nombre*, we see a large sign: *Urbanización Inti Raymi*: one hundred homesites with electricity and water, sewer, and so on. I will hear later that the developer of this land was an indigenous leader, now entrepreneur, selling lots to Cañaris living in New York and New Jersey.

~

One late afternoon a week later, we meet Lourdes in her office in Cuenca. She says the young worker who was drunk on the job on Friday drank all weekend and was nearly dead of alcohol poisoning by Monday. He will not be coming back. Lourdes wants us to go look at hand-forged light fixtures that she insists we will love. She drives us across town during crazy rush hour to the iron-worker's shop, where we find the owner, Miguel, completely disorganized and distracted. He can't find his albums with photos of his lighting fixtures, but he wants to show us photos of a Gaudí-like project for a public park (a serpent going in and out of the ground, absolutely grotesque).

As we walk around his small showroom, waiting to see any fixtures that might be appropriate for our house, his wife sits at a small table, talking on the phone to another client. A dog barks incessantly right outside the door and no one notices. Michael is intense, wanting to know if I like this, or that, of the few models in the room. I don't like anything and I don't like being here and I don't like feeling we have to make a decision.

Lourdes, calm as always, chats with Miguel: "Remember when you did (such and such) for (so and so?) Don't you have a photo of that?"

Finally, Miguel brings out a large rococo fixture that he says could be a light "structure" for the courtyard and tells us to take it and try it out and if we like it, he will wire it. The cost is "about thirty-five dollars if I remember right." Neither of us liked it that afternoon, but we take it in order to get away (I think Miguel was equally eager that we go away). Funnily enough, it ends up as the overhead light in our courtyard.

Back in town, although it is late, Michael and I have other errands. We go to the phone company to send a fax to our bank in Portland, and as we walk away, heading for another light fixture store, Michael asks if I've been to the Banco de Guayaquil to see if they are still "sucking out" funds for a cancelled cell phone account from last year. He's mentioned this "sucking" of funds several times, and I hate how it sounds and I've finally just had it.

"I don't want to hear another word about sucking or financial stuff!" I say as I march ahead of him down the street.

"OK, I'll just get my bag and go home, right now!" he responds angrily.

"What bag?" I ask, turning around. We both stop and stare at one another. It's a funny moment (in retrospect), as Michael realizes he doesn't have a bag, but, rather, a box of groceries that he's left at his chess café, Cafecito. And I was honestly curious about what bag he might have.

The moment passes, but he stays defensive. "Why are you in such a bad mood? Don't you think I'm also sick of looking for lighting fixtures?"

"Yes, but this is about me. This is my meltdown!" I yell as we walk on down the street. But we are distracted from our argument by coming upon the workshop where Michael saw a beautiful San Antonio statue the other day. We go to see the little statue and talk to the *maestro*, who says he has restored it for the owner. It is beautiful, but not for sale.

By then our anger has run out of steam and the day is over. We go back to the Cafecito for *mojitos*, friends again.

~

JOURNAL, JANUARY 22

We go into Cañar for a comfort lunch at Elsa's. The señora there cooks pork the way Michael likes it. Before we left last July, she warned me that if Michael came back to Cañar alone in September he might be "stolen" by another woman. I always knew she liked Michael, but figured I was safe as Elsa is married with three teenage girls. She'd asked him to bring her something from the United States and today he gives her a tiny pair of fold-up scissors. She's delighted.

Sitting at a table just inside the open door, we see our *compadre* José Miguel in the street; he comes in and sits with us to exchange news. He tells us with excitement that his musical group, Los Chaskis, has launched their third album. Music is José Miguel's great passion, and his photography business, Estudio Inti, is mainly a source of income to fund his musical activities. When I first taught him, I saw a great future for him as a documentary photographer, but I know now that was my projection.

Later, we walk up to our lawyer's office, where we find Vicente looking through the thirtieth anniversary issue of *Vistazo*, an Ecuadorian monthly that's a mix of *People* and *Newsweek*, but always with a sexy woman on the cover. Vicente says it features me in an article about "silent heroes" in Ecuador. I'm a little shocked to see it. The journalist did the interview months ago and I'd heard nothing since. I cautiously take a look. I like the photo of me on a mountainside with Tayta Isidoro at Carnival, but the title of the article is embarrassingly presumptive: "Mi Familia Cañari." My Cañari Family. I hope no other of my Cañari friends will see it.

CHAPTER 18

The Devil Is in the Details

~

The crew with Michael

"THE TIME'S GOING TOO FAST," I said plaintively to Lourdes the other day, as we sat in her office. "We only have these six months! How much longer before we can move in?" Lourdes looked thoughtful for a moment before saying "One month, *maximo*!" She peered expectantly across her desk at us with her sweet smile.

Michael and I sat silent a moment before nodding warily. I, the practical optimist, privately calculated at least two months. Michael, always the pessimist, muttered as we left the office, "We'll be lucky to sleep in the house one damn night before we go back to Portland in July."

It's the first week of March, and while the carpenters, painters, tile layers, floor guys, and glaziers are slowly finishing their work, Michael and I impatiently wait for our "real" life to begin. We've come to Cuenca today to talk to Lourdes and buy supplies.

Building a house is a mysterious process, perhaps a bit like a love affair. In the beginning, anything is possible, the unknowns are infinitely intriguing and the glimpses of a prospective future intoxicating. But as day-to-day reality sets in, and maybe the love affair doesn't go so well, those endless possibilities are no longer so enchanting—Do I *really* want to live with this guy forever?/Will the house *ever* be finished?)—the unknowns become worrisome—Why won't he talk about his previous wife?/Why won't Lourdes tell us how much it will all cost?—and the future begins to look downright scary—He'll leave me and I'll be alone again./We won't be happy in our new house.

There's not much we can do right now but walk down to the house site a couple of times a day and check the progress. I plant a few flowers, pull a few weeds, tramp around, take a few photos, and dream about living here. I can't plant a kitchen garden as long as the workers are everywhere around the outside.

Michael takes endless measurements and ponders problems. Yesterday, with his new chainsaw, he chopped enough wood "for one night," he said glumly. It seems ridiculous to be doing such small jobs when there are so many big ones waiting, but everything must happen in a certain order. Michael can't install toilets, sinks, and light fixtures until the floors are finished, the walls are painted, the tile work is done, the windows have glass, and the doors have locks; otherwise, as José María keeps warning us, someone might steal the toilets. Hard to imagine.

Michael and I complain to one another, but building in Cañar has been a breeze compared to a house project we embarked on in Portland fifteen years ago. We'd just moved to Oregon after many years in Latin America, and we were trying to get our North American bearings and put together a life there. This included buying a house. One warm summer evening, on a walk with my sister Sherry, we came upon a two-story yellow Victorian house that looked abandoned. We had wandered into in an old inner-city neighborhood long ago gone industrial, and the house, with an unkempt yard and fliers piled by the door, was one of only three left standing in an otherwise empty block.

Although the neighborhood was hardly inviting, and I'd certainly never imagined living in a Victorian, much less one that was yellow, there was something about this house we immediately liked. It was small, tall, and narrow but graceful and nicely proportioned. We peered through the front door window to see, along with water-damaged wallpaper hanging in strips in the hall, a beautiful wooden window seat and a graceful stairway.

I noted the address on a scrap of paper, called the city, got the owner's name, and gave her a call. Mrs. Potts, an elderly widow, said the house had been empty for months, and she planned to tear it down. Built in 1903, but long a rental, pipes had burst last winter, causing a lot of damage that she hadn't bothered to repair. Mrs. Potts said the commercially zoned property where it sat was worth more without the house. "You can have it," she said cheerfully, "if you'll move it."

"Have it?" I repeated.

Yes, for free!" she said. "So why don't you and your husband come over for martinis and we'll talk it over?"

And so, after a series of improbable events, we *did* move the yellow house one clear, cold November day, about twelve blocks east into a neighborhood the same age as the house. Then we embarked on a hair-raising, year-long, tear-out-and-rebuild project that would probably have finished our relationship had it not been tempered by our several years together, and had we not been so busy trying to survive. While Michael worked full time on the house, I dusted off an old Master of Social Work degree and landed a temporary job as a curriculum writer for a summer program of gang-affected youth. As I tried to learn my way around Portland, visiting youth worksites for my job, I had what I later called a "vocational crisis," bursting into tears whenever I found myself driving across yet another of Portland's ten bridges in the opposite direction from where I wanted to go.

A year later, we emerged from the yellow house project like proud parents after a difficult birth, madly in love with our offspring, forgetting the pain of the delivery, and forgiving one another for all the mean things we'd said during the pregnancy. In fact, the invitation I designed for our housewarming party *was* a birth announcement, with a stork carrying a miniature house. Because the movers had picked up the house with a hydraulic lift, we knew exactly how much it weighed: 110,000 pounds, plus its height, width, and length (23 x 42 x 38 feet).

We held a big housewarming party for everyone who had worked on the house, from the movers, roofers, painters, carpenters, floor finishers, and drywallers, to the concrete contractor who had a nervous breakdown in the midst of pouring the foundation and was incommunicado for several critical weeks, nearly giving Michael a parallel nervous breakdown.

At the time, I was a complete neophyte to home ownership, and, in fact, the Cañar house will be only the second one of my adult life. Even married and with a child, and then single with a child, I had contently lived in rented houses or apartments in Colorado, California, New York, Toronto, Costa Rica, and Ecuador, never feeling the pull of wanting my own home.

But when Michael and I came to Portland after those years abroad, we knew we needed to get established, to build a base from which to launch the rest of our life together, whatever that might turn out to be. We were well into middle age, with a "short horizon," as they say in investment planning circles. This meant buying a house and finding work—which turned out to be exactly the wrong order. When we first went to the bank to ask for a loan for the yellow house project, I barely knew the meaning of "mortgage" and definitely didn't have a grasp of the concept of "equity." The bank manager quickly informed us we couldn't get a loan because we had no jobs, no debts, no credit history, no credit cards, no loans, and no previous mortgages. How un-American could we be?

We completed the house renovation using our savings and family loans, and when we returned to the same bank a year later for a mortgage on our "new" house, we were suddenly preferred customers. The bank couldn't give us *enough* money. In addition to the mortgage, the helpful loan agent asked, didn't we want something extra for furniture? A second car? Another house?

I wrote an article about our experience for a national magazine, launching a side career as a freelance writer.

We still live in, and love, the yellow house (which became taupe for awhile but is now back to its original color). And now, many real estate booms and busts later, I fully appreciate the meaning of equity and the American passion for home ownership. In fact, renting out our Portland house for the six months we're in Ecuador has been key to allowing us to undertake this second and—I sincerely hope—last house project.

~

While we wait, Michael cooks.

One Sunday he comes back happy from an early trip to the outdoor market, where he bought a chicken, shrimp, *camote* (sweet potato), white beans, mango, and pineapple. But he is particularly excited about the giant prawns he's found at his favorite fish vendor's stall. "Only two dollars fifty a pound!" he crows, holding up a giant gray creature with long antennae, an enormous head, and trailing tail. He lays the brute on the countertop next to his tape measure and insists I take a photo: nine inches. Men!

Then Michael organizes his day around his great find, gathering the ingredients to make *camerones a la diabla*—lightly boiled shrimp with a bowl of a chili/paprika sauce. That was lunch. Then, all afternoon, the house is redolent with the smell of dinner as he boils the ground-up heads, tails, and shells to make shrimp bisque, served with toast.

~

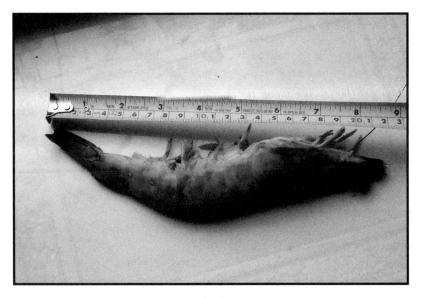

A nine-inch giant prawn

The following week, complications multiply. While we were in Cuenca overnight, two young workers came to finish sanding and varnishing the wood floors in the living/dining room. When they found they didn't have the key to open the double doors to the outside (probably needing fresh air for the fumes), they simply forced open the dead bolt and broke the lock. Michael was furious. "How can they just leave the house open like that?" he rages, although there is nothing inside to steal—not even toilets yet, I say pointedly.

Another worker came from Cuenca to grind the brick floor in my studio with a heavy machine that made a horrendous noise and used water as a medium. For two days, brick-red water was flung onto newly painted white walls and newly finished doors. The water seeped under our bedroom door and stained the new, unvarnished wood floor. A helper scraped the horrible red sludge by hand, sweeping back and forth behind the grinder, and then dumped it in the courtyard on top of the new good dirt we've had delivered. I watched for a couple of hours, but couldn't take it any more, went home and called Lourdes to complain. As usual, she calmly says everything will come clean.

Then, on another day, I realized that the paint color I chose for our bedroom—a subtle rosy shade on the chip—turned out "bordello pink" once on the walls, and I had to ask the painter to redo the bedroom with another color. I was embarrassed, but the painter shrugged, and Lourdes shrugged and said,

"It happens all the time." This time I chose a safe color, "haystack yellow," and it looks just right.

Finally, the glaziers came to install one hundred and thirty-six panes in the windows and doors. The workers were efficient and professional, but they made one mistake, installing clear glass instead of frosted glass in the multi-paned door of the *baño social* in the courtyard, the most public space in the house. While Michael, Lourdes, and I stood talking with the glass contractor, I suggested that we could simply cover the windows with a curtain. "No, we *cannot*," Michael said sharply to me. "We ordered etched glass for that door and that's what I want!" This led to a short, hot argument between us in front of everyone—in English, of course, which no one really understood, but the tone and the tension were very clear.

"Oh, the stress of finishing a house," Lourdes sighed in the pointed silence that followed.

～

JOURNAL, MARCH 10

Michael's *Camarones a la Diabla* (Prawns of the Devil)

PRAWNS:
Pull off heads and peel down to tail, leaving tail. Put heads and shells aside.
Rinse prawns and boil minimum time, about 5 minutes, depending on size.
Throw prawns in bowl of cold water. Save boiling water for sauce.

SAUCE:
In a pan, throw two small or one large tomato, along with garlic, fresh cilantro, cumin, oregano, salt, and pepper. Add one fresh red chili, with or without seeds depending on how hot you like it. Add a little water. Set over low heat to simmer, checking that it doesn't go dry. Add water if necessary. When cooked, add three tablespoons of Spanish paprika. Put mixture in blender, blend until fine, return to pan, and continue to simmer.

Serve prawns chilled or room temperature with small bowl of sauce and fresh lemons.

CHAPTER 19

A Short History of This Place

~

Huasipungueros *(hacienda workers)* *(Foto Navas)*

THE OTHER AFTERNOON, while I was digging behind the house in a spot where I hope to have a kitchen garden one day, I came across a small ceramic shard with a painted edge. I stood staring at it in my hand for a few minutes, thinking about what I know of the history of this place and how old this bit of embellish clay might be. Archeologists and local grave robbers have turned up plenty of evidence around Cañar of gold, copper, and shell ornaments, ceramics, and other artifacts that date as far back as 500 BC. So we know that native peoples had settled this area around three thousand years ago and were planting crops, making pottery, mining, and trading with other groups from the coastal and Amazon regions.

Or this fragment could be of more recent vintage, from the mid-fifteenth century, when the Incas marched up from Peru, conquered the "fierce long-haired" local inhabitants, and brought with them their own distinctive ceramics—hard-finished and polished pots and utensils, decorated with geometric shapes and animals and birds. Historians speculate that the Incas first organized the dispersed settlements of what is now southern Ecuador into their vast empire to create a unified group under their control. Because the local tribes were without a centralized power, the Incas invaded without much resistance and negotiated a peaceful occupation by ruling through local *caciques*, chiefs, rather than imposing their own authorities. Brilliant administrators, the Incas efficiently appropriated what was useful from the local culture and introduced their more advanced technologies of agricultural production based on micro-climates and—most notably—the incredible worked-stone architecture found in ruins throughout the empire and still so well preserved in Cuzco, Peru, their imperial capital.

Perhaps the Incas gave the collective name "Cañaris" to the local tribes, creating a distinct ethnic group, but where the name "Cañar" comes from remains a mystery. Some present-day Cañaris say it derives from the *cañaro* plant that grows in the region. Others propose that it's a combination of "caña," meaning stem or cane, and "ara," which is the genus name for macaw. This conjecture ties in with two local myths of origin. In one myth, the Cañaris descended from a giant serpent living in Lake Culebrillas who enticed a woman to become his wife. The other legend tells the story of a great flood that forced two brothers, the only survivors, to take refuge in a cave in the mountains, where one of the brothers mated with a woman, half macaw, half human. Another version goes that both brothers won macaw-wives. The macaw-wives taught the brothers the secrets of agriculture and became the mothers of all Cañaris. The macaw—a New World parrot called *"guacamaya"* in Spanish—and the snake still have symbolic importance to the Cañaris. At fiestas and processions, I see children dressed in papery costumes meant to represent the feathered macaw, and a coiled serpent remains a popular motif in Andean art.

In a short one hundred years (1438–1533), the Incas created the largest empire in the New World. Called "Tawantinsuyu" ("Land of Four Quarters"), it stretched twenty-five hundred miles along the Andes, encompassing modern-day north and central Chile, northwest Argentina, Bolivia, Peru, Ecuador, and southern Colombia, with an estimated population of 12 million people. Although the Incas controlled the Cañar territory for only about sixty years (1463–1533), they left a large legacy, evidence of which we see everywhere today. They incorporated Cañari sacred sites into their own and built religious complexes with temples to their sun god, Inti, the most famous example in Ecuador being Ingapirca, the archeological ruins a few kilometers from our house that contain both Cañari and Inca graves.

Quichua, the Inca language (called "Quechua" in Peru), supplanted the original language of the Cañari, which is lost. Today, some older Cañaris still speak Quichua exclusively, with a sprinkling of what they say are original Cañari words for place names and local plants. (Interestingly, Quichua/Quechua is more widely spoken today than during Inca times and is not in danger of becoming extinct. In Peru, nearly a quarter of the population speaks Quechua.)

The Incas extended their famous road, Capac Ñan (known in guidebooks as the Inca Trail), through Cañari territory, expanding their vast network of roads, storehouses, and shelters that moved goods, people, and information from one end of their empire to the other. Because the Incas had no writing, *chaskis*, or runners, carried messages using *quipus*, elaborately knotted ropes. A few remnants of the road remain in Ecuador, and some years ago, Michael and I and friends made a three-day hike on the best-preserved section, from Achupallus to Ingapirca.

Everything changed in 1531, when a thin, bearded Spaniard named Francisco Pizarro stepped off his ship on the northern coast of present-day Peru. Pursuing gold, silver, and new territory for the Spanish Crown, Pizarro could not have picked a better time for his visit. A dynastic war between two Inca half-brothers, Huáscar and Atahualpa, had left their empire in chaos. Pizarro marched inland with a small band of soldiers to the town of Cajamarca, where, through trickery and betrayal, he captured, ransomed, and executed Atahualpa in 1533. After that, with primitive firearms and soldiers mounted on horses—an animal the terrified natives had never seen—Pizarro and his small band of soldiers quickly defeated the Inca army of tens of thousands. The Spanish colonization of South America had begun.

A few years before that, the Cañaris had made the fatal mistake of fighting on the wrong side in the war between the two Inca brothers, each claiming succession after the death of their father, Huayna Capac, who had expanded the conquest into present-day Ecuador and died in Tomebamba, today the city of Cuenca. Huáscar lost, and in revenge, Atahualpa brought down a massacre on Cañari men and boys of such biblical proportions that, when the Spanish marched into the territory shortly after, one scribe described finding "fifteen times more women than men." With memories fresh of the Inca massacre, the remaining Cañari leaders greeted the Spaniards as liberators, creating an alliance they would regret for the next five hundred years.

The Spanish soldier and chronicler Pedro Cieza de León wrote the only description of this region from that time:

> The natives of this province, who are called Cañares . . . are handsome in body and face. They wear their hair very long, and wrap it around their heads with a wooden band to hold it, the band as fine as a ring of a sieve, by which they are recognized as Cañares. . . . They dress in wool and cotton clothes, and wear sandals on their feet, which are . . . like clogs.
>
> The women are very beautiful and not a little lusty, friendly toward Spaniards. These women are very hard workers, because they work the fields and plant the crops and reap the harvest, while most of their husbands stay at home weaving and spinning and preparing their weapons and clothing, and making up their faces and doing other effeminate things.

The "lusty women" bit might have been some wishful daydreaming. Cieza de León was writing his chronicle many years later and comfortably back in his native Spain, shortly before his death.

By 1549, the Spanish conquest of South America was complete, bringing with it the wheel, writing, city planning, colonial administration, taxation, and Catholicism, along with oppression, slavery, and European diseases. By the year 1600, more than 70 percent of the indigenous population of South America had died—primarily from infectious disease, but also from starvation and despair.

This is complicated history. With no written records until the Spanish arrived, present-day Cañaris have confusing and conflicting interpretations of their origins. For many, the Incas are seen as honored ancestors when, in fact, they were conquerors and oppressors. But this seems lost in the fog of history as our friends name their children after Inca warriors—including the one responsible for the famous massacre—and Inca princesses—Atahualpa, Rumiñahui, Huáscar, Sisa, Coya, and Pacari—and celebrate Inti Raymi, the Inca festival of the sun in place of their traditional Cañari festival of the moon, Killa Raymi.

So, I think (still standing in my future garden), maybe this bit of pottery came from the early days of the Spanish conquest, when the Crown encouraged soldiers, explorers, and adventurers to settle down and exploit the resources of its new colonies by granting them rights to indigenous labor and products in a particular region. While the Spanish "overlord" did not formally own the land occupied by the native peoples, he had a legal right to force them to work the land, or in the mines, and exact payment in the form of grains, gold, silver, or animals. If the natives refused to work, they could be punished and even killed. The labor system was called "*encomienda*," which comes from "to entrust," but was in reality a brutally efficient form of feudalism and legalized slavery. In return, the Spanish overlord was charged by the Crown to convert the *indígenas* to Catholicism, instruct them in Spanish, and protect them from "warring tribes."

The Spanish were scrupulous record keepers, and so a document exists from June 15, 1540, that granted Gonzalo Pizarro, Francisco's younger half-brother, rights to the natives in Cañar.

> Because the Indians of the province of the Cañares are a warlike people and friends of the Spaniards, and ever since they entered this land to serve His Majesty in the conquest of said province, they [the Cañares] have helped them and served as His Majesty's loyal vassals, and it is good that you, said Captain Gonzalo Pizarro, as governor of said provinces, have them on your head and encomienda—[so that they] live more content and with their help you may serve His Majesty in war.

Given that Gonzalo lived in Quito and was only briefly governor of Cañar before he was beheaded for turning against the Crown, he perhaps never laid eyes on this part of Ecuador. As he is described in a historical document as "one of the most corrupt, brutal and ruthless conquistadors of the New World," I sincerely hope he didn't get this far.

Nonetheless, the hacienda system that grew out of the *encomienda* era dominated Cañar, hand-in-hand with the Catholic Church, for the next five hundred years. As the original conquistadors died, many donated their estates to the Church in hopes of gaining salvation for past sins. Even after independence from Spain in 1822, much of the early colonial properties remained under the control of the Catholic Church. This eventually included our own little bit of earth, which became part of the vast Hacienda Guantug, the Spanish name for the bushy tree *belladonna datura*, which grows around Cañar.

Hacienda Guantug's last owner was a rich spinster from Cuenca, Florencia Astudillo—called "Niña Florencia" or "La Niña" by the Cañaris who worked her estates. Born in 1869, she came from a family so rich that her mother, who had brought the wealth to her marriage, was known as *Juana del Oro* (Juana of the gold). Florencia was an only child who inherited, along with Hacienda Guantug, large properties in other provinces and grand townhouses in Cuenca. The thousands of indigenous and poor mestizo families attached to her haciendas, called "*huasipungueros*," were given a small plot of land where they could build a dwelling, plant their crops, and keep a few animals, but their "souls" and

Hacienda worker with patrón's horse (Foto Navas)

their labor, for a given number of days per week, belonged to La Niña. As with the previous land tenure system of the Spanish, the original inhabitants of the region were little more than indentured servants.

Many of our older Cañari acquaintances remember working on Hacienda Guantug as children, or they recall the stories of their fathers and mothers. A couple of years ago, with the help of the videographer at a cultural center, I recorded Juanito Tenesaca telling stories of hacienda days. (He's the man who sold us straw by the *mula*.) In one, he described how his father was beaten by the *mayordomo*, a white overseer, for gathering firewood, because "everything belonged to the hacienda, even the trees, and it was the job of the *mayordomo* to protect them."

When I asked Juanito about the size of the Hacienda Guantug, he swept his arm to the west and said, "Allllll this, from here to the coast." (In reality, it was about 30,000 hectares, or 74,000 acres.)

In a story much told, La Niña, in her occasional visits to Cañar from her home in Cuenca—about sixty kilometers over a mountain range—traveled in royal style on a platform chair carried by her hacienda workers. "*Los peones* carried her on their shoulders just like a saint," Juanito said. He also described the two- or three-day trips to Cuenca that the workers would make on foot or on horseback to deliver products from the hacienda, including cheese, wheat, barley, and potatoes. "They would spend the night sleeping in the courtyard of one of La Niña's houses in Cuenca before starting the long journey back."

Florencia Astudillo died in 1956 at the age of eighty-seven, "still proudly a virgin" according to local lore. A devout Catholic with many friends in the Church hierarchy in Cuenca, Astudillo left her various haciendas and properties to an order of nuns, the *Hermanas de los Ancianos Desamparados,* who tended homeless old folks. Her bequest made the nuns fabulously rich and the largest landowners in the province of Cañar. (Paiwa's Catholic school is on the grounds of the original hacienda headquarters.)

With the 1964 passage of the Ecuadorian Land Reform, Idle Lands, and Settlement Act, the government, with support from the military, began to break the chains that had bound indigenous people for nearly five hundred years. But real reform was slow taking effect. In the late 1970s, when the appropriation of the haciendas was finally complete, the land—or some land at least—was returned to its rightful owners, the native peoples. Organized into agricultural cooperatives around small communities—or *comunas* such as Chaglaban, near where we live—indigenous and other landless families were granted property deeds.

"As usual, the local mestizos got the larger plots and the best land closest to town," Juanito said in his interview, "while the *indígenas* got very little. Our fields were farther away, and usually on steep hillsides." In fact, land redistribution in the highlands was hardly a success, and many who had formerly worked on the hacienda remained as poor as ever with their own land.

Our *comuna* of Chaglaban consists of about forty families, its center marked by a blue-roofed school and community center—built during the land reform by Plan International, a development charity—and a large adobe house left over from hacienda times. I love its name: Quinta Lolita, painted in big beautiful script on the side of the house. I photographed it many times until last year, when I noticed that the name had been painted over, erasing a last reminder of a bitter past.

~

More likely this piece of ceramic I hold is from recent times: a cooking pot accidentally broken by a Cañari woman preparing lunch for the men in the field; a clay plate shattered by a child as she played nearby, or a cup dropped against a stone by a man after a drink of *chicha* (non-alcoholic corn beer) to celebrate a harvest.

When we first began construction, Michael and I carefully collected all these ceramic bits and pieces in a bowl, imagining each one old and precious. But by now we've lost track of that bowl of shards, and maybe our romantic notions, too. I toss the shard back onto the ground and continue digging.

Five hundred years from now, in a world without us, when the house is gone, and the land forested over, someone (or something) might dig up a fragment of ours, a stainless steel spoon or a piece of Michael's wiring or copper pipe (or, most likely, debris from the roof) and wonder who on earth it belonged to and how we lived.

~

JOURNAL, MARCH 15

Yesterday, walking into town, I stopped to peer into the gate that leads to Mama Jesús's old adobe house, now nearly hidden behind a new three-story unfinished house that her family has built with dollars from a migrant son-in-law. I happened to see Mama Jesús creeping out of her house, barely moving with the help of a stick, her gray hair hanging long. She is now well into her nineties and almost completely blind. I watched as she settled to the ground in a sort of controlled collapse. First she bent at the waist, then her old legs gave way bit by bit until she was sitting against an adobe wall. This is where she passes time now, I imagined, when the sun is out and she wants some fresh air. I'd love to see where she sleeps in her old house, where I photographed her so many years ago, but I know her family would be embarrassed that she—and her house—have grown so old and unkempt.

It was in 1992 or 1993 when I asked Mama Jesús if I could come on a Sunday and take her portrait. She agreed, and on the appointed day I found her dressed elegantly. She carefully posed herself seated in front of her house with a drop spindle and raw wool. "But I'm not going to spin," she warned, "because it's Sunday, and I don't work on Sundays."

CHAPTER 20

Moving Day

Finished house, from street

MOVING DAY, AND LUCK IS WITH US. It's been pouring rain the last few days, but this morning it is dry, if cloudy. José María, his brother Santos, and a visiting American graduate student, Danny, come early to help. Michael's transport buddy, Lucho, arrives at nine o'clock with his big truck, and sits in it while the four men empty our small house with amazing speed: bookshelves, beds, bags, baskets, boxes, cabinets, tables, and chairs. At nine thirty, the truck and men leave for the new house while I stay behind to pack the last of the dishes, clean, and organize those things I don't want to lose track of in the chaos of the move: my laptops, cameras, recorder, and other electronic gear. As I move from room to room, our little rental house reverts to its previous state: a half-finished, poorly constructed, three-room *casita* with water-stained walls and badly fitting windows and doors, devoid of character and warmth. Still, we've lived here almost three years, off and on, we made it our own, and I feel real affection for the place.

Lucho and Michael come back for a second trip at ten o'clock, and I ride back with them to the new house, where I see that the yard is nothing but a great morass of mud, churned up by truck tires. All our belongings are piled at the entrance or in the courtyard, and after Michael pays Lucho, he asks José María, Santos, and Danny to help us move things into the rooms. I'm embarrassed to ask the men to take off their shoes, but I do, as the floors are pristine and their boots are covered with mud. What appeared to be a great amount of stuff in our old house is quickly swallowed by the large rooms of the new. In about thirty minutes we're done.

Michael invites everyone to lunch. We walk into town to Los Maderos, the restaurant near the square where Michael and I had so many meals years ago when we stayed at nearby Hostal Ingapirca. As we finish lunch, we hear thunder and see flashes of lightning out the open door to the restaurant. We hurriedly walk down the hill out of town, black thunderclouds gathering above us as everyone rushes to get home before the downpour.

Drops begin to fall as I step through our front doors and into the courtyard, where I find my least-favorite neighbor from the old neighborhood, Señora Cecilia, a busybody whose sole purpose in life is to know what her neighbors are up to. Somehow, on the very day we've moved, she's come for a look around, bringing her husband, a daughter, and a grandchild. Michael is rushing around arranging things, but remains polite, as always, speaking to the little group as he passes this way and that through the courtyard. I rush around too, but not quite so polite, hoping their visit will be brief. For maybe ten minutes the visitors peer curiously into the rooms and make comments before finally taking their leave. "*Hasta luego, vecina,*" Señora Cecilia calls. See you soon, neighbor.

At last, Michael and I are alone in our new house. He takes off the outdoor shutters, gets the pump going, turns on the water, and assembles our bed. By now the rain is falling heavily on the glass roof, gushing into the rain gutters and down Michael's excellent drainage system to his pipes underneath the courtyard. The lovely sound of the gurgles and splashes makes me feel like I'm in the middle of a rainstorm, and, as I pass from room to room through the courtyard, I keep looking up expecting drops on my head. How wonderful to enjoy the storm, from under glass.

Around four thirty, the electricity goes off. We are standing side by side at the living room windows, watching the heavy clouds float east over the mountains. Chatting amiably, we congratulate ourselves on our view, the choice of the property, the position of the house, the placement of the windows—in short, we are happy with everything. So far.

"Now," Michael says, "I think I'll build a fire." This is a moment we've both worried about. If the fireplace doesn't work, our self-congratulatory mood will plummet with the temperature, as it is our only source of heat. Lourdes promised she'd tried it, and the smear of blackness at the back of the firebox indicates that someone has built a small fire. While I unpack dishes, Michael opens the damper with a long iron handle that sticks out of the dome and cautiously lights a small fire of paper and kindling. Yes! The smoke draws right up. He throws on some small logs from under the porch. Beautiful flames, no smoke! Finally, he piles on enough logs for our first evening.

The lights come back on, and it's cocktail hour. I bring in two plastic outdoor chairs and we sit down with drinks in our new living room. With Bruch's *Scottish Fantasy* on our music system—an iPod with tiny speakers—we turn our chairs this way and that to admire yet another view: the open-beamed ceiling, the kitchen windows, the mountain peaks floating over the tops of the clouds.

"It's a bit like Scotland here, don't you think?" Michael says as the mournful music fills the room. "Yes, a bit like . . . ," I say, remembering my solo bike adventure in the Scottish Highlands years ago, when I came back fantasizing about living there. How sweet that I should realize a version of my dream a continent and hemisphere away in a highland valley of the Andes.

I make popcorn on the tabletop stove, and we watch the lingering light and changing weather. At seven o'clock, it is finally dark. Michael makes a dinner of leftover soup, which we eat on small bedside tables in front of the fire.

"This is what we must do every night," I say, "a fire, drinks, dinner with views and music." We go to bed early our first day in our new house, filled with warm feelings for everyone and everything.

~

The next morning, I am still in bed with my coffee when I hear the voice of our neighbor, Rosa, calling me. I glance up, assuming she's in her cornfield, but then I see she is on *our* side of the fence; in fact, she's at the bedroom window. She motions for me to come speak to her. When I open the window, she says with a dark scowl that she wants Michael. I tell her he's in the kitchen.

Next thing, I hear Rosa yelling at Michael, "You have *not* bought that corn field!"

"But we have the *escritura*," Michael replies evenly. "I'll show you." He marches in to the bedroom and takes the deed out of the filing cabinet, his face set with a look I know too well. I figure it's time to join him and Rosa in the kitchen before things escalate.

"You and my husband have tricked me," Rosa says to Michael, barely glancing at me, or the deed. "I did *not* agree to sell that land."

"But it was you who pointed out the property lines to the surveyor," Michael says, his voice rising. "And you and Juan agreed to the price, accepted the down payment, and signed the final papers."

I can see that logic and hard evidence have no credibility in Rosa's distressed mind. With alternating tears and pleadings on her part, and expressions of sympathy and support on ours (mainly mine), she first demands that we should pay something extra for the land. One of us, probably Michael, answers that the land is already paid for in full, with the last payment in the hands of our lawyer, Vicente. Then, she rejoins, we should at least make sure that some of the money goes to her instead of all to Juan because her husband has misled her, "as he has in the past." I say we will talk to Vicente to see if that is possible, but, I suggest, she should get her own lawyer to deal with her husband.

Rosa changes strategy as she calms down. Will we at least give her three years to plant crops on the land? Michael says that three years is a long time; we've already waited for the corn to mature, and we have some plans of our own for the land.

Dragon downspout with back cornfield

Finally, changing tack again, with one of her confusing non sequiturs, Rosa warns us that we should be careful that our other neighbors don't impinge on our property lines, "because they've tried to do it with me in the past."

This is getting surreal. Michael and I assure her that we will be careful of others around us, and she finally leaves.

I am truly sorry for Rosa. I suspect her husband probably does press her to sell off the land, bit by bit, and maybe he doesn't tell her—or she doesn't fully grasp—what is happening. But she has to know that she agreed to sell this second cornfield because the sale could not have happened without her signature.

A few days later, to add to the confusion, Mama Antuka, an old woman who lives nearby, shows up to say that *she* is the one who planted the corn on our land. Rosa has made her a *partidario*—given her the right to plant in return for sharing the harvest. With the harvest done, Mama Antuka goes on to say that the custom here, known as *la puebla* (literally, "the people"), gives her—Mama Antuka—the right to plant a second crop, specifically a crop of peas! When Michael and I look puzzled, she explains that since she has paid to have the land plowed for the corn, it is only fair that she get her money's worth by planting a second crop.

"*Es el costumbe!*" Mama Antuka repeats several times. It is the custom!

We tell Mama Antuka she can plant her peas. As outsiders wanting to be good neighbors, we feel we cannot argue with a local custom like that.

~

JOURNAL, MARCH 19

A day to organize the new house, but there's just too much to do. I start one job, get distracted, and drift off to another. I set up a little table in the bedroom for my desk and unpack my office things. I'm still waiting for the floors in my studio/office to be finished. In the living room I check the temperature, 55 degrees, and try to imagine my 87-year-old mother here in a few weeks. She'll be freezing, and we must get an electric heater for the guest room.

Michael is already troubleshooting: a running toilet, sticky flusher, drippy kitchen faucet.

José María comes by and works on the outside walkway that runs around the house, cleaning the bricks and applying a wax. I go up to our old house to make some phone calls, then on to a commercial place to make cell calls.

In this crazy place, one cannot call cell phones from a land line, and Michael lost my cell phone on the bus last week.

In the afternoon, I go down to TUCAYTA to show them the Carnival photos and give CDs to the president for their archive. Danny, the graduate student who has been working with the organization, comes with me. He wants to say good-bye as he's leaving for the States tomorrow. It's a sweet meeting, with the staff expressing much appreciation for the collaboration of "Judicita y Danielito."

"Don't go! Don't GO!" they protest to Danny, in the de rigueur Cañari manner of saying farewell. "Stay and work with us! When are you coming back?"

CHAPTER 21

The *Wasipichana*

~

Procession with chacana

Part I: Before the Event

For months now, as Michael and I walked back and forth to the construction site, neighbors living along the way, acquaintances we met in the streets, and even near-strangers stopping in their cars, invariably asked: "When do we come for the *wasipichana*?"—the Quichua word for a housewarming fiesta. If the person was on foot, the question was often accompanied by a sort of friendly leer and the motions of dancing, arms stretched out, hips swaying.

"Oh, not for a long time yet," I always replied, dread and denial adding conviction. "First, we have to finish the house." Michael tended to give a vague nod and say, with a worried look, "Yeah, sometime soon now!"

So imagine that you've finally—undeniably—reached the end of a complicated, eighteen-month construction project that everyone in the surrounding countryside has watched with great interest. Imagine your new house with its pristinely finished adobe exterior, freshly painted walls, newly laid wood floors, newly tiled kitchen and bathrooms . . . new *everything*. Imagine how happy you are to finally be living in this dream house (we moved in just last week), clean and orderly and promising to make your future life peaceful and productive.

Now, imagine that local custom dictates you throw a party for neighbors, friends, and acquaintances, friends of friends, town officials, the press, the mayor, and all those who've been a part of the construction process, from the truck drivers who delivered sand and gravel to the local hardware store owner who has been greatly enriched by your project. In addition, other curious folks you don't even know, who've watched the "house of the gringos" take shape, will want to come. And, of course, your guests will be curious to see *all* of the house, so you must anticipate having visitors examine every room, including bedrooms and bathrooms. (I understand, as I too love houses and always want to see every nook and cranny.)

Imagine too that for this event, which will last all day and into the night, you must provide alcoholic drinks for the adults, colas for the kids, and, of course, food. Lots of food! We're not talking snacks here, but a full-on dinner with roasted guinea pigs and plates of pork with all the trimmings for each person. It is also expected that servings will be large enough for guests to take home food for family members who couldn't come, a custom of the indigenous culture called, in Quichua, "*wanlla*." (Someone has to stay behind to watch the house and the animals.)

Also, for a proper *wasipichana*, there must be live music for dancing, for as long as people can stay upright and move their two legs.

Finally, imagine that this event, a blending of Catholic and native customs, begins with a scary ritual when a beloved spouse, the architect, and the godparents of the house—yes, you will be needing godparents for this event—climb onto the roof to place a marble cross on the roofline. While these folks are up in the air, they will trade alcoholic toasts and throw candy and cookies to the crowd below.

In Cañar, the roof cross is usually a Christian one, with little ceramic doves or dogs on either side. But our cross will be a *chacana*, an Andean cross fashioned after a constellation in the Southern Hemisphere, *Cruz del Sur*, that is believed to be the center of the universe by indigenous peoples.

Wasipichana is a Quichua word combining *wasi*, meaning house, and *pichana*, meaning cleansing or purifying. I doubt such a custom existed before the Spanish came, but, as with many other rituals, the indigenous people saw an opportunity to "repurpose" the Church's custom of blessing a house with an event to suit themselves, while keeping some of the Catholic flavor intact. In place of a priest for a blessing, our old friend, Mama Michi the *curandera*, will perform a purification ceremony to rid our house of any bad spirits or evil influences that might have crept in during the construction.

As I see it, the indigenous *wasipichana* symbolizes the generosity, cooperation, and reciprocity that characterizes the Cañari people. It says, "We have a new house. We want to share our good fortune with you (lest you maybe get jealous). Come celebrate." I later learn that, in building a house, it's a custom to hold two fiestas: one to celebrate the finishing of the roof and the other to celebrate the completion of the house. In past times, no house was built without the help of friends, family, and neighbors, and a big party was a way to repay your helpers. Michael and I skipped the roof fiesta, as we didn't know about it, but there was no way we could avoid the *wasipichana*.

We figure this party will cost us more than a thousand dollars, but we've known from the beginning that we wanted to do it. In fact, it is reminiscent of a similar, though less complicated, party we held in Portland at the end of our yellow house renovation when we invited everyone who had "touched" it the past year, including carpenters, painters, roofers, inspectors, and bankers.

As to *wasipichana* protocol for gringos, we are feeling our way—groping might be a better word—and so we're open to all advice. Knowing we would need "*compadres de la casa*," (godparents of the house), we asked José María, our old friend who worked on the house for the past eighteen months, and his wife Narcisa. José María graciously accepted and quickly informed us that it was his job to find a second set of godparents. He said he would ask Antonio, the masonry *maestro* who built our fireplace, and his wife Luisa. He also let us know, in his gentle way, that it was his job to safeguard the cross for the day and night leading up to the *wasipichana*, keeping it at his house on an altar (a table) with burning candles. We didn't question this, but I suppose, again, it goes back to the Christian tradition of blessing the cross and therefore the house.

We didn't realize it at the time, but asking José María and Narcisa to be godparents of the house tied us to their family as firmly as if one of our children had married one of theirs. We are *compadres* for life, and rather than call one another by name from now on, we will always be *comadre* and *compadre*. While the couple's three daughters are not quite our godchildren, it is understood we will have a special relationship with Lourdes, Sarita, and María.

For the event, I made an invitation with a watercolor rendering of the house and did a walkabout to deliver it to people we know, in town and around the country. Some folks looked puzzled to receive a handmade invite, others seemed amused, but everyone said they would come—and dance! I also visited friends in Cuenca with invites, and I knew Lourdes was asking all her architect friends and colleagues who are eager to see her latest *casa de tierra*.

As the day approached, preparations were daunting, and I admit to having been fairly useless beyond handling the invitations and arranging the house. A few days before, Michael went into town to talk to Señora Elsa, his favorite "pork lady," who sells a roasted pig daily from her tiny hole-in-the-wall restaurant. Elsa agreed to prepare one very large porker for our party, along with one hundred *llapingachos*, a sort of fried potato pancake. In addition, Paiwa's mother, María Esthela, announced that she wanted to contribute ten cooked guinea pigs, or *cuyes*. This was a great gift, but she advised that we would need at least thirty-five more, along with hundreds of servings of potatoes and hominy. She offered to negotiate for us with a woman she knows who could prepare these.

María Esthela also helped us to understand how the food should be served. She said honored guests such as the godparents should receive a plate with a full guinea pig each, while less honored but important guests would get a half guinea pig. Then all other adults will get at least a piece of guinea pig, and the kids get the crunchy little feet and leftover bits and pieces.

Along with the food, we bought untold number of three-liter bottles of cola, two dozen liters of Zhumir, and plastic plates, cups, spoons, and paper napkins for two hundred and fifty guests, just in case. We had absolutely no idea how many people would show up.

Party invitation

~

Part II: After the Event

Well, Michael and I—and the new house—survived the *wasipichana*, but full recovery will take some time. For one thing, the party didn't end when I thought it would. Those who couldn't come on Saturday, or got the date wrong, simply came on Sunday, making it a full weekend of showing the house and providing food and drink for all comers. Thank goodness, we had plenty of leftovers.

Today, Monday, we have hired a neighbor woman to come help us clean. When you serve roasted pig to more than one hundred adults and many children—most sitting on the floor because there aren't enough chairs—you're bound to have greasy handprints on the new adobe walls in the courtyard, and on the white painted walls in the living room, and on glass door and window panes at the level of young fingers. Plus, of course, there were a few spilled glasses of cola and beer here and there.

When guests dance for hours in the loose-earth courtyard with the shuffling Cañari style (moving your feet to and fro without lifting them), you're bound to have dust on every surface in the house. And with an eight-piece band set up in the guest bedroom, complete with microphones, a sound mixer, and heavy speakers, you'd be foolish not to expect a few gouges in the new wood floor.

Finally, when your husband is pressed to take shot after shot of straight 90-proof alcohol from about eleven o'clock in the morning until nine o'clock at night—well, you can imagine the result. Less said about *that*, the better.

But to go back to the beginning. . . . The day of the *wasipichana* dawned cloudy but no rain. An excellent sign, as downpours in the days leading up to the event had been serious enough to close roads between Cuenca and Cañar with landslides.

Michael and I were up early to arrange the house. It didn't take long as we'd just moved in the week before and did not have much furniture. Plus, not even a single mirror. So when it came time to dress for the party, Michael put on his black fedora (from last year's baptism) and asked me if he should wear it. I said, "No, it makes you look rather foolish," but he wore it anyway. Good decision. With the new poncho that José María would present to him a couple of hours later, he would look entirely appropriate.

However, when I put on the hand-embroidered blouse that Narcisa had made for me last year, with sleeves too short, and I asked Michael if I should wear it, he said, distractedly, "Yeah, looks good!" Bad decision. (No mirror, remember?) In the photographs of the day I appear thin and awkward, with my wrists dangling out of the too-small blouse.

The procession of the cross began at José María and Narcisa's house around eleven o'clock. Lourdes had come earlier from Cuenca to join us. Antonio's wife, Luisa, tied a garland of colored ribbons with long tails around the cross and instructed Michael, Lourdes, and me to hold onto the ends of the ribbons as we walked. José María's three little daughters led the procession, and twenty or thirty others followed, mostly family members of the four *compadres*. We climbed up the dirt road from the countryside into our old neighborhood, then back down another rough road to our new house. Two teenage musicians, hired by José María for the day, trailed slowly behind, one with an old accordion, pumping out an aimless tune, and the other dragging a stick over a *raspadora*, a gourd with ridges. The boys looked supremely bored, and the whole scene felt slightly surreal: the countryside, ragtag procession, and plaintive music reminding me of a Fellini film.

Arriving at our house, we found guests already standing around in the yard and inside the house. Most I knew; some I didn't recognize. Mama Michi sat barefoot on the edge of the courtyard, contemplating the scene she had prepared for her ceremony. On a cloth on the ground she had arranged her *mesa ritual*, her ritual table, with objects collected in her travels: feathers, stones, antlers, amulets, seashells and an iron railroad spike. All around the courtyard she had sprinkled flowers, fruits, seeds, and grains (which would be popping up as tender plants for months to come). Burning candles and a smoking incense brazier sat on the ground.

I asked Mama Michi if we should start the ceremony directly and she said we should serve a round of drinks first.

This led to some confusion in the kitchen. I asked Michael if we should serve *chicha*, the non-alcoholic corn beer that José María had made the day before and that was now sitting on the kitchen floor in large containers. Or cola? Or shots of Zhumir? Wasn't it too early for alcohol? And did we have any trays? How could we serve drinks to this many people without trays? We had many eager helpers, much confusion, and no clear procedures. I was obviously helpless as a hostess.

Meanwhile, more guests had crowded into the courtyard, sitting around the edges or standing in doorways. Somehow, we got drinks into everyone's hands. Again, I asked Mama Michi—who by now seemed to be dozing—if we should start the ceremony or make our speeches first. "Make your speeches," she said dryly and closed her eyes again. (Earlier, she'd mentioned that she'd been up all night performing a healing session with patients.)

The day before, Michael and I had prepared short speeches, and in the chaos I'd somehow managed to hang onto our notes. Michael ignored his notes and launched into a long-winded but heart-felt description of why we came to live in Cañar, how we love this place, feel a part of the community, and so on. I nudged him to cut it short, and he wrapped up with an emotional thanks to all.

My speech, following my notes, acknowledged all those involved in the land purchase and construction of the house—our lawyer, the maestros, workers, Lourdes. Short and sweet and totally unimaginative and unemotional. Lourdes followed with an elegant speech about her unique experience as an architect in Cañar and what it meant to collaborate with Cañari workmen on a traditional house in their home territory.

Finally, it was time for Mama Michi's magic. She came awake, stood up, and began by blowing mouthfuls of alcohol in the four directions, then knelt and blew into the ground to invoke *Pachamama*, Mother Earth. The courtyard filled with smoke from the charcoal brazier as the two godfathers appeared from my studio carrying the *chacana*. They stood at attention while Mama Michi sprinkled them and the cross with a leafy branch dipped in a liquid concoction. Someone handed out small candles. We lit them, one from another, and followed Mama Michi in a procession out the front door and clockwise around the house. As we walked, Ranti, Mama Michi's nephew, carried the bucket with the liquid and used the leafy branch to beat the house and sprinkle the guests. The two young musicians, whom I'd forgotten were still with us, brought up the rear with their tuneless tune.

Now came the scary part. Everyone gathered in front of the house, where a wooden ladder had been placed against the eaves to reach the roof. Days before, José María had removed two rows of the fragile terra cotta tiles to make a pathway to the roof ridge.

Michael climbed the ladder first, followed by Antonio carrying the cross; then came the carpenter, Javier, who would mix the mortar to attach the cross, and Ranti, still sprinkling the "holy water." Next came the godmothers, Narcisa and Luisa, with bottles of Zhumir and little plastic glasses to serve drinks. Finally, Lourdes climbed up to make a toast.

By previous arrangement, I stayed on the ground to take photos. (The truth was that I was feeling dizzy from all the days of tension and preparation.)

The *chacana* was placed, drinks were served among those on the roof, and the godmothers threw handfuls of cookies and hard candies into the crowd standing below. Children and adults scrambled to collect them.

The roof-walkers came down and the crowd drifted back inside just as Elsa arrived in a hired truck with her crew. She set up her large portable gas stove in the kitchen and uncovered a full-grown roasted pig in a metal roasting pan. It was now about three o'clock, and everyone must have been starving, judging by the buzz of increased traffic around the kitchen. I was baffled as to how we were to serve lunch to more than one hundred people and intensely uncomfortable when I realized several women were standing by, awaiting instructions from me.

The first challenge was to serve the honored guests, the godparents and Lourdes, already seated at the VIP table in my studio. I was saved when I saw that Elsa and her crew knew just how to heap the plates: big slabs of pork, potatoes, corn, hominy, and salad, with an entire guinea pig laid out over the top. Someone rushed the plates into the studio. Then Elsa served slightly smaller portions for everyone else, with a part of a guinea pig on top. Miraculously, in about thirty minutes everyone was served, right down to the last child.

For the last hour, the music group Los Chaskis had been setting up their sound equipment in the guest bedroom, and just as people finished eating, the eight musicians began to play. The music was very loud, given the small space and the powerful sound system, but it was real live Cañari music meant for dancing. We opened all the double doors into the courtyard, where in the future we hoped to have a fountain and garden, but today it was a perfect earthen dance floor.

Dancing in the patio

Within minutes, old men in ponchos who had been sitting quietly on the sidelines were up on their feet and asking young women to dance. Then it seemed that everyone was crowded into the small space, sliding and twirling and stepping to and fro. Lourdes's friend from Cuenca, Ricardo, danced like a man possessed, snapping his red suspenders. The godfathers, José María and Antonio, circulated, serving endless shots of Zhumir or cola. This was their job, to keep people drinking and dancing. (I was reminded of the time years ago when Michael and I became godparents to Paiwa, with little experience in these affairs. Someone had told us that as godparents our job was to "drink until you drop," and it became quickly obvious that it was the task of one old uncle to make sure we did. I was embarrassed when, in the late hours of the night, he caught me throwing my drinks on the ground.)

Los Chaskis played for two or three hours. The guests danced, drank, and danced some more. By this measure alone, the event was a success.

Then, near dusk, came my favorite moment. All the guests gathered at the back of the house for the lighting of the *globos*—hot-air balloons of multi-colored paper made to order for special occasions. Lourdes had arranged for ours, each with a different banner, saying "Viva Judy & Mike," "Viva Cañar," "Viva Lourdes," and "Viva Chaskis." José María or Antonio held a match to a paraffin-soaked pad attached to the bottom of each *globo* until it filled with hot air. Everyone cheered as the glowing orbs drifted up into the dusky sky and over the fields below. It was an incredibly beautiful sight.

The release of the *globos* marked the official end of the *wasipichana*. Many people left soon after, but a few dancers and drinkers stayed . . . and stayed and stayed. I was exhausted and so ready to be alone, but all I could do was keep dancing. I knew it was shamefully early to end this fiesta, which normally would last all night and into the next day. Michael, meanwhile, was soundly "resting" in our bedroom, having had one too many shots of Zhumir.

By midnight, everyone had left, with the exception of a neighbor, a sweet old widower, Tayta Francisco, who was lying in the courtyard and mumbling in Quichua. There was nothing for me to do but run up to the highway and hire a truck to take him home; luckily, I knew where he lived.

Then, at last, the fiesta was over and I went to bed, exhausted and relieved, but happy. The house was a mess, but with no real damage. All those who came had been served food and drink and had danced to live music. The placing of the *chacana*, Mama Michi's ceremony, and the release of the *globos* had provided the requisite spectacles. Most important, our *wasipichana* had, I think, gained Michael and me a respectable place as members of the Cañar community. Or at least outsiders who have come to stay.

Now we could settle down to the business of settling into our new home.

~

JOURNAL, APRIL 15

I'm reminded daily (if I ever didn't know) that a newly built house continues to be a construction site. I need shelves in my studio, which Michael says he will build. We need another bed to accommodate guests, which he also says he will build. Last week, the carpenter Javier made and installed towel racks and toilet paper holders, with noisy drilling and drifts of dust. Curtain rods ordered from a metal shop have been painted, drilled, and hung; kitchen racks and shelves constructed. My daily routine includes endless sweeping up of wood scraps and sawdust, dirt, and adobe dust, along with scraping dried varnish from the edges of our many windows. We still have almost no furniture except for beds and tables and benches, and our evenings in front of the fire are still spent in red plastic garden chairs with blankets for cushions.

But there is progress. The floors in my studio are finally done and I have a usable workspace. Michael's pots and pans and utensils are hung in the kitchen. We enjoy tepidly warm showers, but no telephone.

Michael announced yesterday that we're ready for the next phase: contouring the earth around the house, creating drainage and irrigating systems, planting trees and grass and flowers. All this we hope to do before we leave on July 1.

"Isn't it great that we'll have projects for the next ten years?" I asked. He groaned. While the thought might give him great pain, it certainly gives me great pleasure.

CHAPTER 22

The Mysteries of the New House
and a Mother's Visit

~

Mom and Michael at home

LIVING IN OUR NEW HOUSE AT LAST, we are now busy unraveling its mysteries. Why does the pump go on in the middle of the night when no one is using water? It wakens us out of a deep sleep a few times every night, as unfamiliar sounds do. There must be a leak somewhere, but Michael can't find it, so now we turn off the pump at night. Also, we didn't expect the damn thing to be so loud! We jump every time it switches on, and it scares the wits out of any visiting children. Michael says he'll have to construct a separate building on the west side of the house where he can install the pump, now situated in the laundry room off the courtyard, alongside the three-hundred-gallon water tank already there. That's a project for next year.

As someone who hasn't given much thought to the systems that run a modern household, I've found that watching this place being built, and now living here, has been a revelation. Our municipal water, for example, comes in a half-inch pipe that connects us to a water main on the road above. The supply is meager, available for only a few hours a day and frequently cut off without notice, so like everyone else in Cañar, we need a water storage tank. Most folks have a *chancho* perched on the roof, a tank that uses gravity feed to deliver water. The height of the *chancho* determines the pressure, and most people live with a trickle because their tanks sit only a few feet above the faucet or outlet. This was Michael's first choice for our water system, but Lourdes and I refused to have a bright blue plastic "pig" sitting on top of our beautiful new tile roof. So instead we have a hulking black tank sitting alongside the west side of the house.

When we have a hot shower, water from the outside tank is pumped through the instantaneous hot water heater in the laundry room, fed by a propane gas tank, and run through the pipes under the courtyard to our bathroom. At first, we had enough pressure, but only tepid water. "Too far to go," Michael speculated, eyeing the distance from tank to bathroom. He made some adjustments and we now have hot showers, but with very low pressure. Michael says we need a second water heater. Another project for next year.

When we flush or wash dishes, the "black" water goes into an eight-foot-deep, brick-walled, porous septic tank buried on one side of the house, with a drain field below. I watched this being hand dug by the workers during construction, but forgetting its location, I planted a tree on top of the tank last week. Michael says the tree will have to go, but not until next year.

"Gray" water from our showers, bathroom sinks, and laundry runs into a large plastic pipe that empties into the back garden to water my flowers and the cornfield below. Rainwater downspouts all around the house empty into the same pipe. Michael's systems are wildly innovative for Cañar, at least in rural areas, where plumbing in most houses, if it exists at all, is rudimentary. It's taken such a long time for poor families to get access to potable water, the idea of using the precious stuff for anything but drinking and cooking is anathema.

Electricity is available to all, but it's relatively expensive, given other utility costs. Most of Ecuador's power comes from hydro dams, and when water levels fall in dry seasons, electricity is rationed to the point of frequent brownouts and blackouts. Sometimes Ecuador is forced to import energy from Colombia. Michael has toyed with the idea of buying a generator, but that seems excessive given our modest needs. Instead, we keep a good supply of candles and flashlights.

Ecuador has natural gas in abundance and makes it affordable to just about everyone in portable propane tanks that, after an initial investment of about thirty dollars per tank, cost only two dollars to fill. One tank is good for a month's worth of cooking for a family of four, so everyone has at least a tabletop "cooker" and indigenous families also have wood-fire cooking areas. Gas tanks are delivered throughout the town and countryside daily by roaming trucks, privately owned, that make a piercingly annoying, whooping sound to let you know they're in the neighborhood. Michael or I lug our empty tanks to the gate and flag down the truck. A helper jumps down, grabs the old tanks, and sets down filled ones. For our small household, we have an excess of tanks: two in the laundry room for hot water and three tanks for cooking (Michael fears running out in the midst of preparing dinner).

We still don't have a telephone. More than a month ago, I put in a formal request to the state phone company, Pacifitel, for a new line, carefully following the company's demanding requirements, including copies of the deed to our land, copies of our national ID cards, and a document from the water company showing the location of our house. Once a week, I check in with a Pacifitel employee, Señora Vilma, at her upstairs office. In contrast to the neglected austerity of the "main office" downstairs, with its three old booths, two idle women behind a glass partition, and a guard at the door, Señora Vilma's office has a small carpet and a couple of comfortable chairs for those waiting. When it is my turn, I move to the chair in front of her desk, always to hear the same cheerful response: "Things are moving along, Señora Judy. Come back next week."

Then, last week, in my usual chair, I heard, "Bad news, Señora. Due to the change of management, we have temporarily suspended all new phone service. Come back in a few weeks."

~

We had only been in the house a couple of weeks before my mother, Adelene, came to visit. This had been planned months ago, back when we thought we'd be well settled in the house. She was worried we wouldn't be ready for a guest, but I persuaded her to come anyway. My mother is eighty-seven, and healthy, but as she always says, "You never know. . . ." With her age, a mild heart condition, and the high elevation of Cañar, we both know this will be her only visit to this part of the world.

Since my father's death fifteen years ago, my mother has taken up traveling the world with an enthusiasm she could never instill in my father, who in later

Mom in Sunday market

years preferred to stay close to his favorite fishing lakes in New Mexico and Colorado. Now, she regularly visits us in Portland, and, with one or the other of my two sisters, she has been to Mexico, Israel, Egypt, Spain, Italy, and France. With her own sisters, she has taken several cruises to the Caribbean and Alaska.

She arrived in Cañar the first week of May and loved every minute of her time with us. Her heart condition restricted her walking, as the hills are steep and we're more than ten thousand feet in altitude, but she was game and up for anything else, including trips to the market and dancing at a fiesta to inaugurate a friend's new hostel.

Although we've not lived close to one another since I left home at eighteen, I feel I intimately know my mother because she is such a great communicator. Before e-mail, she wrote letters once a week, just as her own mother had written her once a week until she went blind from glaucoma at ninety or so. Now she e-mails me almost every day, and I relish knowing the mundane details of her life: how she's feeling, the books she's reading, her plans for the day, news of friends. We talk every Saturday morning.

In Cañar, Mom's basic Spanish was barely recognizable, but she valiantly tried, charming everyone, from my friend Mercedes who admired her earrings and promptly received them as a gift to the truck driver who ferried us around. ("How's your mamacita?" I will be asked for years to come by that driver and others who met her.)

At the end of Mom's two weeks, we planned to go with her to Guayaquil for her flight home the same way we had come—by bus. It hadn't occurred to me to travel otherwise. Ecuadorian buses are generally comfortable, and the newer buses even have tiny bathrooms, albeit kept locked until you weave forward to find the driver's helper with his key, and then maneuver into and out of the baño while riding curvy mountain roads. Oh well. The ride up had been uneventful, if long at five hours, and bumpy, but we expected nothing less going down to Guayaquil.

So, one brilliant May morning, Michael, Mom, and I caught a "first-class" Ejecutivo San Luis bus. An hour or so into the trip, however, the bus rolled to a stop at the side of the road. We had paused briefly twice before on the outskirts of Cañar. "To add oil," the driver's helper had muttered when a passenger asked why. But on this third stop Michael, in the seat behind Mom and me, leaned forward to say, "I think something is seriously wrong." Michael, the worrier, often thinks things are "seriously wrong," so I didn't pay much attention. I could have reminded him of the time in Mexico when he insisted the train car was "wobbly" and that we move to another car, which we did briefly before the porter found us and insisted we return to our original seats.

Still, this time he was right. The driver killed the engine and he and his helper jumped off, leaving the door wide open. Reading that sign, and suspecting this would not be a brief stop, we thirty or so passengers slowly filed off, stepping over two sets of legs sticking out from beneath the bus.

From Cañar we had dropped about one thousand feet, making the temperature warmer, the landscape semi-tropical, and the views toward the coast breathtaking on this clear day. Fanning out along the verge of the highway, we stood and chatted or sat on grassy hummocks and speculated about what would happen next. One woman worried she would not make her afternoon flight in Guayaquil, making me thankful my mother's flight was not until midnight. I settled down on a grassy hummock to read. Michael paced beside the bus and tried to divine what the mechanical problem might be. Mom, always a good sport in situations like this, admired the view and then wondered if there might be a "real bathroom" nearby.

Finally, the driver's helper announced that this bus would go no farther. He said the cooling system had failed and they could not repair it on the side of the road. We would have to wait for another bus.

Then our real troubles began. Thirty minutes later, a bus came roaring in our direction. The driver's helper flagged it down, yelling at us passengers, "Get on! Get on! I'll pay your fare." Everyone rushed to climb on, crowding and urgent, as the driver of the new bus gunned the motor and *his* helper stood on the road alongside the door, yelling, "*¡Muévase, muévase!*" (Move it! Move it!) Interprovincial buses have to keep a strict timetable, and the driver and helper were impatient with this unexpected stop.

My mother was the only passenger who had luggage to go into the cargo hold underneath. Alarmed to see the line waiting to board, and thinking we'd have to fight for seats, I yelled to Michael to stay with Mom and join the line while I managed her two suitcases. The second driver's helper saw me, left his post herding passengers, and hurriedly threw open the hold. I heaved in the two bags and ran to climb on the bus.

Unfortunately, Mom and Michael were last in line, and once they climbed on board he saw immediately that there were no seats. Then, as they fought to get back off, Michael yelled at me, "No seats, don't get on!" while I, in turn, shouted at the helper to get my mother's suitcases out of the cargo hold. Meanwhile, the helper from our first broken-down bus, seeing Michael was getting off, yelled at him that he had already paid our passage. "Get on and stand," he commanded, "others will be getting off soon." I shouted back that my mother is eighty-seven and could not stand on a moving bus, even for a short while.

Meanwhile, the driver gunned the motor and bellowed, "*¡Vámanos!*" Michael and Mom finally got off, and the bus began to inch forward while I was still screaming at the second helper to get the bags from the hold. He finally threw open the hatch, flung the suitcases into the middle of the road, and ran to jump on the moving bus. Checking for traffic, I retrieved the bags and dragged them to the side of the road. There, the first driver's helper was still yelling at Michael, gesturing at the exhaust cloud of the departing bus, "Why didn't you stay on? I've paid your fares. Now you'll have to pay again!"

Then I saw Mom, turning in circles by the roadside, looking confused. "Oh, there you are!" she said, finally seeing me. "And my bags, too!" She beamed. My mother is great in difficult situations if she thinks others are looking out for her welfare.

Quiet descended on the peaceful mountainside as we settled down to wait. I took out my book again and found my hummock. My mother sat down nearby to admire the view, while Michael stewed about the lack of maintenance of motor vehicles in Ecuador. Within fifteen minutes another bus appeared in the distance. The driver saw us, slowed, and stopped. His helper jumped off and calmly put Mom's bags underneath, while we sedately climbed aboard a brand new, air-conditioned bus with only a few passengers. We sunk into spacious seats with more legroom than a first-class flight, and settled in to watch the Jean-Claude van Damme movie playing loudly on the big screen mounted behind the driver.

~

JOURNAL, MAY 17

We see Mom off in Guayaquil and come back to Cañar the next day on a hot, un-air-conditioned, rattletrap bus, and I am in a very bad mood. It must have been those two weeks of being a "good girl"—attending to Mom's needs while at the same time giving Michael some attention, plus getting the house settled—that has taken its emotional toll. Every little thing that Michael does or says annoys me. By the time we get back to Cañar, midday, I'm totally pissed and get off the bus and march home without speaking. We finally have it out at drink/sunset time, airing our respective complaints. I can't remember mine, a bunch of things building up during the week, I suppose. Nor do I remember Michael's, but I explain to him how I'm feeling, and he explains to me how he's feeling. The air is cleared, the sunset is beautiful, Michael makes dinner, and our little world settles back into its usual orbit.

At least for a while. Then it suddenly occurs to me that we have only six weeks left in our new house before we leave for Portland. Too soon!

CHAPTER 23

Mama Michi, *Curandera*

~

Mama Michi and her mesa ritual *(ritual table)*

"THESE PATIENTS WILL BE THE DEATH of me," Mama Michi says wearily one day when I stop in the rutted road outside her house to chat. Since her husband died several years ago, Mercedes Chuma has transformed herself from the tired, oppressed wife of an alcoholic husband and mother of six into Mama Michi, a locally famous *curandera*, or native healer. As we speak, she gestures to the house behind her, where I can see patients sitting on a wooden bench by the open door and others lying on mats in the room beyond, all waiting for attention.

"They come day and night," she shakes her head, but I can hear pride in her voice and satisfaction in her new status. This is a world where folks believe good health depends on a regular *limpieza*, a cleansing or exorcising of the ill effects of *mal aire* (bad air, or negative energy), an *arco iris* (rainbow, negative aura), a *susto* (mild fright), an *espanto* (bad fright), an enemy's curse, or the restless spirit of a recently dead relative. In just a few years, Mama Michi has become well respected for the *limpiezas* that her patients believe restore balance and serenity to their lives.

"May I come and film you at work sometime?" I ask as she turns to go back to her patients. Mama Michi is one of my oldest friends in Cañar, and I figured she would say if it is inappropriate for me to be present during a healing session. She answers yes. "I have a *consultor io* in town on Friday. Why don't you come then?"

Mama Michi is probably in her fifties, but you'd have a hard time guessing her age. Parts of her look older, like her worn face with missing teeth, while other parts seem younger, like her legs, which are surprisingly girlish given a lifetime of walking steep mountains with a heavy load on her back—a baby, a sack of newly harvested potatoes, a load of alfalfa for her guinea pigs. Like most Cañari women, she is roundish and short, well under five feet, with a spherical face and brown, Asian eyes. I've often thought Mama Michi would look right at home in an Inuit village in northern Canada or on the steppes of Mongolia. Her thick black hair hangs to below her waist, the top half bound into a braid with a colored wool strip, the last twelve inches or so swinging loose. It is beautiful hair, without a trace of gray, another part of her that seems young.

Early Friday morning, I walk up the hill into town to the rambling, old colonial-style hospital donated to the indigenous community by the Catholic Church about twenty years ago. There, down a dark corridor, I find Mama Michi's native health clinic, occupying two dimly lit rooms on either side of a hallway. As I step into the room on the left, I see several women already waiting along two walls on a collection of old chairs and wooden benches. Cloth-wrapped bundles and tied-up handfuls of plants and flowers sit on the floor alongside them. One woman perches on the edge of her chair twisting wool onto a drop spindle. Several have babies on their backs, held with shawls tied across their shoulders. A young girl about six stands leaning against her mother, watching me with big serious eyes.

Mama Michi is not here yet. I greet Beatriz, her assistant, who sits facing the room behind a small beat-up metal desk. She uses a stubby pencil and school notebook to keep a list of patients as they come in. Everyone watches with grave interest as I set up my tripod and video camera, but no one says a word. Cañaris are generally silent and watchful with strangers, neither friendly nor unfriendly. I try to imagine what these women are thinking as they peer at me from under their round white hats. Does my presence give Mama Michi even more importance in their eyes? Or are they dismayed to think a stranger will be filming and photographing a transaction between them and their *curandera*— one for which they are paying good money?

I sit down on one of the benches alongside the patients to wait and take a good look around. The room is about eighteen by eighteen feet. Two windows face a glassed-in gallery that runs around two sides of the building and lets in subdued light. This must have been a beautiful place once, a rambling hospital run by nuns and called San Clemente, a labyrinthine series of buildings with arches, interior patios, fountains, and sun porches. But now the place is terribly run down, a white elephant that Cañari organizations have a hard time maintaining and covering services, such as lights and water. Today there are neither . . . .

Behind Beatriz, a glass-fronted cabinet in one corner is filled with jars and tins and packaged remedies for everything from prostate trouble to unrequited love. On the wall poster board, I see photos I took several years ago of a birth in a remote village, attended by Mama Michi and her midwife sister, Mariana.

Shortly after nine o'clock, Mama Michi makes her entrance, swinging a plastic bucket of water. She barely acknowledges the waiting patients as she briskly crosses the room and sets the bucket on the floor under a table. She wears two bright wool embroidered skirts, one on top of the other, and a market sweater over an embroidered blouse. A swath of red beaded necklaces, dangling filigreed earrings, and a white round hat complete her colorful ensemble. Mama Michi, like all Cañaris, wears this hat from the moment she gets up in the morning until she goes to bed at night. It keeps her head warm and dry in this chilly, rainy climate and distinguishes her as a Cañari, an indigenous from this particular part of Ecuador.

Mama Michi exchanges a few words with Beatriz and then turns to nod at her first patient. An elderly Cañari woman steps forward and hands Mama Michi a fresh egg and a handful of bushy plants and flowers. She launches into a litany of complaints: she has pain in her arms, she is tired, and all her bones ache when she works in the fields. She speaks with a mix of Quichua and Spanish, but I can understand because her gestures say it all.

"Then don't work," Mama Michi retorts with her distinctive cackle. She puts the fresh egg and plants on her table and picks up the woman's arm and critically examines the fingers, hand, and wrist, turning her arm this way and that.

"Who else can work but me?" the old woman rejoins in a joking tone. "There's no one, no husband." Both know that Cañari men and women try to work until the day they die, and the day they can't work usually means death is not far off.

All this takes place only a few feet from the roomful of others waiting, who watch attentively and listen and laugh at the exchanges, as though it is a theatrical performance. And I, behind the camera, think it is a bit like reality TV.

Mama Michi gestures for the old woman to step into a flimsy cubicle in one corner of the room and tells her to remove her clothes. As patient number one disappears, Mama Michi turns and nods at a young woman who had been standing against the wall: patient number two. Like any busy clinician, Mama Michi doesn't waste a moment. Patient number two is not indigenous, as is everyone else in the room, but a mestiza from the town, dressed in slacks and a sweater with a shawl wrapped around her shoulders.

The young woman hands a color snapshot to Mama Michi, who carefully studies it while the woman talks softly, barely above a whisper. I can't hear what she says, but I can see the photo—a young man leaning against the cab of a big truck—and I guess the gist of the story. The young man, her brother or husband, is an undocumented immigrant in the United States, and something has gone wrong. He might be ill, or perhaps he has lost his job, or he's had a run of bad luck. This woman, his sister or his wife, has brought the photo to Mama Michi to diagnose and treat the problem, via long distance.

Mama Michi takes an unlit candle from the table and rubs it up and down over the photo several times, looking hard at the image as she mutters a few words, like a prayer, or invocation. Holding the candle on top of the photo with one hand, she takes a mouthful of liquid from a cologne bottle on the table and blows it over both the candle and the photograph, carefully covering it top to bottom, bottom to top, right to left, left to right. She lights the candle, and with a few drips of hot wax sets it upright on the tabletop and props the photo directly behind it. Mama Michi watches the flames intently for a few seconds.

This wooden table is Mama Michi's *mesa ritual*, her center of operations, her diagnostic hub, you could say. A large ceramic Madonna with a blue cape reigns over a mess of candle stubs, large plastic Coke bottles filled with liquids, smaller bottles of cologne, bunches of dried herbs, a little Buddha about six inches tall, a small saint or two, several beaded necklaces, and a packet of cigarettes.

"Hmmmm, he's very nervous," Mama Michi says, still watching the flickering candle, ". . . and desperate." She glances at the young woman. "You should probably come to my house on Friday night so I can do a good *limpieza*."

Every other Friday, people come from near and far to be treated by Mama Michi. Her medicine is stronger at night, she has said, and she has a special room in her house for cleansings and more serious healings. Many patients spend the night on mats on her floor, believing that a recently treated person is more vulnerable to *mal aire* and other malevolent forces that are abroad at night.

"But let's wait and see what else the flames reveal," Mama Michi says as she motions the young woman back to her place against the wall.

Mama Michi sticks her head into the cubicle to see if the old woman is ready for her treatment. Without a door and with only three-quarter walls, the little examination room is far from private. From my vantage point, standing against the far wall with my camera, I can see the old woman is stripped down to her big white underpants, with her arms crossed over her chest. Mama Michi picks up a fresh egg from the table in one hand and with the other raises a plastic jug to her lips. With a deep mouthful, she steps into the cubicle, holds the egg to the old woman's forehead, and sprays her from the top of her head down her torso. The astringent smell of alcohol mixed with cologne and herbs hits my nostrils. The woman blinks with the sudden shock, but stands obediently as Mama Michi quickly rubs the egg over her head, then down her chest and along her arms. "Turn around," the healer says brusquely as she continues rubbing the egg on the woman's back and down her legs. "Now blow!" she holds the egg in front of the old woman's face.

Mama Michi steps out of the cubicle and deftly breaks the egg into a glass of clean water she has dipped out of the bucket. The egg, I've learned over many visits to Mama Michi's clinic, is a diagnostic tool she uses in almost every case. Rubbing it over the patient picks up indicators, or symptoms, of the problem, and once she breaks the egg into the glass of water and it settles, Mama Michi

Mama Michi making a diagnosis with a cuy (guinea pig)

can read the signs. In more serious cases, I've seen her do the same procedure with a live guinea pig, then killing and eviscerating the animal to diagnose the malady.

Mama Michi hardly pauses. She picks up the handful of plants and flowers the old woman had earlier handed her, takes another mouthful of liquid, steps into the cubicle, and, holding the plants in front of the woman's face, blows the liquid through the plants and onto the woman. Then Mama Michi divides the plants, and with a bunch in each hand, she lightly beats the old woman from top to bottom, front and back, chanting sounds like *quich quich*, maybe the Quichua word for "out" or maybe it sounds like it should mean, "get out, go away!"

Finished with the *limpieza*, Mama Michi holds the plants in front of the woman's face and say brusquely: "Now blow! Okay, get dressed." Mama Michi steps out of the cubicle and rapidly crosses the room with the bunch of plants. I follow her with my camera down the short hall, where she throws the plants against an exterior wall. "¡*Contaminado!*" Mama Michi says emphatically as she turns around and passes me on the way back. She means these plants are contaminated with the old woman's complaints, and they must be thrown away so they won't bring harm to anyone else.

Mama Michi walks back into the clinic room and looks around with a mixture of satisfaction and apprehension. The women and children on the benches have watched everything with curious eyes, happily entertained while waiting their turns. Two cases were underway, seven or eight patients are still waiting, and others will come. It is only ten in the morning and Mama Michi has a long day ahead.

"Who's next?"

A young woman approaches leading a small boy by the hand. She has a sleeping baby on her back. "My *gallina* crowed like a rooster three times this morning," she says softly to Mama Michi, "and she wasn't ready to lay an egg. Also, this same hen has been eating her eggs and the eggs of other hens."

"Your house has bad luck," Mama Michi says flatly. "If she crows like that again, you must cut her throat and bury her far from the house. Don't leave a single trace, not a drop of blood." The woman nods and asks Mama Michi if she will give her little boy a cleansing, just in case he has been infected by a *susto*, a fright. Mama Michi nods, but just then the older woman steps out of the cubicle, fully dressed and ready to know what the egg in the glass has revealed about her condition. At the same time, the young woman who brought the photograph steps forward and gestures toward the candle. She is eager to know what the flames reveal about her loved one, the man leaning against the truck.

Mama Michi stands in the middle of the room, surrounded by patients eager to hear her professional divinations and ready to pay for them. She looks around, laughs her inimitable cackle, and says something in Quichua that I don't understand.

~

JOURNAL, JUNE 15

A cold and cloudy day. We decide to go to Elsa's for a comfort lunch of pork *asado* and *llapingachos* (small potato pancakes). She's very busy, so while we wait, I look through a photo album of her daughter Angela's *quinceñera*, fifteenth birthday party, two weeks ago. There she is in her white dress, like a bride, and I count ten "bridesmaids" in blue satin. This party must have cost Elsa at least a thousand dollars, representing how many days of cooking and selling her roasted pigs? The *quinceñera* is akin to a coming-out party, but much more significant for Latin Americans. Traditionally, it marks the transition from girlhood to womanhood and announces that the young woman is now on the marriage market (well, maybe not that different from the purpose of the "coming out" for a debutante?).

In Cañar, however, I'm sure it's simply an elaborate social event that every mestizo teenage girl looks forward to being the star of, with a beautiful dress and attendants, but with no intention of moving toward marriage. Certainly in the photos Elsa's daughter still looks like a girl playing dress-up.

CHAPTER 24

Coming Home to Cañar

~

Narcisa and José María with alfalfa for their animals

"*¡Las aguas han llegado!*" the taxi driver pronounces cheerfully as we leave the Guayaquil airport. "The rains began on New Year's Day and haven't stopped."

It is January 2008, the beginning of our first full six months living in our Cañar house. We land in Guayaquil late at night after a long day of traveling that took us from Portland to Houston to Ecuador. Though not so long as that of the young man next to me on the plane: he had left London the same morning on his way to visit his girlfriend, who is working with street kids in Guayaquil. I like him and invite him and his girlfriend to come visit us in Cañar.

After getting through *migración* and customs, it is past one o'clock in the morning, and I am on that familiar edge of exhaustion/exhilaration—happy we are here, glad we've cleared the airport hurdles, but knowing we can't relax until we've made it safely inside the locked gates of Hostal Tangara. We decide to rest another day and night in Guayaquil before going on to Cañar. This is the first time we've landed in this city together, and from here we have several travel options. We can fly to Cuenca—a quick thirty-minute trip but one involving two airports, followed by a bus ride to Cañar, and a hired truck to our house. Or we can take a bus directly from Guayaquil to Cañar—a five-hour trip that can go well, or be a living hell. Too, since Michael strained his back loading our luggage into the car in Portland, he is in no mood to wrestle bags through the chaos of the Guayaquil bus station while fending off an army of boys demanding to help us. So we decide on a third option: we'll hire a car and driver to take us directly from Hostal Tangara to our front gate in Cañar, a great convenience but, at a hundred dollars, an expensive alternative to the bus, which costs about five dollars.

The next morning, knowing we have an extra day, I stay in bed at the hostel reading *The General in His Labyrinth* by Gabriel García Márquez. The general of the title is Simón Bolívar, the great liberator of South America, and the book is part of my effort to get a better grasp of the regional history. I've also brought a big fat biography of Bolívar to read while I'm in Ecuador, one of a stack of books I've been collecting the past six months for Cañar-time reading.

For lunch, we saunter over to our favorite outdoor crab restaurant. It's always a shock to be in the humidity-saturated air of this tropical coast after leaving near-freezing Portland twenty-four hours before. My hair, fairly straight at home, instantly curls and frizzes. At least the rainy season in Guayaquil means the temperature is nearly comfortable—in the high eighties instead of the high nineties, where it stays most of the year. (According to one history book, the oppressive, fever-inducing climate of this tropical outpost claimed the life of every American consul through the nineteenth century.)

The next day, as we cruise up the twisted and potholed road into the Andes in a new, air-conditioned SUV, I feel a little guilty remembering last May, when I subjected my eighty-seven-year-old mother to the same trip in a jolting, five-hour ride on a local bus. Both ways! "But remember what a good story you got out of it," Michael reminds me.

Today, it takes only three-and-a-half quiet, comfortable hours before the driver pulls up at our gate in Cañar. He has brought his girlfriend along, but they have hardly spoken the entire time. I suspect they are taking a paid mini-vacation today; I hope they enjoy themselves and at least talk on the way back. "Hiring a car like this is a habit we might just get used to," I say to Michael as we climb out.

The house looks exactly as we left it six months ago. Closed wooden shutters on the doors and windows give the impression of a big dun-colored box with a red roof. *Triste*, our Cañar friends would say, sad, because it's a house unoccupied and without life. That will soon change.

I'm shocked, however, to see the front yard completely overgrown with tall peas in bloom, mixed in with a crop of alfalfa. The side yard is also covered with peas and alfalfa.

"Where are my new little trees?" I exclaim as Michael pays the driver. I scan the yard. "What happened to my flowers, the bulbs, the native shrubs I planted before we left last July?" But he doesn't answer, his attention occupied with taking in the house.

We drag our bags down the stone walkway to the entrance. While I wait for Michael to find his keys, I see something written in small, penciled letters on the shutter nearest the door. I lean in to read: "*¿Para que se van?*" Why did they leave? It looks like a child's hand. I imagine it was written by one of our godchildren who forgot we were leaving, or maybe a neighbor child coming to visit and disappointed to find us gone and the house closed up tight.

We step into the courtyard, warm with the midday sun pouring through the glass roof, drop our bags, and eagerly examine the plants we'd put in six months ago. Michael's side, with succulents, cacti and aloe, looks to be thriving and right at home in the sunny dry space. Pleased, he gives me his mild "Told you so!" look. He has always argued that the covered courtyard, with intense solar heat and no rain, is only suitable for desert-loving plants. His precious Meyer lemon tree is about the same size as when we left, maybe twelve inches tall, with a few tiny, green fruits the size of walnuts. Michael gets down on his knees to count them: four.

My side, planted with fuchsias and dahlias and ferns, shows mixed results. One yellow-blooming thing is about four feet tall and propped up with a bamboo pole. It will have to go. Other flowers have dried up and died in these hothouse conditions. The fuchsias obviously love it here; they have grown into towering bushes that will also have to go. The biggest surprise is the four tall tomato plants; one even has unripe fruits. José María, who cares for the house and garden while we're gone, must have planted them, Michael says. "A farmer never misses an opportunity to plant when he sees an open space."

Outside the kitchen door, we find a beautiful vegetable garden that José María and his wife Narcisa have planted—purple cabbage, lettuce, onions, chard, cilantro, and broccoli—all shared today with a clutch of five or six chickens, visiting from one of the neighbors. The cabbages are huge, the chard and cilantro going to seed.

"Didn't I have some flowers around here?" I ask Michael, but he is already back inside and busy with other things.

Our first job is to open the house. Michael fetches a ladder from under the porch and takes down the removable shutters on the big windows facing the mountains while I throw open the smaller shutters around the outside walls and hook them back. We designed this house to be left unoccupied for six months, and it has passed its first test beautifully. I see no damage or evidence of vandalism, other than the sweet little scribble beside the front door. We know we've been lucky this year, leaving the house empty, and we know it will be a continuing risk. But it's one we're willing to take.

Inside, nothing is changed except for cobwebs in every corner and dust on every surface where the high sierra winds blow down the fireplace chimney and through the gaps around the skylights. We have almost no furniture, so cleaning will be an easy matter.

At lunchtime, we stop our work for a sandwich and beer at the little table in the courtyard and talk about our next big project: the addition on the side of the house that will contain the water tank and pump and serve as a toolshed. We are already calling it the "West Wing."

"Here's what I'm really looking forward to," Michael says as he pulls a pen out of his pocket and begins to draw on a paper napkin: a fountain for the center of the courtyard. It's an idea he's had from the beginning, so the wiring and piping are already in place underground. We discuss possibilities: the classic Spanish colonial three-tiered affair or a more modern stone monolith such as the one Michael made for our garden in Portland. He says he's excited to have a more artistic, non-stressful project to work on now that the house is done.

After lunch, I step outside to take a good look around. From our porch facing the mountains, I see our neighbors below us plowing the field with a *yunta*, a team of bulls and a wooden plow. I also see (and hear) an earth-moving machine at work. A *ciudadela*, or housing project, called Inti Raymi, is taking shape beyond the field, with new roads, a water tank, and sewage ditches. We knew when we bought this lot two years ago that the area was slated for *urbanización*, eventually to be part of the municipality of Cañar. Still, it's sad to see rows of eucalyptus that have been part of our view these past two years come down, and fields that have always been corn, beans, barley, wheat, and potatoes disappear into house lots.

Later, as the sun goes down and the chill sets in, Michael builds a fire. He reckons that the wood scraps from the house construction will last another year before we'll need to buy firewood. Once that moment comes, we'll no doubt get a lesson in why fireplaces are uncommon here, and why wood is used only for cooking. Firewood is expensive. But for us, pampered gringos, one of the great pleasures of life in Cañar is settling down at five thirty or so in front of a fire with a glass of wine (me) and a beer (Michael).

We stay by the fire until bedtime at nine thirty, eating dinner and listening to a couple of chapters of *The Turn of the Screw*, by Henry James, an audiobook I downloaded in Portland. I'm not generally a fan of ghost stories or mysteries, but I love Henry James, and I thought it might be fun to listen to something scary in Cañar. I go to bed knowing I'll have insomnia as I always do the first couple of nights at this high altitude.

Next day, after a night of snatches of sleep, life quickly falls into its Cañar rhythm. Awake at six o'clock with first light, Michael is in the kitchen singing and making coffee, while I stay in bed and wait for his call that my *café latte* is ready. I love the early morning sounds here, so different from our urban Portland soundscape. First, of course, there's the crowing of a rooster, or several, followed by the busy twittering of birds the minute the sun hits the peas and nasturtiums. I watch out the bedroom window as small brilliant yellow-and-black birds, called "*chugos*," and iridescent green, long-tailed hummingbirds flit about in the tall broom hedge. (Note to self: buy a bird book next year.)

About seven thirty, Michael sees José María walking by the kitchen window. He goes out to greet him, invites him in for coffee, and I join them at the dining room table.

We tell our *compadre* how much we appreciate his work taking care of the yard, the courtyard, and the house, for which we pay him seventy-five dollars a month. Michael presents him with a gift of a Swiss Army knife, joking, "Now I won't be bothered with you asking to borrow mine." José María tells us he is finishing expanding his adobe house, that it will be ready for the roof in three weeks. He is rushing to finish a room for a graduate student coming from Oregon State University who will live with the family while he does his research.

Later in the morning, I hear the "slap slap" of wet clothes as our thirteen-year-old neighbor on the west side, Teresa, works in a tub on a wobbly wooden table in the patio, doing the family wash. She seems to be the woman of the house now, caring for her younger brother, Ruben, ten, and a little sister, Isabel, about four. When I ask about an older brother, who was maybe twelve last year, Teresa says simply, "He's away working." This probably means he's left school after sixth grade. I ask about her mother, Magdalena, and Teresa, expertly twisting water out of a shirt and hanging it on the barbed wire fence between us, says crisply, "In the market."

All day, a group of eight women have been harvesting peas in the field to the east of us and then in our own field behind the house. I listen to the murmur of

Women and cows gleaning the back field

their conversations in Quichua and Spanish, punctuated by high-pitched laughing. When they stop for a communal lunch, sitting in the middle of the pea field, I yell over the fence to ask if I may take a photo. One of them yells back, "¡*Vecina, venga!*" Neighbor, come! I climb over the fence and take a few shots before one of the women hands me a platter of cooked potatoes and fresh peas. I recognize several of our neighbors, including the troublesome Rosa, who smiles at me. I guess I have been officially welcomed back.

Early the next morning, Michael comes into the bedroom to tell me that two cows have spent the night in our field. "I wonder if they belong to Mama Antuka?" I say. I go to the window and see two piebald cows, staked with long ropes, munching away on the pea plants. The cows glean, chew, and ruminate all that day, all night, and they will still be there three days later. Every so often, I will look out to see white hats bobbing in the field as two Cañari women pull up the stakes and move the cows to new grazing ground.

We don't know who these women are—they never speak to us—or even who owns the cows. We speculate, however, that this is part of *la puebla*, the folk custom that Mama Antuka explained to us last year, that allowed her as a *partidario* (sharecropper) to plant peas after she'd harvested the corn. Does *la puebla* allow cows to glean once the peas are harvested? And since we've seen nothing of Mama Antuka, has she passed on her right to these two women?

We can only admire these agricultural practices that use every bit of a crop, like the cows gleaning the peas, but wonder what other customs might intervene before we can claim the field as our own, What does Mama Antuka have up her sleeve for us?

~

JOURNAL, JANUARY 10

Mercedes, one of the first scholarship recipients in our Cañari Women's Education Foundation, comes by early on Sunday to tell me the great drama of her graduation from law school and the birth of her son, two life-changing events that not only happened on the same day, but also within hours.

Her graduation—after seven hard years at the University of Cuenca—was set for November 29 and the baby's due date was December 15, so Mercedes thought she was safe. With tremendous effort, she had completed her last courses, finished the paperwork for graduation, and paid for her gown, mortarboard, and diploma. She had also decided, a few months earlier, to become a mother on her own, extremely unusual for a Cañari woman. She only told me the father was a friend and would be uninvolved in raising the child.

On the morning of November 29, as Mercedes's family was readying a big fiesta to celebrate her graduation, she woke with mild labor pains. She didn't want to tell her mother, who was in the kitchen peeling a mountain of potatoes, but she did tell her sister, Rosa, once her pains were about an hour apart. Her sister called their brother, Nicolás, and they decided to take Mercedes to the hospital in Azogues, an hour away to the south, where she had earlier arranged to give birth.

Once there, the obstetrician examined her and said she probably had seven or eight hours before the baby would come. She saw no reason why Mercedes couldn't go on to Cuenca (forty-five minutes by bus), get her law degree, then come back to give birth.

This was nine or ten o'clock in the morning. As the four thirty graduation ceremony approached, Mercedes's pains were thirty minutes apart and she didn't think she could carry it off. But she had to inform her family, already waiting in the auditorium.

"As I went through the door, I met the dean of the law school, whom I know well," she said. "I told him I thought I might make it if I could be allowed to graduate ahead of all the others. He said, 'Talk to the woman arranging the lineup.'

"There were about eighty law students graduating, along with thirty social workers, but I was put at the head of the line to march onto the stage and take a chair while the others filed in. Another hard pain came and I hung onto the arms of the chair so tightly that one of the photographers below the stage asked if I was O.K."

Skipping the long and multiple introductions common in these ceremonies (I've attended a few), the master of ceremonies announced that Mercedes Guamán would receive her law degree before everyone else. Mercedes said she stood up, faced the eight dignitaries seated behind a table while the *acto de grado* was read, accepted her diploma, then rushed off the stage, threw off her gown and mortarboard, and ran out the door where her sister and brother were waiting with a taxi.

"I got to the hospital about six o'clock and my son was born at seven thirty."

As Mercedes describes this to me, the little guy in question slept wrapped in a shawl on her back so I don't get to meet him. He doesn't have a name yet; Mercedes says his character has not yet suggested what he wants to be called. But when he's older he will surely be proud to know that this extraordinary woman became his mother *and* the first Cañari woman lawyer on the same day.

CHAPTER 25

Neighbors and Fences

~

José María, Antonio, and Michael measuring for the back fence

THERE IS NOTHING LIKE BUILDING fences to get to know your neighbors.

Early one morning last week, as I sat in bed with my coffee and laptop, I heard a loud muffled voice that sounded like it was coming through bad speakers. It's a common way of advertising events here—someone drives through the neighborhood, blaring speakers atop the cab of their truck, announcing some event or other. Because I can never understand a word, I always ignore it. This morning, however, the noise persisted, then grew stronger, and then became familiar. I recognized that it was my husband's urgent voice I was hearing. I got up and looked out the bedroom window to see Michael standing at the garden fence, talking excitedly with our neighbor, Rosa. His arms were swinging up and down in a gesture that I recognized as extreme agitation.

On her side of the fence, Rosa stood impassively—or maybe defiantly; I couldn't quite read her expression—hands primly folded. I quickly dressed and went out into the yard to mediate, or witness, or just to see what was happening.

"¡*Muy adentro!*" Rosa said as I came up, gesturing brusquely along the fence line through the field below. Meaning literally, "very inside," Rosa was saying that our fence line had crossed onto her property.

"But *you* were *here* when the city engineer measured the property lines!" Michael said, his voice rising, sweeping his arm down the line of posts. "*You* helped him. *You* showed him the markers. It's in the *escritura*," the deed.

"He too knows how to steal," Rosa shook her head, eyebrows lowered, face dark. "And I'd like a copy of that *escritura*. I've never seen it!"

Michael had just discovered that the fence posts he'd set in concrete along one side of our back field, before we left last June, have been crudely broken off and moved into our property by about four feet. He hadn't noticed it until this morning when, with the peas harvested and the cows finally gone, he was able to walk the field for the first time. I looked down into field to see the posts standing at odd angles, clearly stuck directly in the ground.

When Michael put in the posts last year, he'd intended to string barbed wire to make a proper fence. But Rosa and Mama Antuka had begged him to hold off so they could more easily bring in a *yunta*—yoked bulls—to plow the land before planting the peas. Wanting to be a good neighbor (and not wanting bulls charging through our garden), Michael had agreed.

"I did you and Mama Antuka a favor by not stringing barbed wire, and in return you've moved my posts," Michael was now yelling, face red, as he leaned over the fence toward Rosa.

"I wasn't here!" she claimed, backing up. "I was working somewhere else. I don't know what Mama Antuka did . . . ," her voice trailed off in a waver. As I watched Rosa's expression, uncertain and a little scared, I figured she was lying.

"¡*Mira!* Just look how your property line goes—it's too far into mine," she came back with renewed strength. Michael, his face still red, stalked off abruptly to talk to another neighbor, Don Pepe, who had appeared in his cornfield below.

Rosa and I were left facing one another across the fence.

"*Michael está muy alterado*" (changed, disturbed), she said to me, eyes wide.

"Sure," I said, "because he paid to have someone put in the posts, and now they are broken and he'll have to pay to do it again."

"*Muy alterado,*" she repeated, shaking her head as though puzzled that anyone could be upset by having their fence line moved, reducing the size of their land by several hundred square feet.

Trying to hit a sympathetic note, I said, "I'll get you a copy of the *escritura* tomorrow. I know it's hard, selling your land." Rosa saw an opening for her usual lament: "All this was mine," she gestured. "Two *hectarias*! Imagine! What a bad idea to sell . . . first to that impossible man down there (she pointed at Don Pepe, still talking with Michael) and then where all these houses sit. It was *all* mine and now it's gone!"

I've heard this many times before, so when the moment was right I nodded and made motions to go back into the house. Rosa saw this and brought out one of her famous non sequiturs: "But we have our families and our health, thanks to God, and that's the important thing, no?"

Adding up all the problems we've had with Rosa over the past two years, Michael and I have concluded that she really might be a bit psychologically unbalanced. Neighbors around us, all who've bought land from Rosa, have reinforced this theory. "¡*Está loca*!" is the quick and common judgment. She's crazy. One older woman from town who bought a small lot between Rosa and us, planning to build a house, sold it after a year of dealing with Rosa. "¡*Imposible*!" she said when I tracked her down, thinking we might buy the lot. Some opinions are even stronger. "*Es un demonio*," Don Pepe was saying to Michael as they stood talking in the field below.

Later, José María's wife, Narcisa, told Michael that she had witnessed Rosa and a helper breaking off the posts and resetting them one day while she—Narcisa—was working in our garden. But in true reticent Cañari manner, Narcisa and José María had kept silent rather than cause trouble by confronting Rosa or upset us by calling us in Portland with this news.

The next day, Michael was out early with his long tape measure, a can of black paint, and three hired helpers. They measured the original fence line and Michael brushed a long black stripe, a clear demarcation, on the brick wall that runs behind our contiguous properties. (Our field is a lopsided triangle, but we share a portion of the east and north sides with Rosa and Juan.) Then Michael and the helpers reset the posts, poured new concrete, and strung barbed wire. Rosa did not appear all day.

The following day, the workers spent the day preparing to build a fence on the western edge of our property. In the late afternoon, I was standing at the living room windows when I saw Magdalena, our fierce but generally friendly neighbor who lives on the other side of us. She was standing in her back garden and staring down at the cement posts lying on the ground beside the holes the men had dug. When I stepped out onto the porch to greet her, Magdalena pointed to the posts and yelled back, "¡*Muy adentro*!"

Michael went out with his tape measure. Magdalena took him to the road in front of her property, where she pointed out the big rock that she claims marks her property line. This rock has always been suspect as an accurate marker, but

Magdalena with fence posts

Michael long ago accepted it. He ran his tape over the ground to a retaining wall we built last year, then on the downhill side of her lot to her lower boundary. A few minutes later, I heard Michael say to Magdalena in a hearty voice, "I grant you the gift of twenty centimeters!" followed by her high-pitched laugh. Magdalena had apparently accepted that the fence line was in her favor by twenty centimeters.

The third day, as the workers laid out the fence line at the north end of the field, a neighbor called Fernando, whom we've never met, appeared and questioned Michael about the northeast corner marker. When they made careful measurements together, it turned out that Fernando's rock wall bulges into our property by almost a meter. Given that revelation, an agreement was quickly reached: Fernando would accept Michael's northeast corner marker if his wall could stay.

And so we are fenced in, or nearly so, and I'm sorry for that. I loved it when our property was open on all sides and we had unobstructed views. The concrete posts and barbed wire are ugly, but I'll plant climbing roses and vines to cover them and put in more native plants to make hedges. Then at least we'll be hemmed in by green.

The fourth day, Michael came in to say that next year we must build a tall fence and gate on the front of our property. "All the workers say this is necessary for our security," he said.

～

We always knew it would be a risk leaving the house unoccupied for six months, so in the design and construction we made every effort to make it secure. All the windows and doors have wooden shutters that close and padlock, leaving the house looking like a closed box with a roof and porches. The interior courtyard is covered with a steel-frame, tempered-glass roof, but if someone really wanted to break in, they could probably come through any of several skylights by breaking or raising the glass.

Botada—thrown away, or wasted—is how our Cañari friends describe an uninhabited house. I understand. It does seem sad to let a perfectly good house sit vacant, though there are plenty of empty-and-waiting migrant houses around the countryside. Our neighbors also believe that any house without people or dogs is an open invitation for thievery. "Don't you want someone to live here while you're gone and protect your property?" one neighbor asked. He warns us that everything from the toilets to the beds might be hauled away. But then another neighbor, standing by, interjects, "*Por supuesto, Cañar es muy tranquilo.*" Cañar is very tranquil. The "*muy tranquilo*" bit seems to be the common opinion of life in Cañar, which is not to say that everyone we know doesn't take security precautions with fences and locked gates and dogs. But in all our years here we've never had anything major stolen, unless you count my muddy but expensive hiking boots that disappeared from outside the front door last year.

"With the problems I troubleshoot every day," Michael always says, "no one but us can live here." He's probably thinking of our frequent days with no water, about once a week right now because the new water main on the road above was installed too shallow under the road surface, and heavy trucks constantly break it. The street floods, and no one from the city notices until someone goes into town to complain. Then the city cuts off the water and we get the word that we have to uncover our own water line as part of the repair.

"Remember the time a couple of months ago when a tree branch fell across the electrical lines on the road below and we were without lights all day?" Michaels asks. "When the municipal guys finally showed up to do repairs, they asked *me* if they could borrow *my* tools. Who else but me can take care of things like that?" Michael asks.

And I'm remembering when three piglets invaded the yard and made themselves at home rooting up my new plants. We didn't know who they belonged to, how we could catch them, or what we should do with them when we did. I tied one to a post. A neighbor finally showed up, looking amused and not the least bit apologetic, and shooed her piglets home with a switch. Another time, Magdalena's little goat came for a visit and stripped all my new trees of leaves as high as she could reach. When I complained to Magdalena, she said, "It's not my goat, it's my children's. I told them not to buy it!" Without fences or enclosed walls—or a barking dog—I think our neighbors feel we are foolish gringos who bring these animal visits on ourselves.

Our other strategy against theft is to not leave anything in the house we can't afford to lose. My big beloved Hasselblad camera, which I feel is irreplaceable, will board with our friend Lynn in Cuenca this year. All my electronic gear—laptops, hard drive, cameras—travels with me to Portland in my backpack and Michael's.

That leaves some furniture, lamps, books, clothes, bedding and linens, rugs, and art, all of it carefully chosen, but nothing that would break my heart to do without. I pack away as much as possible in trunks, bags, and boxes and lock everything in the small room that will eventually be my darkroom. Michael stores his most valuable power tools deep in a corner of the dark attic. We cover bookcases and big furniture with sheets.

José María, our *compadre* who plants alfalfa around the house and potatoes or corn in the back field, is our caretaker. He and his family come once a week or so to tend their crops or cut alfalfa to feed their animals. They also tend the kitchen garden and water the plants in the courtyard. We've told José María that he will not be held responsible if anything happens, such as a break-in. But we also know from experience that he is disinclined to let us know if any problem does arise.

Not wanting to deliver unpleasant news is a slant on a characteristic I've noticed in our indigenous friends—that is, to feel *pena*, or shame, when anything bad occurs, whether one is at fault or not. We leave José María instructions for a phone call to Portland, and money for contingencies, but my guess is we will not hear from him for six months unless something catastrophic happens. We should probably call him every couple of months, but the truth is that we too are disinclined to hear anything unpleasant, so we don't call.

~

Every morning for several days now, a sight out our kitchen window has fascinated and puzzled Michael and me. Don Pepe, the older mestizo man who owns the cornfield below, spends hours standing on an enormous grass-covered boulder in the middle of the field, something like a hummock. He's there at dawn, when we get up, swinging his head this way and that, then sitting for a while, then standing and looking around again. "He's watching his corn grow," I joke several times as we stand at the window, watching. Sometimes we look out late afternoons and he is still there—or maybe he's left and come back?—silhouetted against the mountains in the fading light.

Then, one morning Michael announces that he knows what Don Pepe is doing: "He's watching for corn-eating birds," he said. "See, he's wearing a sort of apron made of a feed sack. It's full of stones that he throws at the birds." Sure enough, although we are too far away to see details, the gesture of throwing a stone was unmistakable.

We recently listened to the audiobook of *Jude the Obscure* by Thomas Hardy. Jude's first job as a young man was throwing rocks at crows in a neighboring farmer's field. This fruitless task was a metaphor for Jude's later life, which ends in disgrace after years of futile efforts to make something of himself.

Don Pepe is an older man, so I don't worry his actions are pointing toward a futile life, but I'm determined, the next time he's there, to ask a few existential questions. What does he think about all day while standing or sitting on the rock? How long through the growing cycle does he have to be so vigilant? How do the birds damage the corn—do they eat right through the sheath?

But when next I look out, I see only three scarecrows in the field. Maybe Don Pepe's job was to accustom the birds to his human presence, then fool them with the scarecrows. He comes no more to keep vigil. I regret that I hadn't taken a photo of him one of those dawns or dusks. I want to write about him in my next Cañar Chronicle, the monthly e-letter with photos I send out to family and friends, and try to talk Michael into posing on the rock and pretending to throw a stone, but he refuses. "There's no way I could walk onto another man's property," he says indignantly.

~

JOURNAL, JANUARY 18

A peaceful perfect day. The temperature inside the house is about seventy-two degrees, and eighty in the patio. I find the rest of the sheets and towels and make up the guestroom so we're ready for overnight guests. Our friends

Eduardo and Alexandra are coming to spend the weekend. Michael's been cooking for days, of course.

The workers José María, Antonio, and Santos have been here for two weeks already, building a rock wall between our property and that of Magdalena, our neighbor below us to the west. She'd complained several times last year that bits of our land fall into her patio and around her house when it rains. Michael has explained that she needed a retaining wall—in fact, should have made one when she built her house. He offered to help pay for it. But she did nothing, and she's very poor, so we came this year prepared to build the wall ourselves.

I go out to watch the men mixing concrete, placing poles for the wire fencing that will go on top, and handling huge rocks with their bare hands. These three men are old friends; in fact, two of them are godfathers of our house. At the end of the day, Michael walks up to buy a bottle of Zhumir because it is Friday, and he wants to offer them a drink on payday.

CHAPTER 26

La Uyanza: A Gift of Sustenance

~

Mercedes roasting cuyes

LAST WEEK, JOSÉ MARÍA INVITED US to a *uyanza* to celebrate his new roof. I'd not heard this word before so I looked it up. *Uyanza* in Quichua means "*regalo de alimentos,*" or, roughly, gift of sustenance or food. When I saw that, it made sense to celebrate a house-in-progress. In this culture of reciprocity, those who help with the planting and harvesting, or plowing and weeding, are repaid with a portion of the harvest. And, so I assume that when it comes to building a house, those who lend their labor are repaid with a fiesta with abundant food and drink. Michael had helped José María with some plumbing and electrical work, and as he and his wife, Narcisa, are *compadres* of *our* house, it was natural we would be invited.

"Come for *almuerzo medio-día* on Sunday," José María had said, the invite delivered so modestly that "lunch, mid-day" might have meant a brief break for soup and sandwiches. But we knew better.

Since Sunday was market day, Michael and I went to the *feria libre* (open air market) in the morning, he early to buy shrimp from his fish guy, and I later for a dozen roses from my flower señora, along with a large fern and two small rose plants from my plant guy. I'd trudged home with my heavy load around noon to be met with the delicious aroma of freshly cooked shrimp. But Michael said we couldn't eat anything because we were invited for José María's *almuerzo*.

"Are you crazy?" I replied. "We always get invited for *medio-día*, and we never eat before five o'clock or later. I'm starving! Let's have a little something!" Michael was not hard to convince: he soon served up plates of boiled shrimp, with great lemons from Lynn Hirschkind's trees in Yungilla, and toasted home-made bread—all so delectable that we had a hard time holding back.

Afterward, we loaded our backpacks with photo gear, sweaters, down vests, and rain jackets before heading down the mountain. It was about one o'clock by then and the day was sunny and warm, but with clouds already rolling up the valley from the coast.

As usual, we were among the first to arrive, Michael with a bottle of Zhumir for José María, and I with a rose plant for Narcisa. José María proudly led us into the room with the new roof, a *sala* about sixteen feet square that he has added onto the old house, with walls of adobe blocks, window openings covered temporarily with corrugated tin and cardboard, and floors of tamped earth. "We still have a lot of work to do," José María said shyly. "This will be a beautiful room," I replied, meaning it. I knew our architect Lourdes had helped José María with his design. During the months he worked on our house, she came to have great respect for this modest man.

Makeshift benches of bricks and boards, about ten inches high, sat along two sides of the room. It was dark and chilly in there, and when José María invited us to sit down—we were the only ones present—I made an excuse to go back outside. Michael dutifully sat alone for a few minutes, but soon joined me in the patio, warm from the sun.

I had assumed this would be a small party, but when I stepped into the smoky kitchen off the patio, I saw several women already at work over two large wood fires. One was Mercedes, the wife of Santos, José María's brother, who had worked on our house. Mercedes was one of the two women who had dug the canal for our water pipe. She was roasting a guinea pig over a fire, turning it slowly on a long pointed stick. I asked her how many animals they were cooking, and she gestured at the baskets around her. I counted fifteen guinea pigs, eight chickens, and four rabbits. On another fire with a grate, two enormous pots of potatoes were boiling; beside them, a huge basket of *mote* (hominy) was cooling. This was a feast for a big crowd! Off the upper patio, in the gas-stove kitchen, I saw other women preparing chicken soup, salads, and vegetables. The three girls of the family, Lourdes, about ten, Sarita, eight, and María, five, ran from kitchen to kitchen, washing pots in the standpipe in the patio, carrying firewood and utensils, looking thrilled at being part of the grown-up preparations.

I recognized José María's elderly mother and father sitting on stumps outside the kitchen, both beautifully dressed in their traditional clothes. She was peeling potatoes into a large pot on the ground. Amidst it all, a stately pair of adult turkeys strolled serenely around, circling the patios, stepping daintily in and out of the kitchens, looking this way and that, with a sideways cant of their heads, before suddenly swooping to snatch up scraps—a wonderfully comic addition to the scene.

Other guests slowly drifted in—aunts and uncles, nieces and nephews and their young children, along with a few neighbors. Some I knew slightly. There was Rebeca, José María's shy sister, whom I'd met and photographed as a teenager. Dressed in Cañari clothing still, but with a dark green fedora instead of the usual white hat, she was much changed. How did she become so matronly? She couldn't be more than thirty. In a quiet monotone, Rebeca told me that her husband went to Spain eight years ago, came back for a visit, and then left for the United States. He hasn't been back since. It took me a while to realize that two of the kids running around were hers: Ramiro and Verónica, about eleven and thirteen, wore sports clothes and fashion jeans, his hair cut short and hers swinging in a ponytail.

As we sat talking, I tried to imagine Rebeca's husband coming home from his other "Western" world every few years to find this taciturn, plump country woman, whom he must have married as a teenager, now raising their two handsome, animated children who clearly do not identify—at least by their clothes and hair—as indigenous. It's a complicated world.

José María and one of his uncles played hosts, circulating and serving endless drinks—cups of *chicha* (corn beer) and small glasses of *canelazo*, hot tea with alcohol. Manuel, José María's nephew, who had been designated DJ for the day, sat beside the window in the *sala* beside his boom box and speakers, alternating *rockero* and Andean music at high volume.

As the afternoon waned, Michael and I stood around in the patio, sat on the steps, took a walk around outside the compound, and waited and waited. It was hard to keep warm. Michael had a long conversation with José María's father, also named José María. They sat on the ground, their backs against a sun-warmed adobe wall, as the father described his stomach and prostate troubles and problems with his feet that keep him from working in his fields. I saw they were enjoying themselves, helped no doubt by the alcoholic *canelazo* that José María (the son) continued serving.

Two *ancianos* arrived, a very old couple who turned out to be José María's aunt and uncle, Eliseo Duy and Carmen Pomavilla. The aunt looked much older than her husband as she stepped carefully through the gate in her purple fleece house slippers, using a stick to walk. The pair slowly made their way to a wall at the edge of the patio and sat down to watch the action with bright eyes.

Knowing immediately they would be great subjects, I introduced myself and asked if I could take photos. They didn't seem to speak Spanish, but when they saw the camera, Carmen smiled a toothless grin, and old Eliseo looked amused and nodded. (Carmen would die within a couple of weeks and these photos became precious to the family.)

The temperature dropped further as the sun was setting, and finally José María asked us to move into the *sala*, lit now by a couple of bulbs. Our gathering had grown to about thirty people, and once we guests had arranged ourselves on the benches, the two turkeys and six or eight chickens flew into the room and roosted in the rafters above us, as though to join the party. Suddenly, the room felt cozier.

Waiting

The young DJ Manuel was still taking his job seriously, sitting on a chair in the corner with his CD player and speakers, choosing the music and controlling the volume appropriately.

While we waited, I had time to think about the generosity of the Cañari people, and the origins of this particular fiesta. José María and his family are very poor, and the construction on their house is a tremendous financial outlay, even with volunteer help from others. Michael said the cost of the roof alone, made of asbestos cement panels, was probably six or seven hundred dollars. I wondered if they had borrowed money from a relative in the United States, where I know José María has several brothers.

Yet the family goes all out to put on this potlatch of food and drink they cannot possibly afford. (And it's not just the meal itself; custom dictates we all go home with extra food.) I wondered if, in addition to reaffirming relations of reciprocity—"You've helped me, now we'll celebrate and later I'll help you"— another impulse for this largesse might be to mitigate the possible effects of *envidia*, envy, a powerfully negative force in indigenous culture. Perhaps this fiesta conveys: "We have a new roof; please don't be jealous and hold it against us." Or maybe it's simply a desire to share good fortune: "We have a new roof over our heads and we'd like to mark the moment with you." I don't know, and I'm sure if I asked José María he would simply say, "It is our tradition."

Finally, José María and his uncle and a couple of young men began rushing in from the kitchen with large bowls of chicken soup, serving each of us in turn. Then, plates heaped with roasted chicken, rabbit, *cuyes*, and maybe mutton or beef (too dark to tell), on top of boiled potatoes and bits of salad. The food disappeared in about ten minutes, some into hungry mouths, the rest into plastic bags that guests will take home. It's about seven thirty now, but very dark and very cold. Parents with young children began to leave immediately after eating.

Michael and I also wanted to leave, but we knew we couldn't. DJ Manuel brought the music back up, and Michael—who generally hates to dance—suggested that we dance. It was a relief to move and warm up after sitting so long. A few others got up to do the Cañari shuffle, but more people were saying their good-byes. This was not one of Mama Michi's fiestas, where she slams the door and stands in front of it with arms extended so no one can leave.

We danced a few more times: I asked José María, Michael asked Rebeca, but his back was hurting, still not healed from the sciatica caused by lifting our bags. We said good-bye to José María and went looking for Narcisa, who we found in the wood-fire kitchen where she had stayed throughout the evening with the other women who had helped prepare the food. They looked very warm and content. We thanked Narcisa for the wonderful meal. She responded the usual way: "Forgive us, for we have so little."

Michael and I hoisted our packs and started up the road; I lugged an old-fashioned, pale-blue scale that I'd found on the family's dump heap. José María couldn't understand why I wanted something that doesn't work, but I persuaded him that I thought it was beautiful, that I wanted to photograph it once my studio was set up.

Halfway up the mountain we caught a ride with a silent man in a small pickup. He refused payment. We got out at the top of the hill, walked down to our cold house, and jumped directly into bed. It was barely nine o'clock, but it felt just right.

～

JOURNAL, FEBRUARY 11

My birthday. Phone not working, so no Internet, which means it will be a peaceful day, although I know my mother and sisters and my son will be trying to call. Michael forgets my birthday, which is OK since he remembered it a couple of weeks ago when he came home from Cuenca with my present—a goose-necked floor lamp he'd bought at a medical supply place. I'd spotted it one day and mentioned it would be a great reading light for the living room. And yesterday he made my favorite lemon cake.

My best birthday present, however, was the unexpected opportunity to document the plowing of our field—the field that is finally ours now that the corn and peas and cows (and Mama Antuka) are gone. Antonio and Luisa came early with the two oxen, and I jumped up from breakfast to get cameras and recorder ready and ran out to document them tying on the yoke and attaching the plow. José María must have made the arrangements with Antonio to plow, perhaps paying him, or maybe agreeing to share the harvest with him and Luisa. Then, throughout the day, I tried to catch good photos of Antonio plowing (Luisa left soon after he began) and record the special language he uses with the bulls. Michael worked all day on the roof of his West Wing.

CHAPTER 27

Life in Town

~

Street scene, Cañar center

WE ARE HAVING A FEW DAYS of sun after Ecuador's heaviest rainy season in ten years, causing millions of dollars in damages in lost crops, floods, food shortages, landslides, destroyed roads, and a disastrous fishing season. Thirty or forty people have died along the coast due to drowning and collapsing houses, and in the mountains, a landslide buried a bus. President Correa has declared a state of emergency. The source of the wild weather is the climate phenomenon La Niña, an unusual cooling of Pacific Ocean surface temperatures that causes torrential rains for several months. La Niña alternates with its twin weather system, El Niño, which occurs every two to seven years.

Here in Cañar, the effect has been very cold weather almost from the time we arrived in January: daytime temperatures in the fifties, dipping into the forties and thirties at night. This week, however, we've had a break and the weather is brilliant, with sunny days and a newly vivid green landscape after all the rain, reminding me why I love this place.

Like most everyone in Cañar, Michael and I do our errands and pay our bills by walking from place to place and often standing in long lines. Actually not everyone; most middle-class townsfolk wouldn't dream of standing in line, but instead send their handyman or gofer or maid (who welcome the break, I imagine). But I enjoy the routine. It gives me a chance to catch up on what's happening in town, indulge in some prime people-watching, maybe even buy a newspaper if I catch the grumpy guy on the square still selling.

When I climb the hill into town today, everyone seems to be out: school children dawdling in the streets on their way home, mothers and toddlers sitting on the steps watching the action, old people soaking up the sun from second-story open windows or rickety wooden balconies.

I am headed for the state telephone company, Pacifitel, the only place in town where I can send a fax to the United States (remember faxes?). As I walk into the scruffy office on a side street, I see that I am the lone customer. Two middle-aged women sit, bored behind a glass partition, heads on hands, chatting disinterestedly. They look up at me rather wearily when I ask if I can send a fax.

"Yes, we can try," answers one, "but we can't give you a confirmation or receipt because our computer is broken." She gestures at an old monitor on the corner of her desk, dark screen turned to wall, cord coiled on the desktop.

"Let's just try to send it," I say. Unfortunately, my fax is not only "international" but also for an 800-number. When the clerk sees this, she shakes her head doubtfully. "I don't think this will work," she says. It doesn't. She hands back my fax with the same resigned expression.

As I turn to leave, I see that the three built-in phone booths have crudely hand-lettered "closed" signs taped to them. With the computer down, there's no phone service. It's no wonder: the proliferation of new phone kiosks around town offering efficient and inexpensive service have robbed the state telephone company of customers, just as private courier businesses have nearly put out of business the inept state postal system.

~

As we have no mail delivery in Cañar, and so receive no bills in the conventional way, we've had to learn the dates when utility charges are due, how long we have to pay them, and how long before service is cut off: one month for the phone, two months for electricity, and years (apparently) for water.

At the municipal center I inquire about our water bill. "What is your husband's *cédula?*" (national ID number) the poker-faced woman behind the glass asks. "I don't know, but do I really need it to pay our water bill?" Yes, because the account—like all our official business—is in Michael's name. I say I will come back the next day with his *cédula*, but could she tell me if our bill is due and how much. She squints at her computer a moment before saying, "Not for three months." (I'm reminded that when we lived in our storefront in the early 1990s, we discovered that the landlord had not paid the water bill for six years. It was under ten dollars, if I remember right.)

In my daily rounds, I've come to know many people by sight, if not by name: the sweet young brothers who make my photocopies at the school/office supplies store; the two lively women at the property registry office who helped me track down the owner of the tiny lot next door when I thought we might buy it; the postmistress who sits behind her desk in her tiny anonymous storefront on a side street; the old woman flower vendor at the Sunday market with the sad face who sells me "seconds"—a dozen roses for a dollar.

However, when I run into these townsfolk out of context—out from behind their desks, glass partitions, or market stalls—I have trouble remembering who they are. So last Sunday, as I was crossing the Pan-American on my way to the market and a woman yelled my name and came over and gave me a kiss on the cheek, I was completely mystified. Although her face was familiar, I had no idea how I knew her.

"I'm waiting for the bus to go to Quito with my husband," she said, gesturing at a man standing beside the road. "He's returning to Spain."

"Oh, that's . . . good," I answered tentatively, trying to judge if this was the right thing to say. I glanced over to see a well-dressed, middle-aged man standing beside two large suitcases and quickly read the scenario: her husband is a legal migrant in Spain who has come home for a visit with his family in Cañar.

"A letter came for you," the woman continued. "Come by on Tuesday and pick it up."

That's it! She is Eugenia, our ever-elusive postmistress, the single person in charge of all mail that comes in and out of Cañar through the famously inefficient postal system. For years, I didn't even know there *was* a post office in Cañar. Now, trying to get letters out of it has proved a continually frustrating experience. Even on days when the post office is open, Eugenia often leaves, pulling down the rolling metal door but leaving a few inches open at the bottom to indicate that she's not really closed but has gone about her errands. Everyone knows to read those open inches as: "Wait and I'll be back." Several times I've waited, but Eugenia didn't show up. Some days she's simply closed. The last mail I picked up took four visits to town.

Eugenia, postmistress of Cañar

As we stood on the edge of the Pan-American last Sunday, I was happy Eugenia had mentioned Tuesday because I've never understood which are the official days at the post office. Now I know: she is open on Sundays (though not this one), but closed on Mondays. Sunday is the busiest commercial day in Cañar, when country people come in for market and to take care of business, so many trades and services people treat Monday as a holiday.

On Tuesday, I climb the hill into town through the torn-up streets of a never-ending paving project, hoping to find Eugenia there. Yes! She is sitting behind her desk facing an open doorway a few feet from the street, a chair alongside her desk so clients can take a few minutes to gossip or a relative can visit and keep her company. "There you are at last!" she says, as though I am the elusive one.

Eugenia introduces the teenager standing beside her as her daughter, Leidy (pronounced "lady"). "How do you say in English, 'I want to eat!'?" Leidy asks me abruptly. I look puzzled and her mother explains that her daughter is studying to be a tour guide and she is having a hard time with a required English class.

I explain that "I want to eat!" is not a very polite phrase unless, for example, you are on the street with a good friend and passing by a pizza place and have a sudden attack of hunger. I suggest better ways to say it, and Leidy practices a few times.

I give Eugenia my two letters to mail, and she brings forth from a desk drawer a large manila envelope. I know it is from my colleague at the Smithsonian and that it contains DVDs of a project on which we've been working. I've been anxiously awaiting its arrival. But I don't get my hands on the packet yet. First, I must print and sign my name on the daily register of mail received and delivered, and next to my name put my ten-digit Ecuadorian ID number, which I always fake because I cannot remember it. Then, at last, she hands over the booty: no duty, no damage, and it was postmarked Washington, D.C., merely a week ago. I guess I have to take back all the bad things I've said about the Ecuadorian postal system over the years. (Then, the following week, I discover that a letter I sent to Quito never arrived, so I revise my opinion again.)

"How do you say, 'See you later!'?" Leidy asks. We discuss various ways to politely take one's leave, and I walk on down the street.

Picking my way through the workers laying paving stones, I come upon the new storefront of my friend, Martina. She is an indigenous woman who makes and sells clothing for Cañari women: elaborately embroidered wool or velvet skirts called *polleras*, embroidered blouses, wool capes, and accessories such as beaded necklaces. We chat, and I buy a pair of filigreed silver earrings. I know Martina well because I help her with her English lessons, part of a business course she is taking at a local secondary school. Her husband was an early *migrante*, leaving Cañar for New York about ten years ago. He has not come back, and never will, as Martina explained one day with a simple "*El tiene otra mujer.*" He has another woman. But he sends money to give their children university educations, a rare thing in my experience, and perhaps he sends something for Martina as well, which has allowed her to take that course and have this small business.

Nothing marks the changing economy of Cañar more than the proliferation of indigenous businesses. Ten years ago, Estudio Inti, the photography store of my first students, María Esthela and José Miguel, was the only Cañari business in town. Now, spurred by dollars and Euros pouring into Cañar, with houses built and trucks bought, indigenous families are looking for new ways to invest their *remeses*, migrant money. This includes buying up or renting real estate in town that has traditionally been controlled by mestizo families.

Along with the many shops like Martina's selling clothing, I see Cañari proprietors of car parts stores, DVD and CD stalls, cell phone stores, Internet places, and many new restaurants, all run by migrants returned from abroad. Most are small nickel-and-dime operations that can't break a five-dollar bill if you try to buy something. Business names are mysterious and creative: a clothing store called Jesús el Martiro (Jesus the Martyr); a shoe store called Roots (the owner spent years in Canada, home of Roots Shoes); a restaurant called D'Amores, with walls covered with photos of Che Guevara (the owner had been in Cuba). Rents are cheap and labor costs nothing when the owner (or owner's wife or husband or son or daughter) spends all day there. Many stores also double as workshops, where women sit at humming treadle (to save on electricity) sewing machines or string bead necklaces or embroider blouses and shirts. It's also obvious that many of these stores are gathering places for friends and family, prolonging a visit to town where life is so much more exciting than in the country.

Another sign of changing times: newly arrived merchants from mainland China, attracted by the migrant economy, have opened a couple of variety stores near the market, filled with cheap goods. The proprietors don't speak a word of Spanish, but they hire young women from town to tend to customers. I'm not sure, but I imagine older Cañar merchants feel rather proud that their town's commercial life is healthy enough to attract vendors from the other side of the world.

~

In news from the domestic front, Michael's courtyard fountain project has consumed him day and night for about three weeks. During the day, he does hard physical things like getting the six-hundred-pound stone in place (with assistance from four helpers), supervising the concrete and stonework of constructing the fountain base, and wrestling with pipes and pumps and a float and shutoff valves. During the night, making use of different brain functions, he works out complicated mechanical problems. The plumbing, electrical works, and pump are to be hidden in a sunken, brick-lined box next to the fountain, covered with a wooden hatch.

The stone is Andecite, which is probably Andean basalt. We found it in a stone yard about an hour away called Los picapiedras, or The Flintstones, as Michael likes to call it in a loose translation. We'd noticed the rock yard from the bus on our regular bus trips to Cuenca, and a few weeks ago we made a special trip to choose the stone.

Turns out the owner, Héctor, had spent several years in New York working construction, and, I assume, learning English. I saw (too late) that he understood, and was amused by, the little dispute between Michael and me as we tried to agree on a stone. A week later, after a worker spent an entire day hand boring a 1.5-inch hole lengthwise through the center, Hector and a helper brought the stone to our house along with the curved stone pieces for the water base. José María and Antonio spent two Saturdays helping Michael place the stone and build the fountain.

One day, as we have lunch in the courtyard and admire Michael's creation, I imagine archeologists five hundred years from now musing over this strange basalt pillar they've discovered in Cañar (sort of like the monolith scene in *2001: A Space Odyssey*). They will wonder about its ritual significance and ceremonial function, but our little secret is that it was only to provide a couple of crazy twenty-first-century householders the sweet sound of water burbling out the top of a stone.

~

JOURNAL, APRIL 22

On Good Friday afternoon, I saw a notice at the church on the square that a procession to a chapel of San Antonio would begin at eight o'clock Saturday morning. The next day I was a little late getting to the central square, but as I approached, I could hear a woman's clear, beautiful voice, singing. I

Procession to chapel of San Antonio

came up behind the procession to find three or four hundred people slowly walking up the street from the church. A sound truck followed behind with loudspeakers mounted on the cab, and inside I could see the woman with the amazing voice, a microphone at her mouth. I regretted immediately that I hadn't brought my little digital recorder.

I caught up and walked the length of the procession. Midway, I saw, bobbing above the crowd, a glassed-in coffin with a figure of Jesus, carried on the shoulders of four men. Trying to remember my childhood Bible stories, I think this is the day Christ was brought down from the cross and taken to the tomb. In front of the coffin, also carried by four men, was a beautiful figure of the Virgin Mary and, behind her, several other statues swayed. We wound up a steep mountainside to a chapel of San Antonio, overlooking Cañar, where I figured we'd leave the saints. But once there we made a big U-turn in front of the chapel and headed back down the mountain and wound through the streets to the big church on the square.

Inside, Padre Jesús stood waiting. He instructed the men carrying the saints and Christ figure to arrange them alongside the altar. Then, he sternly announced that all who were staying for mass should remain seated. Others should leave immediately, as the church doors were closing and there was to be no coming and going. I, along with many others, rushed out into the sunlight just as the massive doors of the church swung shut.

CHAPTER 28

Living in Two Worlds

~

Parade with Cañar Mayor Belesario Chimborazo,
wife Rosa Camas, festival queens, and city officials

MICHAEL TOOK THE BUS TO CUENCA this morning to buy our tickets
home, putting into motion what is becoming a familiar routine: shutting down
our Cañar life and picking up anew in Portland. Today is the beginning of June.
A month from now, we'll arrive to summer in the Northwest (which usually
doesn't begin until July anyway). The pear trees in front of our Portland house
will be in full leaf, the garden out back a tangle of overgrown weeds, the fruit
on the fig tree just beginning to form. The first day back—within the first *hours*,
in fact—Michael will jump into the old Volvo (if it starts, after sitting for six
months) to rush to Zupan's or New Seasons and spend extravagantly on some
of the delicacies he's missed these past six months: exotic cheeses, anchovies,

crabs, oysters. Then he'll drive on to the Horse Brass Pub for his favorite lunch of bangers and mash with a couple of pints, one gratis from his favorite bartender, Dennis, who'll tell him about the latest science fiction he's reading.

I'll be on the phone in my upstairs office, talking to my mother or one of my sisters, or maybe my son or daughter-in-law. While chatting, I'll begin opening six months' of mail that our tenant Mel has kept in a basket on the window seat. I'll toss all the junk directly into the recycling bin at my feet and set aside a few checks, letters and official-looking documents for later; I can't concentrate on anything serious the first few heady days back. Then I'll neatly stack six months of *New Yorker* magazines in an enticing pile on my bedside table. I always think I'll read them in order, but I know I'll not resist leafing through them at random, high grading, to find the articles that interest me the most.

More than anything, I'll want to be outside, weeding the garden or lying in my Mexican hammock under the cherry tree, near the burbling fountain— another of Michael's creation—and reading a book. I'll be in deliciously fewer clothes than I've worn the last six months, a skimpy T-shirt, cotton skirt, maybe even shorts, and the fresh air against so much exposed skin will feel strangely sensual, almost illicit. Such ease, such warmth and relaxation couldn't be further from our life in Cañar where, this morning as every day, I am dressed in Levis, a wool sweater over a long-sleeved T-shirt, heavy socks, and boots.

I'm looking forward to it all, including the instant media overload: daily newspaper on our doorstep, NPR on the radio, movies at our neighborhood theater, and those red Netflix envelopes coming through our mail slot with all the TV series and films we've missed (although lately I've discovered instant online viewing). And books! I keep a running list while I'm in Cañar, from reviews and friends' recommendations, and once home I'll start ordering books from my library, buying used online from Amazon, or I'll walk across the river to our own amazing Powell's Books. It will be instant gratification, however you look at it. Through my broadband connection, I'll have constant access to the Internet, to instantly answer any question that pops into my mind, to give me breaking news, the weather forecast, and details of all the tragic events and foolish goings-on in the known universe. It's a wired, media-saturated world we're going back to, and I will love and embrace it, at least for a while.

Renting the Portland house while we're gone covers the mortgage and other expenses for that time, but once back Michael and I still have to work. We each have long freelance histories in Portland—he as a contractor, and I as a writer and editor. Disappearing for six months every year, however, is not the best way to maintain consistency in one's contacts and contracts. Plumbing emergencies do not wait for Michael's return, and writing jobs don't land on my doorstep with my arrival in July. It usually takes two to three months before word gets around, jobs materialize, and paychecks begin to come in, but by then we are at the halfway point to leaving in January and constrained from taking longer jobs.

One of the main differences in our bifurcated life is that of household economics. In Cañar, Michael handles all money matters, which he enjoys because Ecuador is largely a cash-only world and Michael's a keep-it-under-the-mattress sort of guy. For my part, I relish knowing nothing about the state of our finances for six months. When it's time to pay the monthly bills, it is Michael who reminds me that one of us has to walk into town and stand in line. It is Michael who counts the cash in the filing cabinet and decides if we have enough to build a retaining wall, or take a trip to Spain. Every few months, as he does an accounting, I'll yell, "Don't tell me how much we've got left," covering my ears in mock denial. And I love the moment when he just smiles and says, "We've got enough." We have a local bank account for money transfer purposes, but rarely use it.

Michael's got it easy because our living expenses in Cañar are minimal. We have no mortgage, as the common practice is to pay for construction as you build. Yearly property taxes are under twenty dollars. Utilities cost a fraction of what they would in the United States, and without a car, we've no insurance, gas, or maintenance expenses. As far as I know, there's no such thing as property insurance. There are no restaurants worth patronizing in Cañar, and even in Cuenca, we rarely spend more than twenty dollars between us on a meal out. Without credit cards, we can confine impulse buying to whatever cash we have in our wallets, and, believe me, one quickly loses the urge to buy when no attractive goods are available (I'm thinking clothes here). Without easy access to the Internet, I cannot impulsively purchase equipment, order that latest book I just read about, or check on those shoes from Spain I happen to like.

In our six months in Portland, where life is considerably more complicated, I'm the one who manages our finances, and Michael remains blissfully uninvolved. I handle banking, bills, taxes, credit cards, monthly services, mortgage, property taxes, and air travel to visit family. Michael carries two credit cards and rarely has cash in his pocket.

In the end, it's the contrast of our two worlds that I relish the most, the differences between our "Cañar life" and our "Portland life" ("the freshness of arriving and the relief of leaving" as Gerald Locklin says in his poem "where we are"). By the time we are ready to leave Portland in six months, I'll be sick of the media overload, my over-scheduled, over-stimulated life, and those alarming monthly Visa bills. I relish that last week when I get to cancel our cell phone service, put away the credit cards, reduce our car insurance to bare minimum, put our home phone service on maintenance (enough to keep our number), cancel all news-paper and magazine subscriptions (except the beloved *New Yorker*), remove my name from all annoying e-mail lists, and stop all the catalogs that I've allowed to creep through our mail slot.

I even enjoy the last colossal housecleaning we do the week before we leave. Simplify, reduce, cancel, cleanse—it's a big cathartic tidying up and dumping out once a year that I would never get around to otherwise.

We rent our Portland house fully furnished and leave it organized and stocked as though it were a residence hotel, just as we would want it. Books, art-work, dishes, cookware, linens—and anything else a guest/tenant would need or enjoy—are left in place. (Plus, it gives me an excuse to buy new things, as in, "Oops, that teapot has a chip in it. I'd better go shopping for a new one at Sur la Table.") But I empty closets, put away personal belongings and family photo-graphs, clear shelves, and leave workspaces ready to use. I even make the beds with the best linens.

I am also in charge of renting the house, and Craigslist is—or was—the secret to my success. (The last time I used it, I had responses with photos from young women offering other services, but I hear Craigslist has cracked down on that.) The first tenants, an elderly couple from Canada, came back two years, then we rented to a doctor relocating from New Orleans, and our present (and favorite) tenant, Mel, is in her third year. She comes from New Hampshire in January to be with her Portland family, and leaves at the end of June, a sched-ule that synchs perfectly with ours. Except for one year, when the first couple left suddenly for a medical emergency and left the house full of their things (a friend later removed them), we've had good luck with our renters, finding the house just as we left it: spotlessly clean and everything in place, with the beds made and ready to fall into.

So, come January, I'll be ready to come back to Cañar for long peaceful days in a quiet house with no newspapers, no TV, no cars, no shopping enticements, and no easy access to the Internet. Without these, I concentrate better, read more carefully, think more deeply. Also, with no paid work (or not much), sometimes no power or water, and a phone that rarely rings, life simply slows way down. When I'm in Cañar, I often feel we're living the "real" life by spending more time on the basics: food, shelter, warmth, walking to everything close, using buses and hired trucks for anything afar, engaging with our neighbors (sometimes easy, sometimes difficult), and immersing ourselves more meaningfully in life's rites of passage: births, baptisms, graduations, marriages, and deaths.

And of course there's our house, our wonderful house that turned out to be so much more inviting, comfortable, and interesting than we anticipated, with

Finished house, facing mountains

its open-beam ceilings, glass-roofed patio, fireplace, skylights, and our glorious view of the Andes. The collaboration between Michael and Lourdes has produced a work of architectural art that the municipality of Cañar will recognize next year with a special plaque that reads, loosely translated: "for the valiant contribution of redeeming the traditional architecture of the Cañari culture in an urban setting."

Still, on this June day when Michael is buying our tickets, it feels way too soon to be leaving Cañar. I feel as though we just arrived, got organized and into the rhythm of things, and suddenly it's time to go. I make a to-do list for the garden: separate the crocosmia irises on the west side of house and extend the row of them along the walkway. Clean the rock and cactus wall of weeds; cut and plant the last of the geraniums at the end of yard. Then I decide it's too cloudy and cold to garden today and begin to clean my office, dressed in two layers of sweaters and fingerless gloves. June is the coldest month of our time in Cañar, and on cloudy days I have to stay constantly in motion to keep warm until the afternoon fire.

Michael comes back from Cuenca with our tickets, announces our departure date, and cleans the stove and fridge. He makes an early fire and by four o'clock, we settle down with a movie on my laptop. It's simply too cold to do anything else.

~

We are the only *extranjeros* living in Cañar, by which I mean there are no other North Americans or Europeans here. Although Michael and I revel in this status, this is not a life for everyone. Cañar is a homely place, with none of the attractions of the nearby city of Cuenca, recently cited by *International Living* magazine as number one on its Global Retirement Index ("the World's Most Affordable Haven"), evidenced by the legions of English-speaking retirees now trying out new lives there. In contrast to Cuenca's climate of "eternal spring" at 8,370 feet altitude, Cañar's could be described as "eternal late fall" at 10,100 feet. But Michael and I both feel invigorated by the weather with its daily swings in temperatures from foggy chilly mornings to a few warm hours during the day, if the sun is out, to cold nights under the goosedown comforter.

Our life here also works because of our long history with this place and the fact that we are both fluent in Spanish. It's been nearly twenty years since we first rented our weekend storefront on the Paseo de los Cañaris, and—as with any hometown—old friends, acquaintances, familiar places, happenings, and gossip provide a fascinating, never-dull daily life. In my work as a documentarian, I am constantly stimulated by the photo opportunities, whether I am going off to shoot a multi-day fiesta or simply taking an afternoon walk and capturing yet another image of a farmer plowing his field with yoked bulls. My recent project, the formal creation of a digital visual archive, Archivo Cultural de Cañar, has given new purpose to the thousands of photos I've taken in my time here, and I anticipate expanding, organizing, and sharing it with the community and other institutions for many years to come.

~

It's down to one week before we leave, and I realize I have some unfinished business. I'd applied for an official tax number from Ecuador's Internal Revenue Service (SRI) in February so that I could be paid for a few copies of my book by a bookstore in Quito. I was vaguely aware that I was supposed to declare my income monthly on an SRI website, even if my earnings were zero, but I had ignored this until the other day, when I heard an alarming story. Immigration officials supposedly keep track of those who do not make their monthly sign-in on the SRI website, and the rule breakers can be detained and fined at the airport when coming back into the country (apparently we can leave freely).

I want to be very careful not to threaten my new residency status, so this morning I walk into town to the SRI office that has recently opened and take my place in the line of plastic chairs ringed around a small room. A woman agent sits behind a desk facing us, and the room is so small that those waiting can watch, listen, and be entertained by everyone else's case. Which is lucky, as I'd neglected to bring anything to read. Looking around at the people with receipt books in their hands, I'd guess all are small businesspeople who have neglected to pay their monthly taxes and are here now to settle and suffer the fine.

A poster on the wall promotes an SRI lottery—YOU WIN, AND SO DO WE. Ecuadorians are historically reluctant to pay taxes, and I guess the government's Internal Revenue Service is trying to promote this novel idea of domestic income tax with an old beloved one: a lottery that might make you rich quick.

The youngish woman behind the desk, with a severe black ponytail and two shades of eye shadow, is dressed in the SRI colors—red, white, and blue. Every twenty minutes or so, a new supplicant moves to an unwelcoming wooden chair beside the desk, and the agent listens to their story without a smile or any sign of friendliness. Her eyes stay on the computer screen and her fingers remain poised above the keyboard. Every now and then, the printer spits out a long form.

After about an hour, it's my turn. I give the agent my *cedula*, national ID card, and she brings up my case on the computer.

"You haven't paid since February," she says sternly, staring at the screen. "That's March-April-May-June."

"But I haven't had any earnings," I say, pretending ignorance.

"Doesn't matter. You have to report every month."

"Can't I report every six months? Or can I just cancel my SRI number?"

"No," she says brusquely. "First you have to pay a fine." She stares into middle distance while the printer warms up with clicks and whirs and spits out a long strip of pages. She efficiently rips them off, separates the copies, and hands one to me.

"How much?" I ask timidly.

"Fifteen cents," she says, with the barest trace of a smile. "You can pay it at any bank." (The story of how long *that* took is a tale for another day.)

~

JOURNAL, JUNE 25

"Do you feel more Ecuadorian, or American?" José María asked me the other day. "Well, I'm also a Canadian," I stalled, "and that's an important part of my history." Then, thinking about it, I explained that by birth, family, friends, and my present life in Portland, I now feel more American. He wanted to know where Oregon is and I brought the atlas from my office to show him a map of the United States, pointing out that Portland is about five thousand kilometers from New York (every Cañari's geographical reference en *el Norte*).

"And my son and family live here," I pointed to San Francisco, "and my mother and sisters here," I pointed to Santa Fe, "and Michael's sister and family here," I pointed to Seattle. José María shook his head in disbelief that we could live so far apart and still be a family.

"But," I continued, placing my hand on South America, "now that we have a house and residency visas here, I also feel half-Ecuadorian."

"*Más mejor,*" he said, nodding, meaning loosely, "Much better."

CHAPTER 29

Epilogue

What on Earth Are We Doing Here?

~

Fiesta rucuyaya (*festival clown*)

JANUARY 15, 2010. The fifth year of our Cañar "second life" begins, and occasionally I still have moments of thinking, "What on earth are we doing here?" One such moment comes early the first morning, when the temperature in the living room reads fifty-six degrees, and the solidly cloudy sky through the courtyard roof tells me there is little prospect of sun or warmth until our afternoon fire. Putting off the moment when I'll have to pile on layers of clothing and stay active all day to be comfortable, I take my coffee and oatmeal back to the bedroom, nominally warmer from our sleep, and climb into bed with one of the new books from the stack I've brought from Portland.

The other moment of "Why this place?" comes later that day, when Michael and I walk up to the Paseo de los Cañaris, the row of shops and small businesses that serves our part of town. When we first saw the Paseo, in 1991, while we were living in Cuenca, it was nothing more than a dirt road leading off the Pan-American Highway into the countryside, lined with a few ramshackle storefronts and taverns.

In 1992, our second year, we rented one of those storefronts to use as a weekend studio and meeting place. Our new Cañari friends laughed when they heard what we were paying in rent—fourteen dollars a month. They said the landlord had really taken advantage of the gringos. But we didn't care. We painted the double exterior doors blue, bought a table, chairs, benches, and a bed at the market, and set up a cooking corner in the main room, which we called the "meeting room." The second room became our sleeping quarters and my studio. A trip to the latrine in the backyard required us to step out into the street, walk a few paces to the east, go through a wooden gate and down a path alongside the building to a small back patio with a squat toilet: a concrete slab with two footprints and a hole (a *baño turco* in local parlance).

Pigeons roosted in the rafters at night, bringing down a light rain of feathers on our bed through the flimsy ceiling, and when it was windy a loose piece of tin roof rattled incessantly, like the amateur theater sound effects of an approaching storm. On Sundays, as part of our volunteer work with an indigenous organization, INTI (National Institute of Indigenous Technology), I taught photography classes at our storefront, while Michael went out with the men to help build terraces on steeply sloped land. He also occasionally cooked with the women, much to the amusement of everyone.

We loved being in Cañar, and the contrast with our easy life in Cuenca made it seem even closer to the authentic experience we'd come looking for in Ecuador. It was with regret we left in 1993 to move to Portland.

Our little place with the blue doors is long gone, and the Paseo de los Cañaris looks very different today. Since the mid-2000s, with waves of money coming from migrants in the United States and Spain, the area has been progressively transformed into a commercial thoroughfare a quarter-mile long, from the Pan-American to the entrance to the large Catholic school where, in previous times, the hacienda headquarters stood. For a few years, the noise of construction along the Paseo was constant, with two- and three-story buildings going up everywhere we looked. All had commercial space at street level and living quarters above or behind. With almost no zoning laws or building codes, many structures were odd shapes or sat at sharp angles on irregular lots, giving the street an ad hoc feel, like something out of Dr. Seuss.

Though some of the enterprises were short-lived—the vegetarian restaurant didn't last long, I notice—others thrived and sold goods that marked a new prosperity for Cañar: car parts, musical instruments, imported clothing, cell phones. The road stayed dusty and the buildings still looked hodgepodge, but until recently there was a palpable feel of a busy business strip.

This year, however, the Paseo appears unusually quiet, almost moribund. Construction has slowed or stopped—in some cases, mid-building. Storefronts that were new a couple of years ago are closed or, if open, look unattended, their bright cheap paint already fading and peeling, signs hanging crookedly, the blue reflective windows dusty and cracked. It doesn't help that the road is completely torn up on both sides by one of the endless municipal projects that keep the town's infrastructure in turmoil. Sidewalks and a sewer system appear to be the present undertaking.

I know without asking that the global financial crisis, combined with high unemployment and new anti-immigrant laws in the United States and Spain, has radically changed the economy of Cañar. The restaurant worker in New York City who once sent one hundred dollars a week to his brother is now without a job, and the car parts store they jointly own in Cañar is faltering. A hotel cleaner in Madrid is laid off and can no longer help support her teenage daughter who lives with her grandmother in Cañar, and so the daughter can no longer buy jeans from that cool little shop that was here last year and now is gone. The truck/taxi driver who gave Michael and me a ride home yesterday said he'd recently returned from sixteen years working in construction in New Jersey. "The work slowed way down up north, and I wanted to see my kids grow up," he said, "but it's almost impossible to make a living here."

My sense that things have changed is confirmed on Sunday, when Michael and I walk up to the *feria libre* on a main avenue, a sort of farmer's market where local vendors sell fresh fruits, vegetables, fish, plants, and flowers, and women with improvised street-side kitchens feed the shoppers. At first, all seemed as usual. Michael, his eyes glazed with happiness to be back in the land of giant prawns for $2.50 a pound (well, they are now $3.50), mangos for twenty cents apiece, and a twenty-two-ounce bottle of beer for sixty-five cents, is greeted by César, the fish vendor. "Hey, Miquito! Where've you been so long? Happy New Year!" Michael bought his prawns and rushed home to cook them while I climbed a long set of stairs into the center of Cañar.

From above, in contrast to the busy market below, the town feels dead, with none of the bustle of a Sunday. Streets usually full of cars and people jockey-ing for space are nearly empty. I see vacant stalls at the municipal market, and some stores on the main streets are closed. I step into the open doorway of one store to chat with the elderly proprietors, whom I know slightly because they own a parcel of land below us. The old woman, looking ill and impassive, sits in a chair leaning against old wooden shelves filled with dusty rolls of cloth, her arms folded, her eyes half closed, a shawl over her shoulders. She doesn't acknowledge me, but her husband, who stands leaning against the wooden counter reading a newspaper, enthusiastically shakes my hand, "*Hola, vecina,*" he says. Hello neighbor. "I'm glad to see you back after such a long time."

I ask him how things had been.

"*Estamos acabando,*" the old woman answers without blinking. "We're finished. Nobody comes, nothing sells."

"Bad, bad, it's really bad," her husband adds. "People only buy what they need to live. . . . The dollars aren't coming anymore." I ask him if he thinks migration out of Cañar had slowed down. "People are still leaving," he says, "but others are coming back. Some are deported, others have given up."

In an alleyway between two buildings, I find María, my "basket woman." She is an itinerant vendor who comes by bus from Cuenca each Sunday and sets out her wares on the pavement, leaving a narrow path for shoppers. For several years I've bought baskets, rush mats, candleholders, ceramic pots, plastic buckets, and miniature wooden stools from María. Today, because she's not busy, she asks me to sit down on one of those stools to chat.

"It's bad in Cuenca, too," she says, when I note that things seemed slow for a Sunday market. "Everywhere! My supplier borrowed money from the bank to buy baskets for the Christmas season, and there were no customers. Nothing. Now the baskets are stored in a damp warehouse, growing moldy and they can't be sold. It was a total loss." María goes on to repeat what I'm hearing everywhere: migrants simply are not sending as much money back home.

While we talked, a Cañari woman comes along to ask the price of a plastic gallon bucket. "A dollar fifty," says María. The woman clucks her tongue. "Too much! A dollar twenty-five," she says in the distinctive cajoling voice reserved for bargaining.

"No," answers María, "It's not too much. That's a good price for that bucket. Here's one for a dollar." She picks up a smaller, beat-up bucket.

"No," said the woman, "that one's ugly. I want this one, but for a dollar twenty-five."

María held her ground, and the Cañari woman reluctantly digs into the hidden pocket in her skirt to bring out the extra quarter.

"And I have to work harder for every sale," María says as I get up to leave.

~

But then all doubts about why we're here disappear a few days later when we walk to town through a mestizo neighborhood near our house. "Hey, neighbors! You were gone too long! I'm glad you're back," Lola calls out from her patio, where she sits shelling beans in her blue-checkered apron. Farther on, we run into Ivon, a little tipsy as always. He tells Michael his "heart had been hurting" while we were away, holding his hand dramatically against his chest. Was Michael free to come and have a drink with him, *right now*?

Lucho, the bearish owner of a truck who delivered many of our construction materials and helped us move three years ago, drives by, sticks his head out the window, and yells, "Miquito, I've been crying for your return," then adds as an afterthought, "¡*Feliz Año!*"

Then on the Paseo we stop by the store of our old friends, Mila and Manuel, to buy bananas and beer. Each gives us a big hug before Mila disappears through the back of the store into their living quarters and comes out with a pan of *humitas* (a type of sweet tamale). She presents them with "¡*Feliz Año!*"

As we near the center of town, I realize with surprise that this place is slowly becoming attractive. Belesario Chimborazo, the first indigenous mayor in the 185-year history of the municipality, has poured money into infrastructure— paving streets, putting in sewers—but also into planting rows of trees along newly paved streets, narrowing streets to one way, widening sidewalks, and refurbishing the main square, which is a small formal park ringed by municipal buildings, banks, lawyers' offices, and the Church complex, which occupies one entire side. Around town, it has long been the practice to tear down the old colonial-style buildings, but today I notice that some are being refurbished, retaining nice details such as small balconies and wooden doors. I doubt the new mayor can take credit for all this, but it's great to see Cañar showing some civic pride and beginning to look appealing.

~

We run into Pedro Solano, a teacher from the village of Junducuchu, and he asks if I'll come and document their annual fiesta of San Antonio the next day. "Delighted," I say, or the equivalent in Spanish, *encantada*.

San Antonio de Padua is the patron saint of Cañar, but no one can tell me how a thirteenth-century Franciscan monk who was born in Portugal, died in Italy (near his adopted city of Padua), and canonized the next year, in 1232, came to be adopted as the patron of this out-of-the-way South American town. Perhaps San Antonio was the favorite of some conquistador who settled here? Or perhaps an early Spanish priest adopted him for his flock in Cañar because

María, Lourdes, and Sarita, left to right

he's one of the patron saints of poor and oppressed people? San Antonio is also venerated as the patron of infertile women, travelers, masons, bakers, and papermakers and credited with miracles involving lost people, so maybe, well . . . who knows? There's a little research project for me some year.

I end up staying all afternoon in Junducuchu, taking photos, drinking *chicha*, accepting a few of shots of Zhumir offered in a beautiful cow-horn cup, and dancing with a tipsy old man in wooly chaps who keeps calling me his *warmi* (Quichua for woman). I am happy, and I feel privileged to be welcomed to this fiesta, even if it is the only time of the year when I can be pinched on the butt by one of the *rukuyayas*, festival fools who wear masks and act lewdly, much to the crowd's delight.

Still, I suppose it was all too much, too soon. The sun was hot, my lungs are small, my white skin tender, and my stamina for the rigors of Cañar life not yet up to speed. By the next day, I was in bed with a slight fever and some aches and pains—maybe a touch of *sorroche*—altitude sickness?

~

Finally, I am reminded why we are here when we have a Sunday evening visit from José María and Narcisa with their three daughters, Lourdes, Sarita, and María. While I send Sarita for colas and cookies, Michael serves José María beer and Narcisa juice. We'd already heard from José María that Lourdes, his oldest girl at twelve, is stable with kidney dialysis three times a week. Although she's a little puffy and as tiny as ever, she is alive and looks happy, a seeming miracle given her many medical crises this past year. While the adults sit around and talk about the weather, the crops, the bad economy, and the past tragedies of their lives (Narcisa's father died of drink and a teenage brother of pesticide exposure; José María lost an eye in a fire), the three girls sit in a row on the couch in front of the fire, reading books.

I look at them and think how they are the enduring hope of Cañar, despite the slowing migrant dollars, fractured families, shaky economy, devastating illnesses, and hard times to come. Hope lives with this intact family, with these sweet girls who go to school, love to read, and who have scant notion yet of the poverty of their parents.

María, who is just seven, shows off shyly by reading aloud from *Jorge el Curioso* (*Curious George*). "George climbed up until he was in the sunshine again, high above the rain cloud."

As I listen, I feel one of those moments coming on, suffused with happiness, so grateful that I have no desire to be anywhere else in the world but here.

ACKNOWLEDGMENTS

~

BECAUSE I SOMETIMES WRITE about undocumented immigrants from Ecuador in the United States, I changed their names, as well as those of their family members and home villages. I also used pseudonyms for a few individuals in Cañar if I felt my descriptions would be embarrassing or prejudicial. Otherwise, places and people are portrayed as known.

Through eighteen months of construction, Michael and I grew to greatly admire the men (and occasionally women) who worked on every aspect of our house, from the stone foundations to the tile roof, especially José María Duy, Santos Duy, Antonio Acero, Juan Alberto Cambi, Javier Dután, and Maestro Miguel, the specialist who came from Cuenca to apply the final finish on the walls. From the beginning, Vicente Tenesaca, Cañari lawyer extraordinaire, was crucial in helping us acquire the property and untangle the endless red tape involved in getting our residency status as *inversionistas*.

Lourdes Abad was not only our exceptional architect and general contractor, but she also became a close friend in the process of building the house in the clouds. She and I continue to collaborate on a Spanish-language booklet on adobe construction, inspired by the many admiring visitors to the house who ask, "How did you do this?"

I owe special thanks to my good friend in Cuenca, anthropologist Lynn Hirschkind, for being my best source on all things historical and anthropological and for reading those chapters for which I needed extra assurance or advice.

Several readers in various countries constitute my virtual book club. Although we may never meet at the same time, we are close friends, fellow writers, good critics, and always there for one another: Nancy Henry, Lynn Hirschkind, Arlene Moscovitch, Maya Muir, Joanne Mulcahy, and Andrew Wilson. By virtue of the wonderful maps she drew for this book, Carla Hansel also belongs to the club, as well as Julie Keefe, who brought her critical eye to my photographs through several Photoshop lessons.

A Fulbright teaching/research grant brought us back to Cañar in 2005, when the scales tipped in favor of making this our permanent "second" home. That year also saw the beginning of two long-term, bilingual projects with Cañari colleagues in collaboration with the Smithsonian's National Museum of the

American Indian (NMAI). In Washington, D.C., Amy Van Allen and Manuel Gancedo guided the Indigenous Geography project, while in Cañar, Ranti Chuma, Magdalena Guamán, Antonio Duchi, Melchor Duchi, José Pichazaca, Sara Pichisaca, Andrés Quindi, Gregorio Quishpilema, and Pedro Solano produced and edited the written materials in Quichua and Spanish for the website and accompanying book: *Los Cañaris y Sus Expresiones Culturales*. At a critical moment, Federico Benítez and Maureen Shaughnessy arrived from Argentina in their van and stayed to do a beautiful job producing the audio and video materials.

Special friends in Cañar who deserve mention are my *comadre*, María Esthela Mainato, who manages the Cañari Women's Education Foundation while I'm in the United States; Mercedes Guamán Mayencela, one of our scholarship graduates, who is now a busy lawyer; the godparents of our house, José María Duy and his wife Narcisa and their three girls, Lourdes, Sarita, and María; and our beloved goddaughter, Paiwa Mainato Acero, who continues to greatly enrich our lives.

In Cañar, I owe additional thanks to the Navas family, who has given me access to the precious collection of glass and early celluloid negatives of their patriarch, photographer Rigoberto Navas, for my Archivo Cultural de Cañar. Two of the Navas photos appear in this book, and I hope the entire collection will one day be part of a permanent archive at the Casa de la Cultura.

Gerald Locklin generously allowed me to use his poem, "where we are," which I came across by accident in Garrison Keillor's *Good Poems* and which so perfectly illuminates the theme of two homes, two lives.

At the University of Texas Press, editor-in-chief Theresa May has been my enthusiastic ally through two books. Thanks also to Leslie Tingle, managing editor, and to Sally Furgeson, who did a great job editing the manuscript.

Finally, there's Michael, my partner in life and all adventures thereof. Building a house and living in a faraway place is not for the faint of heart. I would never be here, in Cañar, Ecuador, in an earthen house on the side of a mountain overlooking the Andes writing this book, if I had not had the good fortune to come across a non-birder like myself in the cloud forest of Costa Rica all those years ago.

JUDY BLANKENSHIP
Cañar, April 2012